Beginning Google Glass Development

Jeff Tang

Apress®

Beginning Google Glass Development

Copyright © 2014 by Jeff Tang

ISBN-13 (pbk): 978-1-4302-6788-1

ISBN-13 (electronic): 978-1-4302-6787-4

Publisher: Heinz Weinheimer
Lead Editor: Michelle Lowman
Development Editor: Douglas Pundick
Technical Reviewer: Andres Calvo
Editorial Board: Steve Anglin, Mark Beckner, Ewan Buckingham, Gary Cornell, Louise Corrigan, Jim DeWolf, Jonathan Gennick, Jonathan Hassell, Robert Hutchinson, Michelle Lowman, James Markham, Matthew Moodie, Jeff Olson, Jeffrey Pepper, Douglas Pundick, Ben Renow-Clarke, Dominic Shakeshaft, Gwenan Spearing, Matt Wade, Steve Weiss
Coordinating Editor: Kevin Shea
Copy Editor: Kim Wimpsett
Compositor: SPi Global
Indexer: SPi Global
Artist: SPi Global
Cover Designer: Anna Ishchenko

Distributed to the book trade worldwide by Springer Science+Business Media New York, 233 Spring Street, 6th Floor, New York, NY 10013. Phone 1-800-SPRINGER, fax (201) 348-4505, e-mail orders-ny@springer-sbm.com, or visit www.springeronline.com. Apress Media, LLC is a California LLC and the sole member (owner) is Springer Science + Business Media Finance Inc (SSBM Finance Inc). SSBM Finance Inc is a Delaware corporation.

For information on translations, please e-mail rights@apress.com, or visit www.apress.com.

Apress and friends of ED books may be purchased in bulk for academic, corporate, or promotional use. eBook versions and licenses are also available for most titles. For more information, reference our Special Bulk Sales–eBook Licensing web page at www.apress.com/bulk-sales.

Any source code or other supplementary material referenced by the author in this text is available to readers at www.apress.com. For detailed information about how to locate your book's source code, go to www.apress.com/source-code/.

To my mother, whose smile, kindness, courage, and words left unspoken will continue to be my guiding star.

Contents at a Glance

Contents

About the Author

Jeff Tang has successfully developed mobile, web, and enterprise apps on many platforms. He became a Microsoft Certified Developer and a Sun Certified Java Developer last century; had Apple-featured, top-selling iOS apps in App Store; and was recognized by Google as a Top Android Market Developer. Jeff has a master's degree in computer science with an emphasis on artificial intelligence and believes in lifelong learning. He loves playing basketball (he once made 11 three-pointers and 28 free throws in a row), reading Ernest Hemingway and Mario Puzo, and fantasizing about traveling around the world.

About the Technical Reviewer

Andres Calvo is a software engineer who has worked with wearable and mobile devices for more than five years. He works for Ball Aerospace as a contractor at Air Force Research Laboratory, where he acquired an interest (read: obsession) with usability and user experience. Since he joined the initial group of Glass Explorers in 2013, Andres has been fascinated by the potential of Glass to provide unprecedented user experiences. During his free time, Andres develops applications for Android and Glass both for fun and as a freelancer. He has received bachelor degrees in computer science and computer engineering from the University of Dayton. Visit his blog at http://ocddevelopers.com and contact him at andresacalvo@gmail.com.

Acknowledgments

This book could not have been written without the great people at Apress. Steve Weiss responded within hours to my e-mail inquiry, two days after the Google Development Kit (GDK) Sneak Peek was released in November 2013, about writing a Google Glass development book. Michelle Lowman, the lead editor for iOS/electronics and robotics, offered great support and understanding throughout the book planning and writing. Louise Corrigan helped tremendously on the book proposal and contract. Kevin Shea, the book's coordinating editor, did a wonderful job communicating and scheduling each milestone. Douglas Pundick, the developmental editor, helped with a lot of terrific feedback on how to improve the book content. Thank you so much, Michelle, Kevin, and Douglas, for keeping the book on the right track. Kim Wimpsett, the book's copy editor, did an amazing job of correcting so many mistakes in my writing. Anna Ishchenko, the cover designer, magically turned the poor picture I took of my Glass into something beautiful, among other things. To all the great folks at Apress, you have my deep, heartfelt appreciation for helping make one of my big dreams come true.

A very special thank-you goes to the greatly talented technical reviewer, Andres Calvo. Andres provided countless excellent suggestions and comments and tested all the GDK and Mirror API code in the book. I feel so lucky to have Andres as the book's technical reviewer.

John Rodley also did a good job reviewing the first two chapters of the book. James Wu reviewed and tested the iOS code in Chapter 7. Thanks, John and James, for your comments and help.

My 82-year-old father, who introduced me to the computer programming world so many years ago, collected and forwarded to me, using the popular WeChat app, many great articles on Google Glass and wearable computing. Dad, thanks for showing me what "Never too old to learn" means.

Finally, thanks to Lisa, Mark, and Sophia for their unwavering support during my book-writing months. Now I'm about to be running out of excuses for skipping parties, hiking, shopping, games, and travel. First, bring in the 2014 World Cup Brazil!

Introduction

Google Glass is a wearable computer developed by Google. Although Glass is based on Android, it is fundamentally different from existing mobile platforms. The best line to describe Glass is "There when you need it. Out of the way when you don't." Glass is designed to complement a smartwatch, smartphone, tablet, or computer.

In April 2013, the Google Glass Explorer Edition was made available, for the first time, to Google I/O 2013 developers. There were four Glass-related sessions at Google I/O 2013 held in May 2013:

- *Developing for Glass:*
  `https://developers.google.com/events/io/sessions/332490621`

- *Building Glass Services with the Mirror API:*
  `https://developers.google.com/events/io/sessions/332733833`

- *Voiding Your Warranty: Hacking Glass:*
  `https://developers.google.com/events/io/sessions/332704837`

- *Fireside Chat with the Glass Team:*
  `https://developers.google.com/events/io/sessions/332695704`

Since then, several important events have happened:

- On November 19, 2013, Google officially released the native Android-based Glass Development Kit (GDK) Sneak Peek, so developers can now build native apps in Android 4.0.4 (API Level 15) for Glass.

- On April 15, 2014, Google announced a major upgrade for Glass to Android 4.4.2 (API Level 19).

- On May 15, 2014, Google made the Glass Explorer Edition available to any U.S. resident older than 18 and with a U.S. shipping address.

It is almost mid-June 2014 now, and Google I/O 2014 is only a couple of weeks away. More Glass-related sessions on how to design and develop Glass apps (also known as Glassware) and on the Glass platform details have been scheduled (see `https://www.google.com/events/io/schedule`).

This is a great time to start learning Glass development; if you need more reasons, see the "Why Glass?" section in Chapter 1. You should definitely check out those Google I/O 2013 and 2014 videos on Glass if you are interested in Glass development. In addition, Google Glass's developer site at https://developers.google.com/glass/ has great documentation on designing, developing, and distributing for Glass. But none of this compares to having step-by-step tutorials with working code examples on every major Glass development topic, using both GDK and the Mirror API. That is exactly what this book is provides.

What's in This Book

There are ten chapters in this book, covering every major Glass development topic.

Chapter 1, "Getting Started": In this chapter, I'll discuss several general topics about Glass and Glassware: Why Glass? What is Glass and Glassware? What can you do with GDK Glassware and Mirror Glassware? Why this book? Who is the book for? I'll also list popular Glass development web resources.

Chapter 2, "Hello, Glass! Your First GDK App": I'll first cover the detailed steps of how to set up your GDK Glassware development environments, whether your favorite is Mac, Windows, or Linux. Then I'll discuss how to set up Glass to get it ready for development and how to run sample GDK apps on it. Finally, I'll introduce the generic template Glassware, which you'll use to create new GDK apps, and show you a step-by-step tutorial of building HelloGlass, your first GDK app, with nice features such as menu actions, text-to-speech, and speech-recognition versions of HelloGlass.

Chapter 3, "Glass User Interface": In this chapter, you'll enter the exciting world of Glass and learn what kinds of UI elements can be built with GDK for a Glass app. The main Glass UI elements—the timeline, Glass-styled cards, live cards, immersions, menu items, and gestures—will be discussed in detail with fully tested sample code that shows you how to render standard UI content, content from an XML layout, and content created using Android's Canvas 2D and OpenGL ES 1.0 and 2.0. By end of this chapter, you'll have a basic understanding of what kinds of apps you can build with GDK and when to use which or a combination of them.

Chapter 4, "Camera and Image Processing": In this chapter, you'll start with how to use the Glass camera to take pictures, both in the easy way and in the custom way, which allows you to preview and zoom before taking a picture. Then I'll briefly cover how to browse the photos in any directory of your Glass. After that, I'll discuss step-by-step many common practical image-processing tasks, including barcode and QR code recognition, OCR, image web search, and OpenCV. I'll cover how to integrate the best open source libraries out there, if needed, to your own app and how to call their APIs from within your app. By the end of this chapter, you'll be well prepared for exploring your own great app ideas using all kinds of image-processing techniques.

Chapter 5, "Video: Basics and Applications": In this chapter, you'll start with the basic video capture and custom video capture with preview and then look at how video can play on Glass. Then I'll discuss how to use OpenCV to add image effects on frames extracted from video. A more powerful video-processing library, FFmpeg, will be introduced with detailed instructions of how to integrate it with your own app. Commands for various video filtering effects will be presented. Finally, a YouTube video search and play app will be covered in detail, which can be used as the foundation of a full-fledged karaoke app.

Chapter 6, "Voice and Audio": In this chapter, I'll cover a lot of voice- and audio-related topics, from the standard Glass voice input, both high-level and low-level audio capture and playback, to various audio-processing examples, including musical note detection, DTMF touchtone detection, and, finally, song identification. Voice and audio are essential parts of our communication with each other and with devices, so you can expect to see many innovative apps in this area, developed by people like you.

Chapter 7, "Networking, Bluetooth, and Social": In this chapter, I'll first cover how to implement the basic HTTP GET, POST, and file uploading operations using the recommended HttpURLConnection class. Then I'll discuss how to accomplish low-level socket programming and let Glass talk with another Android or iOS device for data exchange, both as a client and as a server. After that, I'll illustrate in detail how to use Classic Bluetooth for communication between Glass and another Android device, without the need of wi-fi. I'll then introduce the exciting topic of BLE support and how to let Glass act as a BLE client and also how to use the Samsung Galaxy S4 smartphone or an iOS device as a bridge between Glass and BLE devices. Finally, I'll show you how to use Apple's push technology to let you share your new picture taken on Glass with your WhatsApp or WeChat friends in seconds.

Chapter 8, "Location, Map, and Sensors": In this chapter, I'll discuss in detail how to get your current location and show its address and map, how to zoom in and out the map, and how to find nearby business information based on your location information. Then I'll cover the eight sensors Glass supports and how to detect head movement and direction, how to detect Glass shake, how to develop a metal detector, and how to add the compass support easily to your app. Finally, I'll outline the steps to build a planet-finder Glass app.

Chapter 9, "Graphics, Animation, and Games": In this chapter, I'll cover common graphics and animation APIs and show many demos running on Glass, which you can use in your own simple Glass apps. Then I'll discuss in great detail how to set up and run three popular open source game engines (Cocos2d-x, libgdx, and AndEngine) on Glass. You'll learn how to run and interact with many examples for the three game engines, as well as how to create new apps using the engines. Finally, you'll learn how to use the Glass rotation vector sensor to control your game with head movement. By the end of this chapter, you'll be well armed with these powerful tools before you continue your own exciting game development journey.

Chapter 10, "The Mirror API": In this chapter, I'll discuss in detail how to set up your environment for Mirror API app development and how to deploy the Glass Mirror API quick-start PHP project to your own server and the Java project to Google App Engine. Then I'll go through the main building blocks of the Mirror API in detail with many examples, including timeline and static cards, contacts, subscriptions, and locations. I'll also show you how to build a hybrid app launching the GDK app from the Mirror app and pass information from the Mirror app to the GDK app if needed. You'll also reuse the Java image-uploading code from Chapter 7 in your Mirror app to upload a picture to a server for further processing. Finally, I'll demonstrate a complete Mirror API app that lets you view and search for any player in the 16 NBA playoff teams.

Before Getting Started

I actually wrote this Introduction after I finished writing the book. It took me about six long months of weekday evenings and weekends to learn and get up to speed on the GDK and Mirror API, to develop and test dozens of examples that illustrate what Glass can truly do (as summarized in the previous section), to write step-by-step tutorials on how to run and use the examples, and to review and fix any known issues.

No matter what your background and interests are, there should be some examples in the wide range of Glass development topics covered in the book that will inspire you and help you have a quick start on developing your own great Glass apps. I hope the hundreds of hours I spent on the book will save you a lot of time when developing for the exciting Glass platform.

Have a wonderful trip in the Glass development world! If you have any questions or comments on the trip, just email me anytime at `jeff.x.tang@gmail.com`, and you'll receive my response within 24 hours.

Getting Started

Welcome to the exciting new world of Google Glass! If you are reading this book, either you are most likely a Google Glass owner or you do not own Glass yet but are intrigued by it. Chances are that you are a mobile, web, or enterprise application developer looking for the next big thing and platform and trying to understand what great apps can be built on the new Glass platform. Or maybe you just want to understand the potential of Glass and see what Glass can truly do.

Before you start the journey of Glass development, let's first discuss some big questions in this chapter: Why Glass? What is Glass and Glassware? What can Glass do? What kinds of Glassware can you develop? I'll also cover Google's Glassware Policies and resources for Glass development at the end of this chapter.

Why Glass

The first generation of iPhone was released in June 2007, and Apple's App Store was launched a year later. Android Market (renamed to Google Play later) was released in October 2008. It is absolutely amazing how many successful apps and companies have been built on and for the iOS and Android platforms.

Could Google Glass be the next big thing, in terms of mobile computing platform? Nobody knows for sure. But the attention that Glass has garnered in 2013 and 2014 is bigger than any other mobile products except iPhone or iPad, so here are several questions to ask yourself:

- What if it becomes a big thing and everyone seems to wear their Google Glasses in a few years like they use their iPhones or Android phones now? You probably don't want to miss the opportunity to jump on Glass and at least learn what it takes to build apps for it. The year 2014 is definitely a great time to experiment, if you missed 2013.

- Can you imagine the use of Glass in cases where smartphones are not appropriate or convenient, especially where hands-free devices are required or when the moment would be over if you had to take the time to reach for your smartphone to take a picture or video? Or imagine you need to access some quick information or have answers to some quick questions while your hands are busy with, for example, cooking, fixing something, playing with your kids, washing your pets, playing cards, or even doing a surgery.

- How do others bet on Glass? You can do lots of research on the Internet and see how many new search results for *Google Glass* come up every day. You may also want to check out `http://glasscollective.com` to find out how some of the most visionary Silicon Valley investors back up the Glass development. Mary Meeker, "Queen of the Net," predicted in her 2013 Internet Trends Report that "Wearable computing is emerging as the type of significant technology shift that will drive innovation in the way personal computing did in the 1980s or mobile computing and tablets are doing currently." Forrester Research, one of the leading technology and market research companies, also noted that Google Glass could be the next big thing and estimated that up to 21.6 million Americans would be willing to wear Glass daily if it were available in stores right now.

> **Note** You may want to create an alert with the query *google glass* at `www.google.com/alerts` to get daily e-mail updates when there are any new search results for that query. As of May 2014, there are many exciting new results every day. Also, you can check out the web sites for the Glass community and developers detailed in the "Resources" section later in this chapter.

So, if you want to bet on Glass yourself and plan to learn about Glass development, this book is right for you! My goal is to reduce your learning curve as much as possible by providing clear and concise tutorials with fully tested samples for every topic in Glass development.

What Is Glass and Glassware?

Glass is a new, potentially paradigm-shifting mobile computing platform, or wearable computer, developed by Google. Glassware is the term for the apps that developers build to run on Glass.

According to the Wikipedia page at `http://en.wikipedia.org/wiki/Google_Glass`, Glass began testing in April 2012 and was further demonstrated by Google founder Sergery Brin in June 2012 at Google I/O that year, where attendees were invited to the Glass Explorer Program. Glass was first available to testers and developers in early 2013 through the program; people who were interested in buying the device for $1,500 were required to tweet a message using #ifihadglass specifying how they intended to use Glass if they had it. The people who were selected by Google and went to buy Glass are called the *Glass Explorers*. In October 2013, those first explorers received e-mails from Google saying they could invite up to three people to join the Glass Explorer Program. The invited people would then receive an e-mail from Google with information on how to order Glass and become new explorers. Weeks after that, the new explorers also received an e-mail from Google stating that they could invite up to three more people. People can also go to the Glass web site and register their e-mails to request Glass from Google.

On April 15, 2014, Google made the Glass Explorer Edition publicly available for purchase, but only for that day. By the next day, all five Glass models (Charcoal, Tangerine, Cotton, Shale, and Sky) sold out. In May 2014, anyone can become a Glass Explorer by purchasing the Glass Explorer Edition at `http://www.google.com/glass`. With the anticipated consumer version release date coming in late 2014, it should become cheaper for developers and others to get Glass.

In case you don't have Glass yet, just search for *google glass* at `http://images.google.com` to see how it looks. Glass keeps getting updated, so for an update of how it looks, you should check out `www.google.com/glass/start/how-it-looks/`.

To effectively use Glass and develop apps, you need to understand the *timeline*, which is the Glass user interface with which the user interacts with Glass. You should definitely check out `https://developers.google.com/glass/design/ui` to get a general idea of how the timeline works.

Here's a quick overview of how you use Glass: After your Glass is turned on, you can either tap the glass or tilt your head up to go to the home screen, also called the *OK Glass* screen, where you see the words *ok glass* with the current time. There you can either tap Glass again or say "OK Glass" to enter the voice menu, which includes the actions Google, Take Picture, Record Video, Get Directions, Message, Video Call, Take Note, and other Glassware you have added. If you don't tap or speak to enter the OK Glass menu, you can swipe Glass forward or backward on the touchpad to see the timeline cards, and on each card, you can tap to see its specific menu actions. You may also want to check out Google's video of the basics of how to use Glass at `www.youtube.com/watch?v=4EvNxWhskf8`.

> **Note**   The order of the voice menu actions after entering the OK Glass screen for the Glass XE 16 update (released on April 15, 2014) and later is different from that for the Glass XE 12 update (released in December 2013). XE 16 or 17 sorts the menu actions by use frequency and recency, while XE 12 and older show the actions always in the same order.

Before late November 2013, there was only one official way to develop Glassware: the Mirror API way. Basically, you build web-based services that talk to Google's cloud API, which in turn talks to Glass. Glassware built with the Mirror API can send updated information to Glass, subscribe to notifications of when users take actions on your updated information or when their location changes, and let users share information with others or other Glassware.

While the Mirror API was the only official way to develop Glassware before November 2013, since Glass is based on Android (some people think of Glass as just another Android device), early Glass developers actually were able to develop and test native Android-based Glass apps—with a little hack, of course. You'll see in some projects of this book that this hacky sprit will continue to solve some hard problems. After all, we're called Glass Explorers, and we're supposed to do something officially not quite ready.

It was not until the release of the Glass Development Kit (GDK) Sneak Peak Rev. 1 on November 20, 2013, that the power to developers was officially presented. The GDK is built on top of Android, with rich and fuller user interaction that, unlike the Mirror API, does not always require network connectivity. Imagine that you can run OpenCV, a popular and powerful open source image processing library, or optical character recognition (OCR) completely in your Glass. You can also have access to low-level Glass hardware with the GDK. Unlike the Glassware built with the Mirror API, which runs on a server, the GDK Glassware runs natively on Glass. This book is mainly focused on the GDK but will also cover the Mirror API and how it can interact with the GDK in a complete but quick way.

> **Note**   The GDK Sneak Peak was based on Android 4.0.3 (API Level 15). On April 15, 2014, the next major GDK update, called the Glass Development Kit Preview, based on the latest Android 4.4.2, was released. This massive version bump means a lot to developers because they can now use APIs available for Android API Levels 15 up to 19. For example, the important Bluetooth Low Energy APIs were introduced in Android 4.3 (API Level 18), so they were not available with the GDK Sneak Peak (Android 4.0.3, API Level 15) but are available now with the GDK Preview (Android 4.4.2, API Level 19).

What Can Glass Do?

There are a lot of things Glass already can do and some other things you may not even know it can do.

Feature-wise, Glass offers the following built-in features:

- Take a picture, in one of three ways: with a voice command, the press of a button, or a wink of your right eye
- Record video hands-free and send live streaming video to others of what you're seeing
- Activate speech recognition, speech synthesis, and voice dictation
- Perform a Google search using voice
- Connect to your Android or iOS device via Bluetooth to get location updates and directions
- Browse text, image, and video content, as well as share them with others via wi-fi
- Seamlessly integrate with Gmail, Google Now, and Google+
- Install Glassware developed in the Mirror API or GDK

Application-wise, you can use Glass to accomplish tasks such as the following:

- Get updated text, photo, or video from Glassware such as from YouTube, Facebook, Twitter, Evernote, Path, CNN, and the New York Times sites
- Share and upload notes, photos, and videos on Facebook, Path, and Evernote

- Play innovative games unique to Glass (check out the samples at
https://developers.google.com/glass/samples/mini-games);

- Find and submit favorite recipes

- Translate printed words you see on Glass to many other languages

For a complete list of active Glassware available for you to install on Glass, visit
https://glass.google.com/u/0/myglass.

From a developer's perspective, you can build all kinds of apps for Glass with the GDK and the
Mirror API, such as the following:

- Interactive voice apps with Android's speech recognition and synthesis APIs

- Image- or video-processing apps using the OpenCV, barcode, OCR, and
FFmpeg libraries

- Audio- and voice-processing apps for pitch, touchtone, or song recognitions

- HTTP, socket, and both Bluetooth Classic and Bluetooth Low-Energy
communication apps

- Location-based services with the Location APIs, with support for both a network
location provider, which uses cell tower and wi-fi signals to determine user
location, and a full-blown GPS provider, which requires you to pair Glass with a
smartphone or tablet with the MyGlass app installed

- Apps taking advantage of low-level hardware and sensors, including the
accelerometer, gravity, gyroscope, magnetic field, light, orientation, and
rotation vector

- Graphics, animation, and game apps with Canvas 2D and OpenGL ES drawing,
and game engines such as Cocos2d-x, libgdx, and AndEngine

- Apps that send updated information to users and let users share text, image,
or video to your own Glassware or other social apps

- Enterprise apps in sports, education, healthcare, and many other fields

You'll see lots of working sample code related to the previously mentioned apps throughout the
book, and depending on whether you're an end user or a developer, you can either install and use
the apps developed in the book or make further improvement and use them in your own apps.

Finally, here are some important quick tech specs on Glass:

- 5MP photos and 720p videos

- 12GB of usable memory, 16GB flash total

- 682MB RAM available for development, 1GB total

- Wi-fi and Bluetooth connectivity

- Android 4.4.2 (API Level 19), as of June 8, 2014

You should visit https://support.google.com/glass/answer/3064128?hl=en for the complete tech
specs and https://developers.google.com/glass/release-notes for the detailed release notes.

What Kinds of Glassware Can You Develop?

Before November 2013, the only official way to develop Glassware was using the web-based Mirror API. In November 2013, Google officially released the native Glass Development Kit.

Mirror API–Based Glassware

Mirror API–based Glassware consists of web-based services developed with the Mirror API. You can use many programming languages—on Google's web site (`https://developers.google.com/glass/samples/mirror`) , sample start projects in Java, PHP, Python, Ruby, .NET, and Go are provided—to develop such web services to interact with the Mirror API running on Google's server, which further interacts with your Glass on behalf of your Glassware. Figure 1-1 illustrates these interactions.

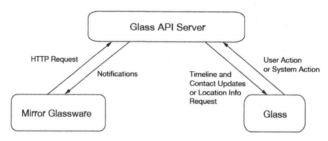

Figure 1-1. Interactions between your Mirror API–based Glassware, Google Mirror APIs, and Glass

Before the GDK, the timeline consisted of only static cards; the other type of cards are *live cards* and will be covered in the next section. Cards are the core of the Glass user experience. The size of each card, static or live, is 640 pixels in width and 360 pixels in height. Static cards can display text, images, videos, and HTML content.

Actions that can be completed on timeline cards include creating, updating, deleting, getting, listing, and patching. You can also associate menu items with timeline cards to let users perform built-in actions and/or your app-specific actions.

Timeline cards can also be shared with another person or Glassware. This is accomplished via subscribing to timeline notifications (using the Mirror API, of course). After the subscription, whenever a user selects a menu item or shares a timeline card content, or there is any insertion, deletion, and update in the timeline, the Mirror API can send notifications to your Glassware via a callback URL (to your Glassware web service) specified in the subscription API call. This is called timeline notification.

The other type of notification is location; you can get users' location updates about every ten minutes after subscribing to the notification. You may also request for the location information for a specific timeline card or attach a location and menu item to a timeline card so the user can navigate to it when choosing the menu item.

One powerful feature of the Mirror API is that you can launch native GDK apps from a static card.

That is all you can do with the Mirror API. On one hand, you can build amazing services with the building blocks offered by the Mirror API. Here are some examples:

- The Mirror API–based Glassware Facebook, Twitter, Evernote, and Path allow you to easily share a picture or video (in the case of Evernote, you can also create a new note with voice dictation and upload it to your Evernote account handily). If you're a developer of a web site that allows people to upload photos or videos, you can develop a Mirror API–based Glassware to let users easily share their Glass pictures or videos to your site too.

- The Path Glassware can send you a new timeline card when there's a new picture or video uploaded by your Path friends. You can then choose an action on the item: Love, Smile, Laugh, Surprise, Frown, Comment, or Get Directions. Imagine a Mirror Glassware that uses the similar interaction: Send to the user's Glass some interesting content, get notified by the user's action on the content, and keep the fun and engaging interaction going!

- Face recognition seems to be a hot and natural topic for Glass. Basically, a picture of someone taken with the Glass camera is sent to a server to search for Facebook, Twitter, Google+, LinkedIn, and Instagram profiles (or even profiles of hundreds of thousands of sex offenders). If a match is found, the person's name and other profile information can be sent back to Glass. Although Google specifically forbids the development of face recognition Glassware (see the section "Google's Glassware Policies" for details), this policy could change under certain circumstances. Or, it's not hard to imagine other types of computer vision–based services. For example, how about recognition of all kinds of interesting physical objects, such as plants, animals, or architecture?

- The Mirror API Playground (`https://developers.google.com/glass/tools-downloads/playground`) shows a list of elegantly designed static card templates that you can easily use in your Mirror API apps. Those beautiful templates can also inspire you to see what kinds of apps can be built with the Mirror API.

On the other hand, there is some serious limitation of the Mirror API in terms of what kinds of Glassware you can build with it: The timeline cards created via the Mirror API can't access the camera, sensors, and other low-level hardware, and an online web server and always-on network connectivity are required for most of the application features. Enter the more sophisticated world of GDK Glassware.

GDK Glassware

The GDK is an Android SDK add-on that you can use to build powerful Glassware that runs directly on Glass. (Remember, the Mirror API–based Glassware runs on your own web server and interacts indirectly with your Glass via Google's API server.)

Most of the Android APIs and Java language features can be used directly in Glass, which grants your GDK Glassware great power. For example, Android's APIs for speech recognition, text-to-speech, hardware sensors, Bluetooth, media controller, location, and JNI and Java's networking and threading features can all be used directly in your GDK Glassware. A word of caution, though: Some Android APIs running on Glass will return different results because Glass, as an Android-based device, has its own unique hardware support. All the details that can save you time will be covered in the later chapters. Here I'll present a quick overview of the GDK APIs.

As described in the previous section, the timeline and timeline cards are the key elements of the Glass user experience. The following building blocks are what's unique in the GDK and not available in the Mirror API:

- *Live cards*: Unlike static cards that display information relevant to the user at the time of delivery and do not require immediate user attention, live cards display information that is relevant to the user at the current time and require immediate user attention. Also, live cards can access the low-level hardware such sensors, GPS, and 3D graphics.

- *Immersions*: These are created using Android activities when Glassware requires more custom and interactive user interfaces than a timeline live or static card offers. Games and sophisticated apps can be created using immersions.

- *Voice input and output*: There are two official ways to let your GDK Glassware accept voice input: from the OK Glass voice menu or from any activity within your Glassware that launches the Android's RecognizerIntent. Text-to-speech can also be accomplished in any Glassware using Android's TextToSpeech class. Both speech recognition and synthesis can be done in offline mode, which can be quite useful for some Glassware.

- *Sensors*: Glass supports most of the common sensors such as the accelerometer, gravity, gyroscope, and magnetic field. Innovative apps such as games shown at https://developers.google.com/glass/samples/mini-games can be built using these sensors and Android's APIs.

- *Camera*: Image or video can be captured, accessed, and processed locally in Glassware. This makes offline OCR, computer vision (using the OpenCV Android library), and image processing possible.

- *Network and Bluetooth connectivity*: Low-level socket programming can be used for developing advanced networking apps; both Bluetooth Classic and Bluetooth Low-Energy can be used to connect with other smart devices.

- *Graphics and animations*: Canvas 2D and OpenGL ES 2D and 3D graphics and all kinds of animations and game engines can be used to build apps.

By exposing the Glass API as an add-on to the Android API, the GDK no doubt has opened up limitless opportunities for developers to build innovative Glassware.

When to Use Which

This is similar to a question that arises when building mobile apps: Do you use the native APIs or the web-based solution? GDK allows you to access Glass's hardware and develop advanced features available for offline use and with rich user interaction. But the learning curve is also steeper, especially if you don't have Android development experience. The Mirror API uses Glass's built-in functionality and can be developed with many common web development languages, but you need a web server running for the Mirror API, and there's a courtesy limit of 1,000 requests per day per app for using the Mirror API.

If your app is mainly information-oriented and does not require an advanced user interface or if a server is required for content updates or data processing, then the Mirror API is more appropriate. If your app requires low-level hardware access or offline processing or rich user interaction or the user input data can be processed in the Glass itself, then the GDK is the right choice.

In some cases, you may want to build a hybrid app that uses both the Mirror API and the GDK. This is made possible because the static timeline card inserted by your Mirror API–based Glassware can invoke the GDK Glassware with a menu item associated with the card. I'll show you a sample project that does this in Chapter 10.

You can also find a good summary on when to use each one at Glass's developer site: `https://developers.google.com/glass/develop/overview`.

Google's Glassware Policies

Understanding Google's policies on Glass development can be important because as a developer, you need to know what you can and can't do; you don't want to spend lots of time developing an app such as facial recognition but find out later that it's against Google's policy. Here is a brief summary of the Google's Glassware policies that are most likely related to your development effort:

- You can't use the camera or microphone to present personal information identifying anyone other than the Glass user. This means Glassware that does Facebook or Twitter profile searching based on facial recognition and voice print will not be approved by Google.

- Don't disable or turn off the display when using the camera to take a picture or record a video.

- Don't develop Glassware with content or services that facilitate online gambling, such as online casinos, sports betting, and lotteries.

- You may not charge end users any fees or collect any payments or virtual goods to use your Glassware. This can be a little demotivating to developers. But if you think of the history of Apple's App Store, for the first year after the release of the iPhone, the SDK was not even available. With Glass, the Mirror API and the GDK were available even before the public release of Glass. This shows how important a role Google thinks developers will play in the success of Glass. One way or another, Google will figure out something that makes developers' investment in time and effort worthwhile.

There are a lot of other details in terms of Glassware policies. You should check Google Glass's web site for any updates because the policies may be revised now and then.

Why This Book?

The goal of this book is to help developers jump-start the Glass development, no matter what their backgrounds are or whether they already own the Glass. I still remember in the first months of my learning iPhone programming, I was not aware of the book *Beginning iPhone Development: Exploring the iPhone SDK,* which is full of working code and step-by-step tutorials, so the learning curve with online documentation and samples with no clear tutorial-like explanations was pretty steep for me. When I first came across the book months later, I still remember my reaction: How I had wished I could have had the book the moment I started iPhone programming; it'd have saved me a lot of time.

The moral of the story is more than just "Be aware." I'm trying to do the same thing in this book for those interested in Glass development: to help save a lot of your time and to provide you with lots of working code with clear explanations on every Glass development topic.

Who Is This Book For?

The book is mainly for mobile Android/iOS and web app developers, but other developers such as enterprise app developers can also easily follow the step-by-step tutorials and get up to speed quickly. However, I do assume you are familiar with some modern programming language.

In his book *Social Psychology*, David Myers, one of my favorite authors, stated, "I continue to envision this text as solidly scientific and warmly human, factually rigorous and intellectually provocative." It may seem interesting that in this book for developers, I try to achieve the exact same goal. Glass is an amazing device built with solid and sophisticated technology; all the topics related to the Glass development need to be presented accurately and be "factually rigorous." On the other hand, what really amazes me about Glass is that it can touch our human feelings by never missing a precious moment and by letting us feel Glassware is especially designed for us human. Check out the Glass design principles at `https://developers.google.com/glass/design/principles` and you'll see how Glass and great Glassware can touch us at a deep level. I hope you'll find that this book provides plenty of "intellectually provocative" samples and projects to inspire you.

For Beginning Android Developers

Most of this book requires you to be comfortable with Android, which is what the GDK and Glass are built upon. A good book to help you on that is *Pro Android 4* by Satya Komatineni and Dave MacLean, published by Apress. The Android developer site also has great Training lessons (`http://developer.android.com/training/index.html`) that cover every major Android development topic.

Fully tested working sample code is included in step-by-step tutorials in each chapter for you to quickly learn every topic related to the GDK and the Mirror API.

For Intermediate or Advanced Android Developers

Advanced sample code with potential for real-world apps is also covered extensively in the book for you to apply as easily as possible to your own real projects.

For iOS Developers

If you are entering the Glassware development world as an iOS developer, you'll be glad to find a unique treat in Chapter 7, Networking, Bluetooth and Social: I'll show you how Glassware can be integrated with iOS apps to create more innovative apps.

For Web Developers

If you want to use only the Mirror API to develop your Glassware, you can go to Chapter 10 directly. The code examples there are mainly in PHP and Java, but you should be able to easily understand them and port them to your familiar web programming language. It is true that even with just the Mirror API, you can develop practical and innovative Glassware (see the "What Kinds of Glassware Can You Develop?" section earlier in this chapter). After you become familiar with Java and Android, you can come back to learn how to develop GDK Glassware and hybrid apps.

For Other Programmers

If you don't know how to program in Java (for the GDK or the Mirror API) or PHP (for the Mirror API), you should be able to learn the basics of it quickly online or from Apress books such as *Learn Java for Android Development* by Jeff Friesen or *Beginning PHP and MySQL* by Jason Gilmore. Before you do that, however, you may want to be strongly motivated by skimming through the book quickly to see what kind of Glassware you can develop and what it takes to build amazing Glassware.

For Nonprogrammers

Glass has been considered a paradigm-shifting mobile computing platform with great business potential. Naturally, if you're a nontechnical entrepreneur with, for example, a design or business background, you'll also want to know what is possible with Glass. You can take a quick look at the many examples in the book, get inspired, and be better prepared when teaming up with a developer to build your own Glass-based startup. If you want to test some cool GDK Glassware without having to let the developer physically access your Glass, you can also learn how to install all the apps developed in the book on your Glass.

Resources

1. Google's Glass Developers' site at `https://developers.google.com/glass` obviously has the most authoritative documentation on Glass development, with API references, quick starts, developer guides, samples, and design best practices. You should definitely check it out regularly. But what's missing there—the how-to recipes for common problems, the detailed tutorials on each complicated topic, and fully implemented and tested working code—is what this book is about.

2. `http://stackoverflow.com/questions/tagged/google-glass` and `http://stackoverflow.com/questions/tagged/google-gdk` have lots of questions and answers on common Glass development issues.

3. The Glass GDK and Mirror API Bug Reports and Feature Requests site is at `https://code.google.com/p/google-glass-api/`.

4. The Glass Explorers Community on Google+ is at `www.glass-community.com/`.

5. The Glass Developers Community on Google is at `https://developers.google.com/glass/community`.

Questions and Feedback

I always love to hear from readers. If you have any questions or feedback, please send me an e-mail at jeff@morkout.com or connect with me on Google+ with jeff.x.tang@gmail.com.

Summary

This chapter discussed several general topics about Glass and Glassware: Why Glass? What is Glass and Glassware? What can you do with GDK Glassware and Mirror Glassware? Why this book? Who is the book for? I hope by now you are eager to start the exciting Glass development journey ahead, no matter what your development background is. In Chapter 2, I'll show you how to get your development environment set up and your first GDK Glassware up and running in no time.

Hello, Glass! Your First GDK App

In this chapter, I'll first discuss how to set up your environment for GDK development, whether you use Mac, Linux, or Windows. I'll then show you how to get your Glass ready for development, how to use the Android command-line tool adb to perform common operations on Glass, and how to run GDK samples on Glass. After that, I'll walk you through a complete tutorial of the GDK app template and how to use it to quickly create your first GDK app. You will use the template in most of the following chapters to create all the new GDK apps.

Setting Up the Development Environment

In this section, I'll discuss the system requirements for Glass development and how to install the Android Developer Tools (ADT) Bundle, which includes Eclipse + ADT plugin, Android SDK tools and platform tools. If you already have an Android development environment up and running, you can skip this section.

System Requirements

You can develop GDK Glassware with the ADT or Eclipse IDE on a computer running Windows, Mac, or Linux with the following requirements (see http://developer.android.com/sdk/index.html for more details):

- Intel-based Mac OS X 10.5.8 or newer
- Windows XP (32-bit), Vista (32/64-bit), or Windows 7 (32/64-bit) or newer
- Linux (preferably Ubuntu Linux 8.04 or newer)

Android Developer Tools

The ADT Bundle is Google's recommended tool for developing Android and GDK apps quickly. If you're an experienced developer, you should be able to follow the instructions at `http://developer.android.com/sdk` and get it installed in less than an hour. If you experience any issues and can't find the right answers on Google, you can refer to the following steps.

ADT on Mac

After you download the ADT bundle for Mac from `http://developer.android.com/sdk`, unzip it, and you'll see two subfolders, as shown in Figure 2-1.

Figure 2-1. *File structure of ADT on Mac*

Eclipse.app is the IDE you'll use to develop all your GDK Glassware. Simply double-click it to launch the app. You may need to update the ADT plug-in to successfully import the template project later in the chapter; you can select Help ➤ Check for Updates or Install New Software in Eclipse/ADT and then add `https://dl-ssl.google.com/android/eclipse/` to update the ADT plug-in.

ADT on Windows

Follow these steps to install and set up ADT on Windows:

1. Download the ADT bundle for Windows at `http://developer.android.com/sdk`.

2. Unzip the downloaded file. The unzipped ADT bundle folder on Windows also has two subfolders, `eclipse` and `sdk`, with similar files in them as on Mac. There is an additional `SDK Manager.exe` file in the unzipped ADT folder on Windows. The first time you run `eclipse.exe` in ADT's `eclipse` folder, you may see a dialog box like the one shown in Figure 2-2.

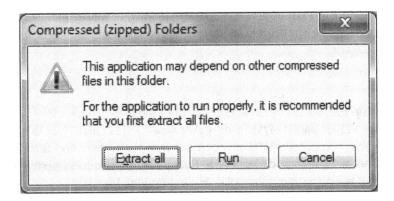

Figure 2-2. Setting up Eclipse ADT on Windows

If you see this dialog box, just click "Extract all." This may take about 30 minutes and more than 1GB to uncompress all the files. After that, you can just double-click the `eclipse.exe` file again to start the IDE. If you don't have the JRE or JDK installed on your computer, you'll see message similar to Figure 2-3. (Note that on March 21, 2014, "20131030" in the `adt` package name was upgraded to "20140321," which may be changed again by the time you're reading the book.)

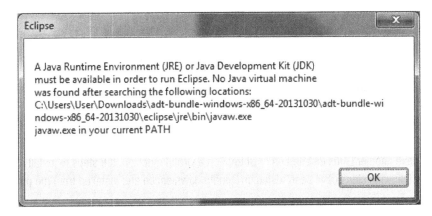

Figure 2-3. Installing JRE or JDK for Eclipse to start on Windows

3. If you see message shown in Figure 2-3, you need to go to Oracle's web site at www.oracle.com/technetwork/java/javase/downloads to download the JDK (you don't need to download the JDK; the JRE is enough to work with ADT). Remember to click the download link for Windows x86 if your Windows is 32-bit or the download link for Windows x64 if your Windows is 64-bit. You may have to register with Oracle or log in to be able to download it.

> **Note**   Although http://developer.android.com/sdk/index.html says that "JRE alone is not sufficient," in my test on a clean Windows machine with no JDK or JRE installed, I found that you don't have to download the JDK; JRE 6 or 7 is enough to work with ADT. This may be a little surprising, but the Eclipse message in Figure 2-3 does suggest that the JRE may be good enough. Also, the latest JDK/JRE 8 should work, but I haven't tested it.

4. Run the setup EXE file and then add the path to the JRE bin directory (C:\Program Files\Java\jre7\bin or C:\Program Files\Java\jre6\bin by default) to your computer's PATH environment variable by selecting Start ➤ Control Panel ➤ System and Security ➤ System ➤ Advanced system settings ➤ Advanced ➤ Environment Variables ➤ System Variables.

5. Run eclipse.exe again, and you should see the ADT IDE up and running!

> **Note**   If you accidently downloaded the 32-bit JRE EXE (all those x86 ones) for your 64-bit Windows, or vice versa, you may see an error message "Failed to load the JNI shared library 'C:\Program Files (x86)\Java\jre6\client\jvm.dll.'" You can fix this by downloading and installing the right JRE for your Windows version.

ADT on Linux

If you have a Windows PC but prefer to run Ubuntu Linux, you can download the Ubuntu Windows installer at www.ubuntu.com/download/desktop/windows-installer and follow the installation steps at www.ubuntu.com/download/desktop/install-ubuntu-with-windows. After the installation is completed, simply restart and boot your computer to Ubuntu.

> **Note**   If you have another Linux distribution or Ubuntu on a virtual machine, the steps to install ADT should be similar. The following steps have been tested on Ubuntu downloaded and installed from the previous URLs.

The steps to install and set up ADT on Ubuntu Linux are as follows:

1. Download the ADT bundle called `Linux 64-bit adt-bundle-linux-x86_64-20140321.zip` or the latest ADT bundle at `http://developer.android.com/sdk` under Download for Other Platforms. (Notice that the browser on your Ubuntu distribution may automatically detect that you're using Linux and therefore show a Download the SDK button.)

2. Download the JRE for Linux x64 file, named `jre-7u45-linux-x64.tar.gz`, at `www.oracle.com/technetwork/java/javase/downloads/jre7-downloads-1880261.html`.

3. Uncompress both archives and move the `jre-7u45-linux-x64` folder to the `eclipse` directory of the ADT folder; you should see something like Figure 2-4. (I renamed the `jre-7u45-linux-x64` folder to `jre`. If you prefer, you can also leave the `jre-7u45-linux-x64` folder where it is and modify `eclipse.ini`; see `http://wiki.eclipse.org/FAQ_How_do_I_run_Eclipse%3F#eclipse.ini` for details.)

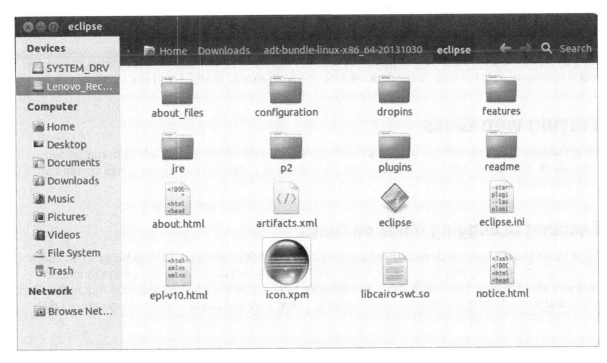

Figure 2-4. File structure of Eclipse ADT on Ubuntu Linux

4. Edit your `.bashrc` file in your home directory to update your PATH variable:

```
PATH=$PATH:<path-to-adt-folder>/eclipse/jre/bin
```

5. If you run the Eclipse program now and see the error message "./android: java: not found," you can fix it by running a command similar to this:

```
sudo ln -s <path-to-adt-folder>/eclipse/jre/bin/java /usr/bin/java
```

6. Another possible error message, "platform-tools/adb: No such file or directory," implies there is a missing shared library needed by adb (the powerful Android Debug Bridge command-line tool, which I'll discuss in more detail in the next section) and can be fixed by running this:

```
apt-get install ia32-libs
```

> **Note**   As you can tell, installing Oracle's JRE/JDK on Ubuntu is a nontrivial process. The earlier instructions have been tested on my Windows PC with Ubuntu Windows, but your environment may be different. For example, if you already have OpenJDK installed, then you can check out resources such as www.liberiangeek.net/2012/04/install-oracle-java-jdk-7-in-ubuntu-12-04-precise-pangolin. In other cases, Google should be your best friend for fixing installation-related issue.

Now that you have the ADT bundle (Eclipse plus the ADT plug-in) installed on your computer, you're ready to start having fun with Glass as a developer—well, almost ready, if you use Windows.

Playing with Glass

In this section, I'll cover how to use the powerful Android command-line tool adb to communicate with Glass, how to run GDK sample apps on your Glass, and, finally, how to see Glass screens on your computer.

Enabling Debugging Mode on Glass

To get your Glass ready for development purpose, you need first to enable USB debugging on Glass. After you turn on Glass and see the OK Glass menu, swipe your Glass backward on the touchpad until you see Settings; then, tap it and swipe forward to find "Device info," as shown in Figure 2-5. Tap again and swipe to find and select "Turn on debug." Now connect Glass to your computer via USB.

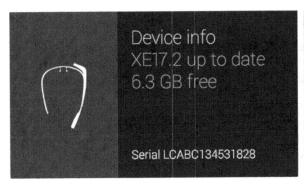

Figure 2-5. Tap "Device info" to find and select "Turn on debug" on Glass

The adb Command

Android Debug Bridge (adb) is a handy command-line tool that you'll use to communicate with Glass. Its main uses are listing connected Android devices (adb devices), browsing the device folders (adb shell), installing and uninstalling apps (adb install and adb uninstall), and copying files (adb pull and adb push). As a Glass developer, you should definitely check out its documentation at http://developer.android.com/tools/help/adb.html and get familiar with it.

Before you can run the adb command, you need to add the path to ADT's platform-tools directory to your system's PATH variable. If you use Windows, update the PATH variable at Start ➤ Control Panel ➤ System and Security ➤ System ➤ Advanced system settings ➤ Advanced ➤ Environment Variables ➤ System Variables. If you use Mac or Linux, update your PATH variable in ~/.bashrc to be like this:

```
PATH=$PATH:<path-to-adt-folder>/sdk/platform-tools
```

Now launch a terminal window on Mac or Linux, and run the following command; you'll see your Glass listed as shown here:

```
adb devices
List of devices attached
015xxxxxxxx17xxx device
```

Installing the USB Driver on Windows

Unfortunately on Windows, most likely you won't see any devices listed with the adb devices command. This is because if you're developing on Mac or Linux, you don't need to install a USB driver, but on Windows, you need to manually install the right USB driver. The steps are as follows:

1. Download the Google USB Driver package for Windows at http://developer.android.com/sdk/win-usb.html; you can either download the ZIP file at the URL directly or use ADT's Android SDK Manager and select the Google USB Driver package to download, as shown in Figure 2-6.

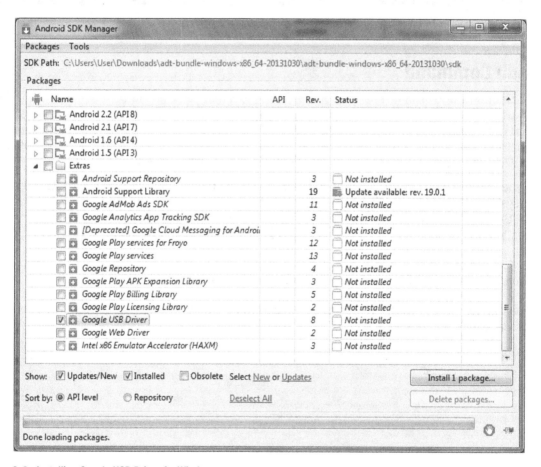

Figure 2-6. Installing Google USB Driver for Windows

2. Unzip the file to a location you choose and find the usb_driver folder; or if you use the Android SDK Manager to download the driver, you can find your auto-unzipped files in ADT's sdk\extras\google\usb_driver folder.

3. Double-click the `android_winusb.inf` file in the `usb_driver` folder and add the following lines to the [`Google.NTx86`] and [`Google.NTamd64`] sections:

```
;Google Glass
%SingleAdbInterface% = USB_Install, USB\VID_18D1&PID_9001&REV_0216
%CompositeAdbInterface% = USB_Install, USB\VID_18D1&PID_9001&MI_01
```

You may want to verify those seemingly magic values by these steps: Right-click Computer and select Manage. Then select Device Manager, and on the right panel under Other Devices, right-click Glass 1 and switch to the Details tab. Finally, select Hardware Ids Property; now you should see something like Figure 2-7 and Figure 2-8. (You need to make the previous code lines the same as the values in Figure 2-8.)

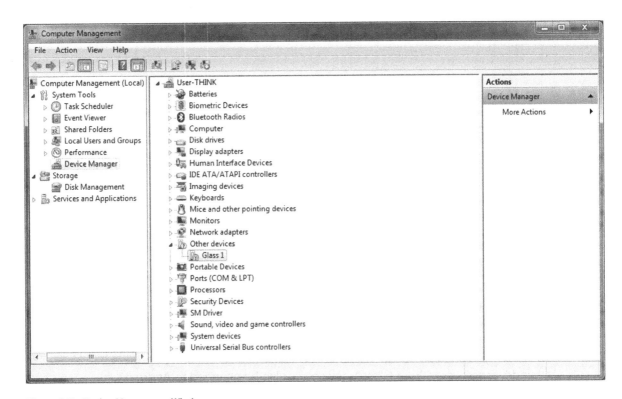

Figure 2-7. Device Manager on Windows

Figure 2-8. Values for Google Glass USB setup info file on Windows

4. Save the android_winusb.inf file, right-click Glass 1, and choose Update
    Driver Software ➤ Browse my computer for driver software. Choose the
    path to the usb_driver folder described in step 2 and dismiss the warning
    message; you should see the message "Windows has successfully updated
    your driver software." Your Glass1 device will also be changed to Android
    Composite ADB Interface.

Note   Steps 3 and 4 were tested on Windows 7. For Windows XP and Vista, you may want to check the
document at http://developer.android.com/tools/extras/oem-usb.html#InstallingDriver
for more details.

5. Open a command prompt window on Windows and run `adb devices` to verify your Glass is listed. You may have to run the command `adb kill-server` first and then `adb devices` to see your Glass listed. If you see a message saying "'adb' is not recognized as an internal or external commands," you should check your PATH variable as described earlier in "The adb Command."

Showing the Glass Screen on a Bigger Screen

You can use tools to show your Glass screen on your computer running Mac, Windows, or Linux. This can make your development easier because you can look at the bigger computer screen most of the time instead of the small Glass screen. It can also make your demo, presentation, or training sessions much easier.

Before you continue, you should verify that the adb command, discussed in the previous section, works fine and shows your Glass in the "List of devices attached" area or the following tools won't work.

There are at least two good tools to use here. You can download the latest Droid@Screen version at `http://droid-at-screen.ribomation.com/download` or Android Screen Monitor at `https://code.google.com/p/android-screen-monitor`. Droid@Screen has a better UI, but Android Screen Monitor has better frame rate. After downloading one of them (and unzipping it for Android Screen Manager), you can run one of the following commands to see on your computer something like Figure 2-9 and Figure 2-10:

```
java -jar droidAtScreen-1.0.2.jar
```

```
java -jar ASM_2_50/asm.jar
```

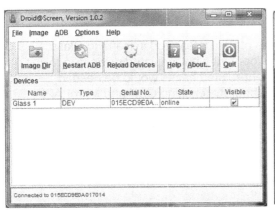

Figure 2-9. Glass screens on your computer

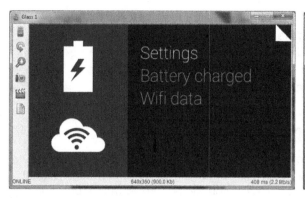 

Figure 2-10. More Glass screens on your computer

Another great way to see your Glass screen content on a bigger screen is to install the MyGlass app on any Android and iOS device (preferably tablets) and use its Screencast feature. There are two ways to activate Screencast: You can pair with Glass via Bluetooth and turn on Personal Hotspot, or you can connect Glass and your Android/iOS devices to the same wi-fi network.

Developing with Simulated Devices or Emulators

If you have some experience with Android or iOS app development, most likely you have used simulators to speed up your development. The bad news is that there is no official support from Google for the Glass development with emulators or Android devices; the good news is that because Glass is an Android device, theoretically you can just extract the `.apk` files from the system image of Glass and install them to your non-Glass Android. The web page `www.elekslabs.com/2013/11/google-glass-development-without-glass.html` is a summary but hasn't been updated for the GDK release as of May 2014.

Although there are some developers who don't own Glass but are interested in learning Glass development, I decided not to cover the GDK Glass development with simulated devices in this book for two main reasons. A lot of non-Glass-development-related hacks would be needed, and the time spent there can be better used for learning about the exciting GDK and Mirror API development. In addition, by the time you are reading this book, chances are Google will have made, or soon make, Glass publicly available at an acceptable price of several hundred dollars. Google will likely also release an official way to do Glass development on emulators or other Android devices.

Testing with GDK Samples

Finally, you're ready to see some samples working on Glass, whether you use Mac, Linux, or Windows. Compared to what it takes to get the development environment set up correctly, especially on Windows and Linux, and configure the Glass USB Driver package on Windows, testing the GDK samples is a lot easier. (After all, there's a balance in everything.) Whether you're an Android expert or beginner, just follow the well-documented GDK Quick Start instructions at https://developers.google.com/glass/develop/gdk/quick-start to install the Android 4.4.2 (API 19) SDK, the Glass Development Kit Preview add-on, and the three GDK samples (Compass, Stopwatch, and Timer).

After you select a sample from Eclipse to run as an Android app, if you have Glass connected to your computer via USB, you'll see your Glass shown as a running Android device, as in Figure 2-11.

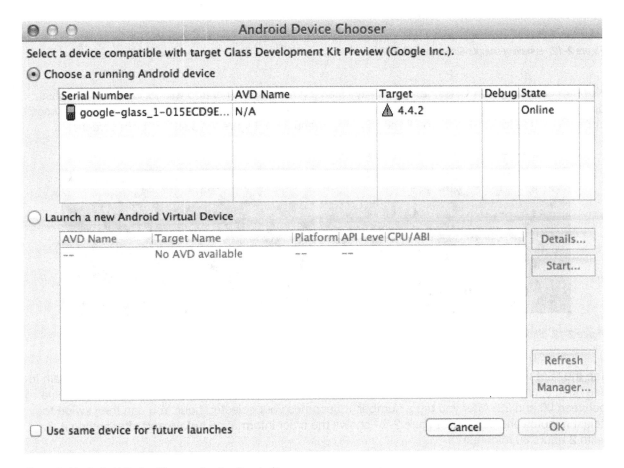

Figure 2-11. Android Device Chooser showing Google Glass

Select the google-glass_1-xxx device and click OK; you'll see the sample app gets installed to your Glass. Figure 2-12 shows the console output after running the Timer sample.

```
Console ⊠   LogCat   Search
Android
[2014-04-02 22:30:03 - Timer] Uploading Timer.apk onto device '015ECD9E0A017014'
[2014-04-02 22:30:03 - Timer] Installing Timer.apk...
[2014-04-02 22:30:07 - Timer] Success!
[2014-04-02 22:30:07 - Timer] /Timer/bin/Timer.apk installed on device
[2014-04-02 22:30:07 - Timer] Done!
```

Figure 2-12. Installing sample Glass app called Timer

Now tap Glass, say "OK Glass," and then say "Start a timer." The Timer app will get launched on Glass, displaying 00:00:00 for hour:minute:second. Tap the Glass touchpad, and the first menu item, "Set timer," appears. Swipe forward, and you'll see the Stop menu item. Figure 2-13 shows both screens.

Figure 2-13. Showing menu items for the Timer sample

Tap the "Set timer" menu item; you'll see the hours text with the first two 0s highlighted. Tap again to see 00 in a large font size centered in a new screen. You can swipe left and right to choose a value between 00 and 23. After you tap a number, it becomes your selected hour. You can then swipe to select minutes and seconds. Figure 2-14 shows the timer information before and after setting it (with 2 hours 30 minutes).

Figure 2-14. Before and after timer setting

Now swipe down on the touchpad, and you'll see the set timer 02:30:00; tap again, and this time a new menu item, Start, appears. Tap it, and you'll see the timer gets updated every second. Tapping one more time will show the new menu items Pause, Reset, Change time, and Stop. Figure 2-15 shows two of these menu items.

Figure 2-15. Timer in action with menu items

To play more with Glass, you can run the other two samples Compass and Stopwatch in the same way. You should also look into the samples' source code. If you're like me when I started to learn Glass GDK development, you probably hope there's a step-by-step tutorial on how to create such a GDK app. That is exactly what you'll get in the next section of this chapter.

The HelloGlass Glassware

In this section, I'll answer two important questions to get you ready for the exciting journey ahead: Can you use a template for creating new GDK apps? How do you create a new GDK app project?

Step-by-Step Tutorial

Follow these steps to build a generic GDK template app that will be used as the basis to build your first HelloGlass app and all the GDK apps in the coming chapters:

1. Launch Eclipse.

2. In ADT's Package Explorer, right-click to show the menu and then select Import. (You can also select File ➤ Import.)

3. Select Android ➤ Existing Android Code Into Workspace and then click Next.

4. In the Import Projects window, click Browse and select the GlasswareTemplate folder in the source code directory that comes with the book. Keep all the other defaults (the window should look like Figure 2-16) and click Finish.

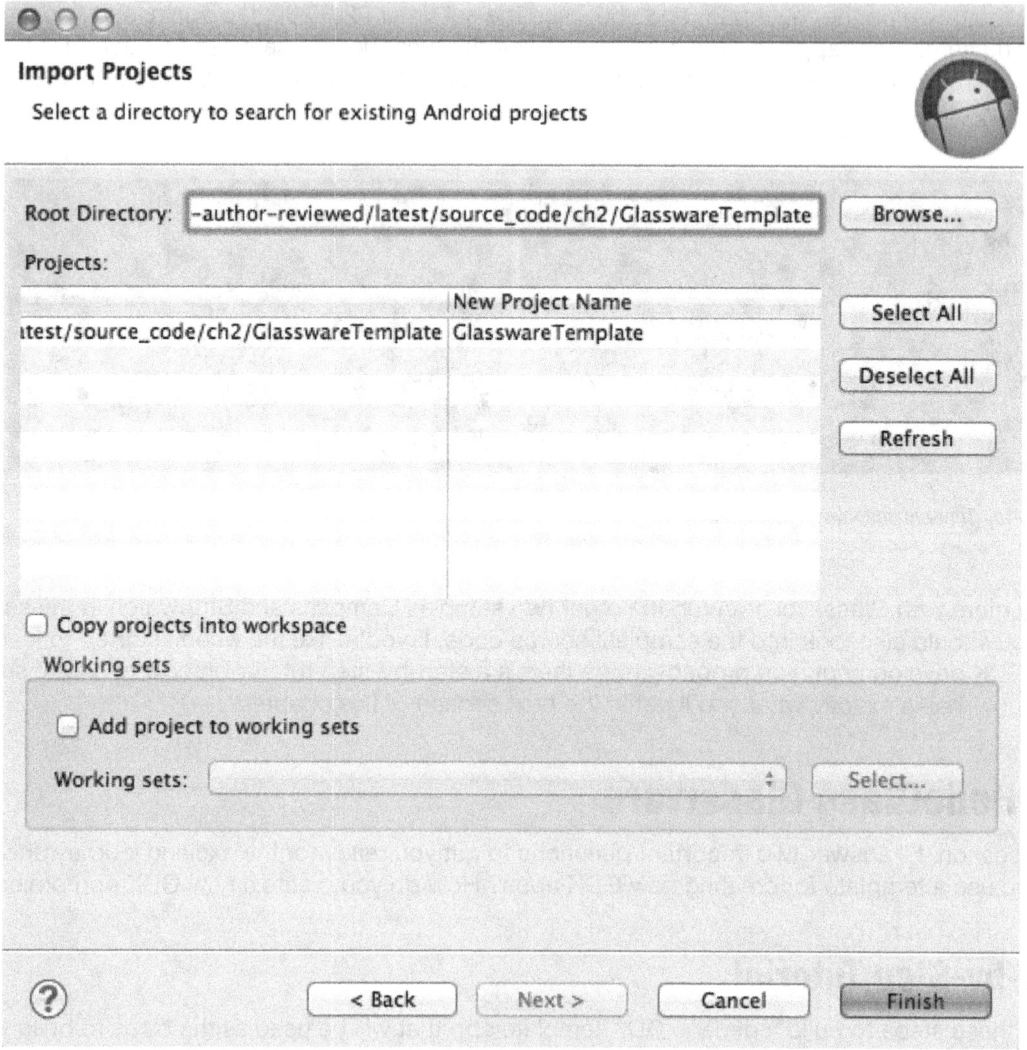

Figure 2-16. Importing GlasswareTemplate project to ADT

Note   You may notice some slight differences between your Eclipse screens and the following screenshots. This is because the ADT looks on Mac, Windows, and Linux are not 100 percent the same, but the difference is so insignificant (for example, the order of Cancel and Finish buttons is different) that you shouldn't have any trouble following the tutorial.

5. An error may occur because an incorrect target could be set as Project Build Target when the project was imported. To fix this, simply right-click GlasswareTemplate in ADT's left Package Explorer panel, select Properties, and then change Project Build Target to Glass Development Kit Preview, as shown in Figure 2-17. Click OK, and you're ready to run the template Glassware.

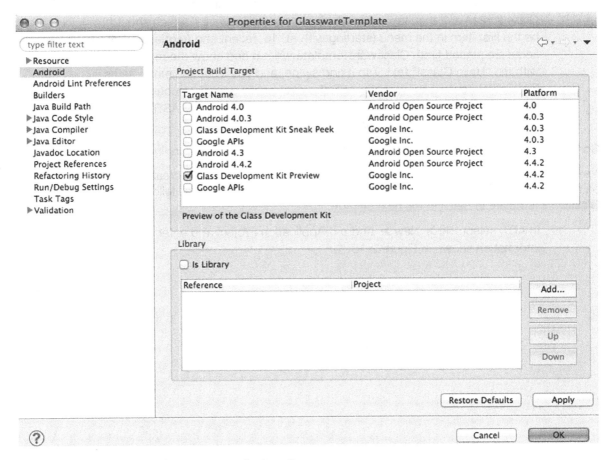

Figure 2-17. Fixing possible project target error after importing

6. Connect Glass to your computer and turn it on if you haven't (you may want to verify your Glass is connected by running adb devices). Right-click GlasswareTemplate and select Run As ➤ Android Application. You'll see the Android Device Chooser window with your Glass; select it and click OK.

7. You should see a message that says "/GlasswareTemplate/bin/ GlasswareTemplate.apk installed on device" in ADT's console.

> **Note**   Sometimes after you import the GDK template app to Eclipse or create a new project based on it, you may get an error message when building the app: "Unable to execute dex: java.nio.BufferOverflowException." You can fix this by right-clicking the project and then selecting Android Tools and Add Support Library.

8. Tap your Glass, say "OK Glass," and then say "Glassware." Or tap the OK Glass screen and then tap again when you see #glassware#, which should be the first item in the menu (starting with XE 16, recent and frequently visited items are placed first). GlasswareTemplate will run and show the main screen with the "Hello Glass!" text. Tap it and swipe, and you'll see the menu items STOP, TTS (for text-to-speech), ASR (for automated-speech-recognition). Tap STOP to close the app; tap TTS to listen to "Hello Glass!"; tap ASR and say "Hello Glass." Glass will recognize your speech!

Congratulations! You have the generic Glassware template app up and running.

Next, follow these steps to build and test HelloGlass, your first GDK app created based on the template app. I'll then explain the project, files, and code for both HelloGlass and GlasswareTemplate in detail in the next section.

1. In ADT, select File ➤ New ➤ Android Application Project and enter the information shown in Figure 2-18.

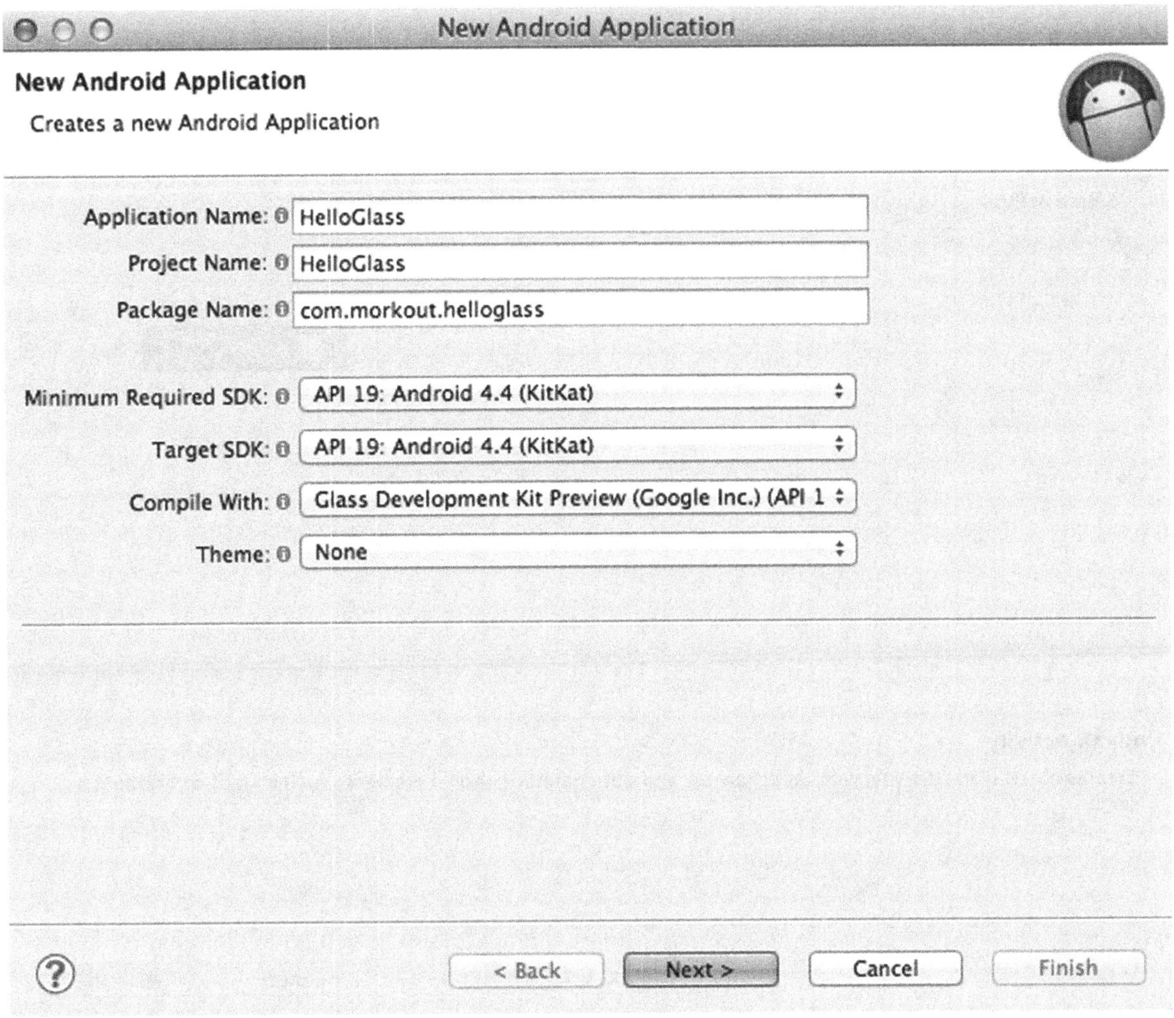

Figure 2-18. Creating your HelloGlass GDK app based on the template app

2. Click Next three times and keep all the default settings.

3. Uncheck Create Activity on the Create Activity screen, as shown in Figure 2-19, and then click Finish.

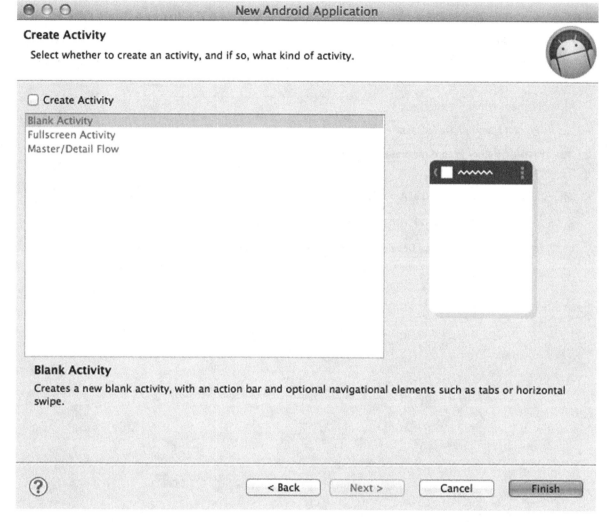

Figure 2-19. Changed setting for your HelloGlass app

4. Open GlasswareTemplate, as shown in Figure 2-20; the files showing are to be copied to your HelloGlass app.

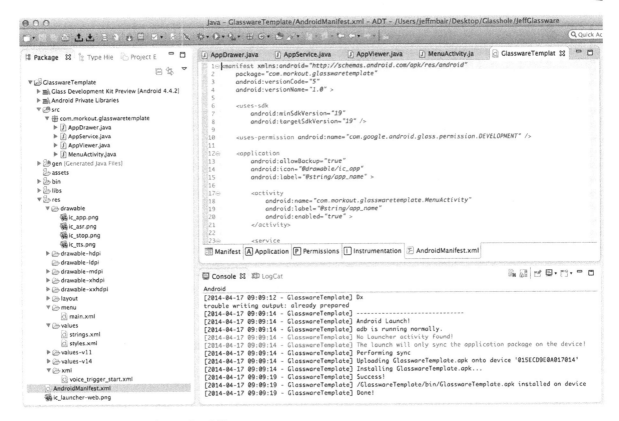

Figure 2-20. GlasswareTemplate project folders

5. Right-click the HelloGlass app's `src`, folder, select New ➤ Package, and enter the name shown in Figure 2-21 (or change the package name to be other name you like better); click Finish.

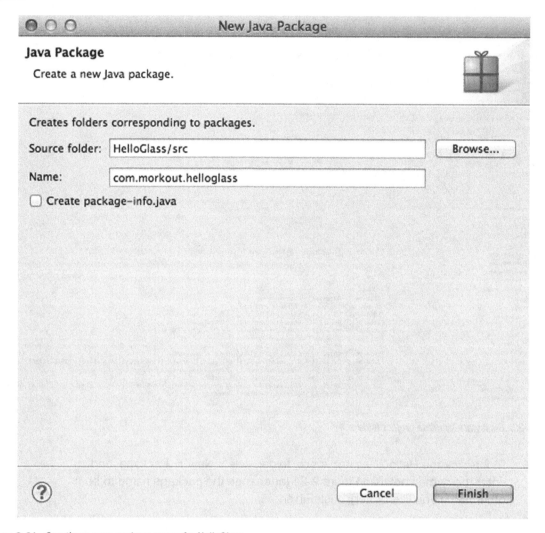

Figure 2-21. Creating a new package name for HelloGlass

6. In Eclipse, copy the four files from GlasswareTemplate's `src` folder and paste them to HelloGlass's `src` folder. The first line in the four files of HelloGlass's `src` folder should have been changed automatically by Eclipse from `com.morkout.glasswaretemplate` to `com.morkout.helloglass`; if not, change them manually. Ignore the errors in the HelloGlass project; they'll all be fixed soon in the following steps.

7. In Eclipse, copy the drawable, menu, and xml folders in GlasswareTemplate's res folder and paste them to HelloGlass's res folder; then copy the files in GlasswareTemplate's res, layout, and values folders and paste them to HelloGlass's res, layout, and values folders (you need to overwrite the strings.xml and styles.xml files in the HelloGlass res, layout, and values folders when you copy and paste). Replace the whole <application> ... </application> section in HelloGlass's AndroidManifest.xml with that in GlasswareTemplate's AndroidManifest.xml. Change android:name's value in the service tag from com.morkout.glasswaretemplate.AppService to com.morkout.helloglass.AppService, and change android:name's value in the activity tag from com.morkout.glasswaretemple.MenuActivity to com.morkout.helloglass.MenuActivity.

8. Copy the line <uses-permission android:name="com.google.android.glass. permission.DEVELOPMENT" />from GlasswareTemplate's AndroidManifest.xml file to HelloGlass's AndroidManifest.xml file. This is something new in XE 16 or later and is required when you develop your GDK apps; see https://developers.google.com/glass/develop/gdk/starting-glassware for more details.

9. Finally, change the string value for say_glasswaretemplate in HelloGlass's res/values/strings.xml file to #helloglass#. Run HelloGlass as an Android application while Glass is connected and turned on. You'll see on your computer something like Figure 2-11 and Figure 2-12. Then on your Glass, you'll see your #helloglass# app in the app list on the OK Glass screen. Tap the app to start it and see "Hello Glass," where you can tap and then swipe to see the menu like in the GlasswareTemplate app.

> **Note** You may wonder why you went through all the previous steps to create a new app based on the template app without adding any exciting new features to the app. You'll soon see in the coming chapters that the steps are repeated for each new category of apps, such as UI elements, image processing, video processing, audio processing, and so on. Creating a new app this way instead of importing and modifying the template app directly will help you organize your apps effectively.

What's Going On

Now that you have both the template Glassware and HelloGlass app running, it's time to delve into the details of the projects. Let's first take a look at the big picture.

The Big Picture

A typical GDK app starts with a service (AppService) that runs when the app's voice command is uttered or the app is tapped in the OK Glass app list. When the service is started, it creates a live card. A *live card* is one of the essential Glass UI elements that I'll discuss in detail next chapter; for now you can just think of it as a card that gets created on the left side of the OK Glass item as the initial Timer card shown in Figure 2-14. (For a quick review of the Glass UI and live cards, you can also check out https://developers.google.com/glass/design/ui and https://developers.google.com/glass/develop/gdk/live-cards.) The live card then adds an instance of a class (AppDrawer) that implements SurfaceHolder.Callback for rendering, as well as a menu activity action (MenuActivity). AppDrawer creates an instance of a View subclass (AppViewer) that does the real rendering, sets the view's layout, and requests the view to draw the content. AppViewer is similar to common Android app view class, drawing UI elements based on a layout XML; in the example, it simply sets the content for a TextView.

Figure 2-22 shows how the classes in the template Glassware interact with each other.

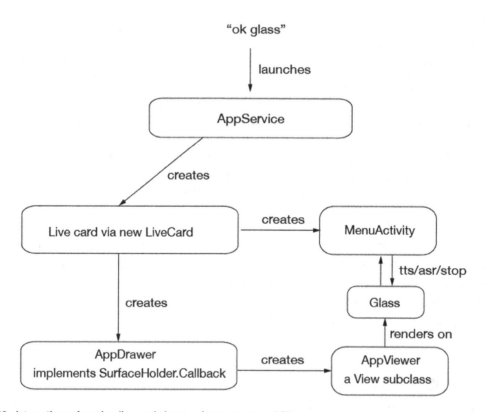

Figure 2-22. Interactions of service, live card, drawer, viewer, menu, and Glass

Source Code

In the HelloGlass project's src folder, there are four files copied from GlasswareTemplate's src folder:

- AppDrawer.java
- AppService.java
- AppViewer.java
- MenuActivity.java

Detailed explanations for these files follow.

AppDrawer.java

The AppDrawer.java file in Listing 2-1 defines the class AppDrawer that implements the SurfaceHolder.Callback interface (SurfaceHolder allows you to access and control a display surface's size and format and monitor its changes), which has three public abstract methods: surfaceChanged, surfaceCreated, and surfaceDestroyed.

Listing 2-1. AppDrawer.java

```java
package com.morkout.glasswaretemplate;

import android.content.Context;
import android.graphics.Canvas;
import android.util.Log;
import android.view.SurfaceHolder;
import android.view.View;

public class AppDrawer implements SurfaceHolder.Callback {
    private static final String TAG = "AppDrawer";
    private final AppViewer mView;
    private SurfaceHolder mHolder;

    public AppDrawer(Context context) {
        mView = new AppViewer(context);
    }

    @Override
    public void surfaceChanged(SurfaceHolder holder, int format, int width, int height) {
        // Measure and layout the view with the canvas dimensions.
        int measuredWidth = View.MeasureSpec.makeMeasureSpec(width, View.MeasureSpec.EXACTLY);
        int measuredHeight = View.MeasureSpec.makeMeasureSpec(height, View.MeasureSpec.EXACTLY);
        mView.measure(measuredWidth, measuredHeight);
        mView.layout(0, 0, mView.getMeasuredWidth(), mView.getMeasuredHeight());
        draw(mView);
    }
```

```
    @Override
    public void surfaceCreated(SurfaceHolder holder) {
        mHolder = holder;
        mView.start();
        draw(mView);
    }

    @Override
    public void surfaceDestroyed(SurfaceHolder holder) {
        mHolder = null;
    }

    private void draw(View view) {
        Canvas canvas;
        try {
            canvas = mHolder.lockCanvas();
        } catch (Exception e) {
            return;
        }
        if (canvas != null) {
            view.draw(canvas);
            mHolder.unlockCanvasAndPost(canvas);
        }
    }
}
```

AppDrawer first creates an instance of AppViewer, a View subclass, and then goes through the two-pass layout process (measure and layout), in surfaceChanged before actually drawing the view. The width and height passed to the surfaceChanged method are 640 and 360 pixels, the size of the Glass display. The view draw request is made between the canvas lock and unlock.

AppService.java

The AppService.java file in Listing 2-2 defines a Service subclass AppService, which in its onStartCommand method creates a live card if the card hasn't been created. After that, an AppDrawer instance is created and set as the callback of the live card's surface, on which drawing will happen; note that the direct rendering has to be enabled on the live card in order for it to return a valid surface holder and for the live card to be displayed. Another condition for the live card to be displayed is to provide it with an action; in the code here, the action is an activity that displays an options menu when the card is selected (after the app is started), but the action can also be any other activity.

Listing 2-2. AppService.java

```
package com.morkout.glasswaretemplate;

import android.app.PendingIntent;
import android.app.Service;
import android.content.Intent;
import android.os.IBinder;
import android.util.Log;
```

```java
import com.google.android.glass.timeline.LiveCard;
import com.google.android.glass.timeline.LiveCard.PublishMode;

public class AppService extends Service {

    private static final String TAG = "AppService";
    private static final String LIVE_CARD_ID = "HelloGlass";

    private AppDrawer mCallback;
    private LiveCard mLiveCard;

    @Override
    public void onCreate() {
        super.onCreate();
    }

    @Override
    public IBinder onBind(Intent intent) {
        return null;
    }

    @Override
    public int onStartCommand(Intent intent, int flags, int startId) {
        if (mLiveCard == null) {
            mLiveCard = new LiveCard(this, LIVE_CARD_ID);
            mCallback = new AppDrawer(this);
            mLiveCard.setDirectRenderingEnabled(true).getSurfaceHolder().addCallback(mCallback);
            Intent menuIntent = new Intent(this, MenuActivity.class);
            mLiveCard.setAction(PendingIntent.getActivity(this, 0, menuIntent, 0));

            mLiveCard.publish(PublishMode.REVEAL);
        }

        return START_STICKY;
    }

    @Override
    public void onDestroy() {
        if (mLiveCard != null && mLiveCard.isPublished()) {
            if (mCallback != null) {
                mLiveCard.getSurfaceHolder().removeCallback(mCallback);
            }
            mLiveCard.unpublish();
            mLiveCard = null;
        }
        super.onDestroy();
    }

}
```

After the live card is published to the timeline, AppDrawer will receive the SurfaceHolder's callbacks to draw its content via AppViewer. When the service is being destroyed, the AppDrawer callback interface needs to be removed from the surface holder and the live card unpublished.

AppViewer.java

AppViewer.java in Listing 2-3 defines a simple View subclass that instantiates the layout XML file and sets the "Hello Glass!" text in its TextView.

Listing 2-3. AppViewer.java

```java
package com.morkout.glasswaretemplate;

import android.content.Context;
import android.util.AttributeSet;
import android.view.LayoutInflater;
import android.widget.FrameLayout;
import android.widget.TextView;

public class AppViewer extends FrameLayout {
    private final TextView mTextView;

    public AppViewer(Context context) {
        this(context, null, 0);
    }

    public AppViewer(Context context, AttributeSet attrs) {
        this(context, attrs, 0);
    }

    public void start() {
    }

    public AppViewer(Context context, AttributeSet attrs, int style) {
        super(context, attrs, style);
        LayoutInflater.from(context).inflate(R.layout.start, this);

        mTextView =  (TextView) findViewById(R.id.hello_view);
        mTextView.setText("Hello Glass!");
    }

}
```

MenuActivity.java

MenuActivity in Listing 2-4 creates an activity with three options: the common Stop option that exits the app; an option to do text-to-speech (TTS) of "Hello Glass!"; and an option to do automated speech recognition (ASR) of any utterance, including of course "Hello, Glass." The intent of this activity is to show you the standard way to close your GDK app and to give you a first glimpse at the power of GDK Glassware with just a few lines of Android code. You'll soon see how to create your own custom menu options and associate your own unique activity with each option; this will open up all kinds of app features and opportunities.

Listing 2-4. MenuActivity.java

```java
package com.morkout.glasswaretemplate;

import java.util.Locale;
import android.app.Activity;
import android.content.Intent;
import android.os.Bundle;
import android.speech.RecognizerIntent;
import android.speech.tts.TextToSpeech;
import android.speech.tts.TextToSpeech.OnInitListener;
import android.view.Menu;
import android.view.MenuInflater;
import android.view.MenuItem;

public class MenuActivity extends Activity implements OnInitListener {
    private TextToSpeech tts;
    private boolean mAttachedToWindow;
    private boolean mTTSSelected;

    @Override
    protected void onCreate(Bundle savedInstanceState) {
        super.onCreate(savedInstanceState);
        mTTSSelected = false;
    }

    @Override
    public void onAttachedToWindow() {
        super.onAttachedToWindow();
        mAttachedToWindow = true;
        openOptionsMenu();
    }

    @Override
    public void onDetachedFromWindow() {
        super.onDetachedFromWindow();
        mAttachedToWindow = false;
    }

    @Override
    public void openOptionsMenu() {
        if (mAttachedToWindow) {
            super.openOptionsMenu();
        }
    }

    @Override
    public boolean onCreateOptionsMenu(Menu menu) {
        MenuInflater inflater = getMenuInflater();
        inflater.inflate(R.menu.main, menu);
        return true;
    }
```

```
@Override
public boolean onOptionsItemSelected(MenuItem item) {
    switch (item.getItemId()) {
    case R.id.stop:
        stopService(new Intent(this, AppService.class));
        return true;

    case R.id.tts:
                mTTSSelected = true;
                tts = new TextToSpeech(this, this);
                tts.setOnUtteranceProgressListener(new UtteranceProgressListener() {
                // 1
                    @Override
                    public void onDone(String utteranceId) {
                        if (tts != null) {
                            tts.stop();
                            tts.shutdown();
                        }
                        finish();
                    }

                    @Override
                    public void onError(String utteranceId) {
                    }

                    @Override
                    public void onStart(String utteranceId) {
                    }
                });
        return true;

    case R.id.asr:
        Intent i = new Intent(RecognizerIntent.ACTION_RECOGNIZE_SPEECH);
        startActivityForResult(i, 0);
        return true;

    default:
        return super.onOptionsItemSelected(item);
    }
}

@Override
public void onOptionsMenuClosed(Menu menu) {
    if (!mTTSSelected)
        finish();
}

@Override
public void onInit(int status) {
    if (status == TextToSpeech.SUCCESS) {
        int result = tts.setLanguage(Locale.US);
```

```
                if (result == TextToSpeech.LANG_MISSING_DATA || result == TextToSpeech.LANG_NOT_SUPPORTED) {
                } else {
                                HashMap<String, String> map = new HashMap<String, String>();
                                map.put(TextToSpeech.Engine.KEY_PARAM_UTTERANCE_ID,"helloID");
                                // 2
                                   tts.speak("Hello Glass!", TextToSpeech.QUEUE_FLUSH, map);
                                // 3
                }
        }
    }
}
```

A quick note on the handling of TTS: Because TextToSpeech's speak (#3) is an asynchronous call, which returns before TTS ends or even starts, you need to set up an UtteranceProgressListener (#1) to capture the speak completion event so you can close the menu activity and return to the live card screen (you don't have to do that, but just assume in some cases you need to) when the speech is done. For UtteranceProgressListener to capture the onDone, onStart, or onError event, a dictionary with a used-defined ID (#2) needs to be provided as the third parameter of the speak method.

Resource Files

The following folders and files define the icons, layout, menu, string, and voice command XML files.

drawable

The icon files copied to drawable from GlasswareTemplate are for the app when shown in the "OK Glass" app list and for the menu items when you tap the app after it's launched and when you swipe to show menu options. There's nothing special here; you just need to create your own icon assets for your own Glassware.

start.xml in layout

Listing 2-5 shows the layout file used in AppViewer.java. A TextView is created within FrameLayout.

Listing 2-5. start.xml

```xml
<?xml version="1.0" encoding="utf-8"?>
<FrameLayout xmlns:android="http://schemas.android.com/apk/res/android"
    android:layout_width="match_parent"
    android:layout_height="match_parent"
    android:background="@color/black" >

    <TextView
        android:id="@+id/hello_view"
        android:layout_width="match_parent"
        android:layout_height="match_parent"
        android:layout_gravity="center"
        android:layout_marginTop="-10px"
        android:gravity="center"
        android:textSize="100px" />
</FrameLayout>
```

main.xml in menu

Listing 2-6 is the XML file for menu item definitions. Title and icon in each item need to be defined in `strings.xml` in Listing 2-7 and exist in the `drawable` folder.

Listing 2-6. main.xml

```xml
<?xml version="1.0" encoding="utf-8"?>

<menu xmlns:android="http://schemas.android.com/apk/res/android">
    <item
        android:id="@+id/stop"
        android:title="@string/stop"
        android:icon="@drawable/ic_stop" />

    <item
        android:id="@+id/tts"
        android:title="@string/tts"
        android:icon="@drawable/ic_tts" />

    <item
        android:id="@+id/asr"
        android:title="@string/asr"
        android:icon="@drawable/ic_asr" />
</menu>
```

strings.xml in values

Listing 2-7 defines all the strings used in the app, including the app name, voice command (used after "OK Glass" to launch your app), voice prompt (which I'll discuss in detail in Chapter 6), and menu items.

Listing 2-7. strings.xml

```xml
<?xml version="1.0" encoding="utf-8"?>

<resources>
    <string name="app_name">Glassware!!!</string>
    <string name="say_glasswaretemplate">#Glassware#</string>
    <string name="glass_voice_prompt">Say Glassware Template to trigger the glassware</string>
    <string name="stop">STOP</string>
    <string name="tts">TTS</string>
    <string name="asr">ASR</string>
</resources>
```

voice_trigger_start.xml in xml

Listing 2-8 defines the voice command Glass users can use to launch your app.

Listing 2-8. voice_trigger_start.xml

```
<?xml version="1.0" encoding="utf-8"?>

<trigger keyword="@string/say_glasswaretemplate" >
</trigger>
```

AndroidManifest.xml

This file describes essential information about an Android app. Listing 2-9 specifies a minimum SDK version and target SDK version, activities, and the service defined in the app. The service is the starting point of the app. The com.google.android.glass.action.VOICE_TRIGGER action and com. google.android.glass.VoiceTrigger metadata name are unique for each Glass app, allowing you to launch your app using a voice command, as defined in Listing 2-7 and Listing 2-8.

Listing 2-9. AndroidManifest.xml

```
<manifest xmlns:android="http://schemas.android.com/apk/res/android"
    package="com.morkout.glasswaretemplate"
    android:versionCode="5"
    android:versionName="1.0" >

    <uses-sdk
        android:minSdkVersion="19"
        android:targetSdkVersion="19" />

        <uses-permission android:name="com.google.android.glass.permission.DEVELOPMENT" />

    <application
        android:allowBackup="true"
        android:icon="@drawable/ic_app"
        android:label="@string/app_name" >
        <activity
            android:name="com.morkout.glasswaretemplate.MenuActivity"
            android:enabled="true"
            android:label="@string/app_name" >
        </activity>

        <service
            android:name="com.morkout.glasswaretemplate.AppService"
            android:enabled="true"
            android:exported="true"
            android:icon="@drawable/ic_app"
            android:label="@string/app_name" >
            <intent-filter>
                <action android:name="com.google.android.glass.action.VOICE_TRIGGER" />
            </intent-filter>
```

```
        <meta-data
            android:name="com.google.android.glass.VoiceTrigger"
            android:resource="@xml/voice_trigger_start" />
    </service>
  </application>

</manifest>
```

If you don't understand some of the concepts or code here, don't worry. In the coming chapters, you'll see a lot of examples on every Glass UI and development topic and get comfortable with Glass development quickly. What's important, now that you have reached this point, is that you're well prepared for exploring all kinds of Glass development topics.

Summary

In this chapter, I first covered the detailed steps of how to set up your GDK Glassware development environments, whether your favorite is Mac, Windows, or Linux. Then I discussed how to set up Glass to get it ready for development and how to run sample GDK apps on it. Finally, I introduced the generic template Glassware, which you'll use to create new GDK apps, and I showed a step-by-step tutorial of building HelloGlass, your first GDK app, with nice features such as menu actions. I also presented the TTS and ASR versions of HelloGlass. All the code has been updated and tested for the Glass XE 16 and 17 with the Glassware Development Kit Preview, released on April 15, 2014, based on Android 4.4.2 (API Level 19).

Chapter 3

Glass User Interface

In this chapter, I'll present a complete discussion of the Glass user interface (UI) supported by the GDK (starting with Android 4.4.2), with sample working code for all the major Glass UI elements, including the timeline, Glass-styled card, live card, immersion, menu items, and gestures.

Overview

`https://developers.google.com/glass/design/ui` has a good review on the timeline, immersions, menu items, and the relationship of static cards, live cards, and timeline. Here is a summary of the main UI elements that GDK supports:

- *Timeline*: The central Glass UI is a bunch of static and live cards of 640x360 pixels that you can swipe forward and backward to view information on a card or perform an action on the card. The OK Glass item is the home screen of Glass and located at the center of the timeline, showing the current time.

- *Glass-styled cards*: These are well-formed cards with main text, a left-aligned footer, and one or more images displayed on the left side of the card. (See Figure 3-1 in the next section for an example.) You can use a card wherever you can a view—in activities, in layouts, or in a `CardScrollView`. For more details, check out `https://developers.google.com/glass/develop/gdk/ui-widgets#glass-styled_cards`.

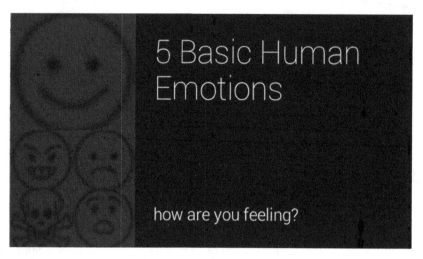

Figure 3-1. Inserted static card

- *Live cards*: These are located in the left (current) part of the timeline for summary information important to the user at present. Live cards can access low-level Glass hardware such as sensors and GPS and most Android APIs up to 4.4.2, and only the GDK can create live cards. There are two types of live cards: *high-frequency live cards* that render many times a second for rich 2D or 3D content and *low-frequency live cards* that render once every few seconds, mainly for text and image. Live cards cannot process swipe forward or backward gestures because they're used by the timeline to navigate through the static and live cards.

- *Immersions*: These are for customized UI elements to temporarily take over the timeline to provide rich content and high user interaction. Immersions are just Android activities and can consume all user gestures. Like live cards, immersions can also access all low-level hardware and Android 4.4.2 or older APIs, but unlike live cards, immersions can consume swipe forward and backward gestures (swipe down takes you back to timeline) if your app needs to support high user interaction, giving the user total control of the Glass environment from within the app.

Note   If you're familiar with the psychology theory of flow, the word *immersion* probably would remind you of flow: "a single-minded immersion, in which a person performing an activity is fully immersed in a feeling of energized focus, full involvement, and enjoyment in the process of the activity." How appropriate it is to have immersion implemented as an Android activity in Glass. You may want to at least check out `http://en.wikipedia.org/wiki/Flow_(psychology)` when you develop Glass immersion, or want to be happier, or both.

- *Menus*: Static cards, live cards, and immersions can all have menu items for the user to tap to select actions to perform. You saw menus in the GDK Timer sample and the HelloGlass app.

- *Voice input*: Glass can accept voice commands to launch an app and contextual voice commands on specific cards after an app is launched. Free-form speech input is also supported from within an app.

- *Gestures*: Glass supports both touch gestures (one-finger, two-finger, and three-finger tap and swipe) and head gestures (head panning, look up, and nudge).

> **Note**   As of GDK Preview, released on April 15, 2014, static cards in the GDK API support only text and image content, but not menu content. Static cards in the Mirror API can support audio and video, in addition to text and image, and the user can choose in a menu to share, delete, reply, read aloud, or perform many other actions. But you'll soon see that live cards and immersions provided by the GDK API offer much more.

In the following sections, I'll show you step-by-step instructions and sample code of how to create the following:

- Glass-styled card

- Low-frequency live card

- High-frequency live card that inflates the layout using standard controls

- High-frequency live card that uses 2D canvas drawing

- Immersion that uses 2D canvas drawing or standard Android views

- Immersion that uses 3D OpenGL 1.0/2.0 drawing

Menu and gestures will also be discussed in more detail along the way.

My goal is to show you the potential of GDK apps and how to get the template app up and running so you can appropriately and quickly set up your projects and plan for your next big app. I'll add the code for each of the app type previously based on the Glassware template in Chapter 2. You can follow the steps there on how the HelloGlass project was built to create a new project for the sample code in this chapter. For your convenience, here is a summary of the steps:

1. In ADT, select File ➤ New ➤ Android Application Project, enter **GlassUIElements** for Application Name (Project Name will be filled in automatically), and change Package Name to **com.morkout. glassuielements**.

2. Set both Minimum Required SDK and Target SDK to API 19, Compile With to Glass Development Kit Preview, and Theme to None.

3. Click Next three times, uncheck Create Activity, and then click Finish.

4. Right-click the newly created project GlassUIElements's `src` folder, select New ➤ Package, and enter **com.morkout.glassuielements** or another package name; then click Finish.

5. Copy the four files in GlasswareTemplate's `src` folder to GlassUIElements's `src` folder. Copy the `drawable`, `menu`, and `xml` folders from GlasswareTemplate's `res` folder to GlassUIElements's `res` folder. Copy `start.xml` from GlasswareTemplate's `res/layout` folder to GlassUIElements's `res/layout` folder, and finally copy `strings.xml` from GlasswareTemplate's `res/values` folder and overwrite `strings.xml` in GlassUIElements's `res/values` folder.

6. Copy the `<application...></application>` element from GlasswareTemplate's `AndroidManifest.xml` file to the `<application...></application>` element of GlassUIElements's `AndroidManifest.xml` file, and change `glasswaretemplate` in the `android:name` element of `activity` and `service` to `glassuielements`.

The whole process seems long, but with a few more tries, you can create a new project within a minute. Now you're ready for exploring the details of all the UI elements in GDK Glassware.

> **Note**   To be accurate, now that you have a better understanding of cards and immersions, the template app GlasswareTemplate and the app created based on it, GlassUIElements, are actually high-frequency live card apps. You'll see shortly how to extend the template and app to support low-frequency live cards, high-frequency live cards, and immersions that use different content-rendering mechanisms and, of course, static cards.

Glass-Styled Cards

`https://developers.google.com/glass/develop/gdk/reference/com/google/android/glass/app/Card` is the GDK reference for the `Card` class, and you should definitely check it out. In XE 12, static cards can be created using the `Card` class and then inserted to the timeline (and updated, deleted, or queried after that) using another class called `TimelineManager`. Starting XE 16, the `TimelineManager` class and support of operating static cards in the timeline have been completely removed; you should use only the Mirror API to create static cards and use the GDK to create Glass-styled `Card` objects and then use `Card`'s `getView()` method to convert the card to a view and use it where a view is expected. For example, you can add cards to `CardScrollView`, a class that allows you to create swipeable cards by converting each card to an Android view with the `getView()` method.

Figure 3-1 shows a Glass-styled card with "5 Basic Human Emotions" as the main body text, five images positioned on the left, and "how are you feeling?" as the footnote.

To test the code on your Glass, first add a new class called `GlassStyledCardActivity` derived from `Activity` to your project, as shown in Listing 3-1 (you can find the PNG files for joy, anger, sadness, fear, and surprise in the source code of Chapter 3).

Listing 3-1. Creating a Glass-Styled Card

```java
public class GlassStyledCardActivity extends Activity {
    @Override
    protected void onCreate(Bundle savedInstanceState) {
        super.onCreate(savedInstanceState);

        Card card = new Card(this);
        card.setText("5 Basic Human Emotions");
        card.setFootnote("how are you feeling?");
        card.addImage(R.drawable.joy);
        card.addImage(R.drawable.anger);
        card.addImage(R.drawable.sadness);
        card.addImage(R.drawable.fear);
        card.addImage(R.drawable.surprise);
        card.setImageLayout(Card.ImageLayout.LEFT);

        setContentView(card.getView());
    }
}
```

Then in `AppService.java`, add a new method called `createGlassStyledCard()` and replace the AppService's onStartCommand implementation with the code in Listing 3-2.

Listing 3-2. Launching Activity That Creates Glass-Styled Card

```java
private void createGlassStyledCard() {
    Intent intent = new Intent(this, GlassStyledCardActivity.class);
    intent.addFlags(Intent.FLAG_ACTIVITY_NEW_TASK);
    startActivity(intent);
}

public int onStartCommand(Intent intent, int flags, int startId) {
    createGlassStyledCard();
    return START_STICKY;
}
```

Finally, specify the `GlassStyledCardActivity` in `AndroidManifest.xml`. Connect your Glass, run and install the app, and launch the app by saying "OK Glass" and then "Chapter 3," which is defined as `<string name="say_glasswaretemplate">chapter three</string>` in the `strings.xml` file in the res/values folder. You'll see a Glass-styled card, as shown in Figure 3-1.

Later in the chapter, you'll see how `Card` objects are used in `CardScrollView`.

Menu

If you're already familiar with Glass as an end user, you should have noticed that a menu is available for most cards on the timeline. For example, tap a Gmail message card, and you'll see Read more, Reply, Archive, Read Aloud, Star, and Delete menu options. Tap a CNN news card, and you'll see Play, Read more, and Read aloud options. And you've seen the menu options Love, Smile, Laugh, Surprise, Frown, and Comment for a new item shared by your Path friends. Naturally you'd probably love to do the same thing on the cards you create in your GDK app.

Unfortunately, it's not possible as of XE 17 for the GDK to create menu items for static (or more accurately, Glass-Styled) cards; only the Mirror API can do so. But Google will likely fix this in a future update of the GDK. Even if that doesn't happen anytime soon, you'll be happy to know that you can easily create menus for live cards and immersions, which are the real strengths of GDK, using standard Android menu APIs. So, let's enter the more exciting world of live cards and immersions. Later in the book, I'll also discuss the Mirror API in great detail.

Live Cards

You can create live cards in two ways: by inflating a layout resource, called *low-frequency live cards*, or by rendering directly onto the app's drawing surface, called *high-frequency live cards*. Which way to use to create a live card depends on how frequently you need to update the card content and if you are primarily rendering widgets for status and information updates or free-form graphics using 2D canvas or 3D OpenGL.

Low-Frequency Live Cards

You create low-frequency live cards by inflating a layout of standard widgets using the Android RemoteViews class. The timeline runs in a different process from your app, so in order for the timeline to render a layout in your app, you need to use RemoteViews, which supports layouts and views documented at https://developers.google.com/glass/develop/gdk/ui/live-cards.

Listing 3-3 shows some sample code with comments to create a low-frequency live card.

Listing 3-3. Creating Low-Frequency Live Card

```java
private RemoteViews mRemoteViews; // add this before AppService's constructor

// add the following two methods method in AppService.java
private void createLowFrequencyLiveCard() {
    mLiveCard = new LiveCard(this, LIVE_CARD_ID)
    mRemoteViews = new RemoteViews(this.getPackageName(), R.layout.start);
    mRemoteViews.setTextViewText(R.id.hello_view, (new Date()).toString());
    mRemoteViews.setViewVisibility(R.id.ex_progress_bar, View.INVISIBLE);
    mLiveCard.setViews(mRemoteViews);

    addMenuToLiveCard();
}

private void addMenuToLiveCard() {
    Intent menuIntent = new Intent(this, MenuActivity.class);
    mLiveCard.setAction(PendingIntent.getActivity(this, 0, menuIntent, 0));

    mLiveCard.publish(PublishMode.REVEAL);
}
```

```
// change onStartCommand in AppService to create the low-frequency live card
public int onStartCommand(Intent intent, int flags, int startId) {
    if (mLiveCard == null)
        createLowFrequencyLiveCard();

    return START_STICKY;
}
```

Run and launch the app (using the same 'OK Glass" and then "Chapter 3" voice command), and you'll see on your Glass the current date and time information, something like Figure 3-2.

Figure 3-2. Created low-frequency live card

Navigate the timeline, and you'll notice the card is located on the left side of the timeline, unlike static cards, which are normally located on the right side of the timeline.

Note   All live cards, low-frequency or high-frequency, must have a Stop-like menu item to dismiss the card. This is why the addMenuToLiveCard method is created and why mLiveCard.publish(PublishMode.REVEAL), which obviously is also required for creating a live card, is added there. If you comment out the first two lines of the addMenuToLiveCard method, you won't see the live card after the voice command, but just the "Chapter 3" screen.

Tap the live card, and you'll see the menu options, as in the HelloGlass app of Chapter 2.

To update the content of a created low-frequency live card, you can call RemoteViews' set methods corresponding to the widget's set methods. For example, to update the TextView shown earlier, you can call the two lines of code in Listing 3-4 from one of your menu options.

Listing 3-4. Updating Low-Frequency Live Card

```
mRemoteViews.setTextViewText(R.id.hello_view, (new Date()).toString());
mLiveCard.setViews(mRemoteViews);
```

Note that the live card's setViews method has to be called; otherwise, the content won't be updated. To make it more interesting, follow these steps to use a progress bar and keep updating it:

1. Update your start.xml layout file and add a ProgressBar element after the TextView element.

    ```
    <ProgressBar android:id="@+id/ex_progress_bar"
            style="@android:style/Widget.ProgressBar.Horizontal"
            android:layout_width="640px"
            android:layout_height="10px"
            android:layout_marginTop="300px"
            android:background = "#0000FF"
            android:progress="0"
            android:secondaryProgress="0" />
    ```

2. You also need to add android:background="@color/black" at the end of your FrameLayout element in start.xml. Otherwise, when you update the TextView, the previous values may not be cleared, causing both new values and old values to be shown at the same time. So, make your Framelayout look like this:

    ```
    <FrameLayout xmlns:android="http://schemas.android.com/apk/res/android"
        android:layout_width="match_parent"
        android:layout_height="match_parent"
        android:background="@color/black">
    ```

3. Add the code in Listing 3-5 to the AppService class.

    Listing 3-5. Showing Changed Text and Progress Bar in Low-Frequency Live Card

    ```
    private final Handler mHandler = new Handler();
    private final Runnable mUpdateProgressRunnable = new Runnable() {
      @Override
      public void run() {
        if (++percent_done > 100) {
          mRemoteViews.setTextViewText(R.id.hello_view, "DONE!");
          mRemoteViews.setViewVisibility(R.id.ex_progress_bar, View.INVISIBLE);
          mLiveCard.setViews(mRemoteViews);
          return;
        }
        updateLowFrequencyLiveCard();
        mHandler.postDelayed(mUpdateProgressRunnable, 100);
      }
    };
    ```

```
public void updateProgress() {
    mRemoteViews.setViewVisibility(R.id.ex_progress_bar, View.VISIBLE);
    mHandler.postDelayed(mUpdateProgressRunnable, 4000);
}

public void updateLowFrequencyLiveCard() {
    mRemoteViews.setTextViewText(R.id.hello_view, ""+percent_done + "%");
    mRemoteViews.setProgressBar(R.id.ex_progress_bar, 100, percent_done, false);
    if (mLiveCard != null) mLiveCard.setViews(mRemoteViews);
}
```

4. Call `updateProgress();` at the end of the `createLowFrequencyLiveCard` method implementation.

5. Run the app, and you'll see Figure 3-2 first, with the progress bar set to invisible. Because of the animation effect in XE 16 and 17, it'll take about two seconds to see the home screen of a launched app. So, after Figure 3-2, it'll take another two seconds or so before the progress bar gets changed to visible and both the text view showing the completed percentage and the progress bar showing the updated progress get updated about ten times per second. After it reaches 100 percent, the progress bar is reset to invisible, and the text view gets changed to DONE! Figure 3-3 shows two screenshots of this.

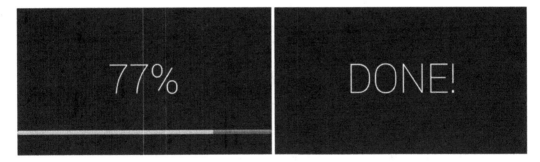

Figure 3-3. Updating low-frequency live card

Now you should be able to quickly try other layouts and views supported by Glass for creating low-frequency live cards, which are documented, as mentioned earlier, at `https://developers.google.com/glass/develop/gdk/ui/live-cards`.

High-Frequency Live Cards

High-frequency live cards are created using a background service, and its content gets rendered with the `surfaceCreated` method, defined in the `SurfaceHolder.Callback` interface. If this looks familiar to you, it could be that the HelloGlass or GlasswareTemplate app actually creates a high-frequency live card from the `onStartCommand` method of `AppService` when the service is launched. Now let's see how to create high-frequency live cards in two different ways.

Inflating Layout

To create a high-frequency live card by inflating a layout, simply add the method createHighFrequencyLiveCardForLayoutInflating and make some changes to onStartCommand in AppService.java, as shown in Listing 3-6.

Listing 3-6. Creating a High-Frequency Live Card by Inflating Layout

```
private void createHighFrequencyLiveCardForLayoutInflating() {
        mLiveCard = new LiveCard(this, LIVE_CARD_ID);
        mCallback = new AppDrawer(this);
        mLiveCard.setDirectRenderingEnabled(true).getSurfaceHolder().addCallback(mCallback);
        addMenuToLiveCard();
}

public int onStartCommand(Intent intent, int flags, int startId) {
    if (mLiveCard == null)
        createHighFrequencyLiveCardForLayoutInflating();

        return START_STICKY;
}
```

You can keep the same AppDrawer.java and AppViewer.java files shown in the previous chapter. Run the app, and you'll see the text "App Template" displayed on Glass, along with a progress bar.

Again, to make the app more interesting, you can show the progress bar by changing the AppDrawer constructor to set an AppViewer listener and updating both the text view and the progress bar as shown in Listing 3-7.

Listing 3-7. Showing Changed Text and Progress Bar in High-Frequency Live Card

```
// in AppDrawer.java:
public AppDrawer(Context context) {
   mView = new AppViewer(context);

   mView.setListener(new AppViewer.ChangeListener() {
      @Override
      public void onChange() {
         if (mHolder != null) {
            draw(mView);
         }
      }});
   );
}

// in AppViewer.java

// add this before the AppViewer constructor:
    private static ProgressBar m_progressBar; //UI reference
    int percent_done = 0;
```

```
private ChangeListener mChangeListener;
public interface ChangeListener {
    public void onChange();
}

public void setListener(ChangeListener listener) {
    mChangeListener = listener;
}

// add this at the end of public AppViewer(Context context, AttributeSet attrs, int style)
m_progressBar = (ProgressBar) findViewById(R.id.ex_progress_bar);
percent_done = 0;
m_progressBar.setProgress(percent_done);

// add updateProgress(); inside the start method and add the following code:
private final Handler mHandler = new Handler();
private final Runnable mUpdateTextRunnable = new Runnable() {
    public void run() {
        if (++percent_done > 100) {
          mTextView.setText("DONE!");

          m_progressBar.setVisibility(View.INVISIBLE);
          if (mChangeListener != null) {
             mChangeListener.onChange();
          }
          return;
        }

        mTextView.setText(""+percent_done + "%");
        m_progressBar.setProgress(percent_done);

        if (mChangeListener != null) {
            mChangeListener.onChange();
        }
        mHandler.postDelayed(mUpdateTextRunnable, 100);
    }
};

    public void start() {
        updateProgress();
    }

    public void updateProgress() {
        mHandler.post(mUpdateTextRunnable);
    }
```

Now run the app, and you should see the same content as in Figure 3-3.

You can see that what's used for the low-frequency live card rendering (inflating a layout) can also be used for high-frequency live card rendering. But not vice versa: Frequent 2D canvas or 3D drawing is available only for high-frequency live card rendering.

2D Canvas Drawing

The second way to create a high-frequency live card is to use a class that implements the GDK DirectRenderingCallback interface, which just adds another callback called renderingPaused to the Android SurfaceHolder.Callback interface.

> **Note**   The renderingPaused method is used to save resources on Glass; it's called when the surface is not visible to the user, so there's no need to update the surface. In the previous sample, you use SurfaceHolder.Callback instead of the DirectRenderingCallback in AppDrawer, so if the Glass screen turns off while the progress bar gets updated, the update continues. In this example, as shown in Listing 3-5, you use DirectRenderingCallback so you can call updateRendering, which stops the rendering thread to save Glass resources (and restarts the thread if needed), from the renderingPaused callback. Normally, you should implement the DirectRenderingCallback interface for high-frequency live card update.

The class LiveCardRenderer in Listing 3-8 is based on the GDK developer site's sample for creating live-frequency cards at https://developers.google.com/glass/develop/gdk/ui/live-cards, but it has a bug fixed and a bouncing-ball canvas drawing code added, and it is also integrated with the tested app for you to try right away.

Listing 3-8. Creating a High-Frequency Live Card with Canvas Drawing

```
// add in AppService.java
    private void createHighFrequencyLiveCardForCanvasDrawing() {
        mLiveCard = new LiveCard(this, LIVE_CARD_ID);
        mCallbackCanvas = new LiveCard2DRenderer();
        mLiveCard.setDirectRenderingEnabled(true).getSurfaceHolder().addCallback(mCallbackCanvas);
        addMenuToLiveCard();
    }

// change the onStartCommand calling code
    public int onStartCommand(Intent intent, int flags, int startId) {
    if (mLiveCard == null)
      createHighFrequencyLiveCardForCanvasDrawing();

      return START_STICKY;
    }

// create a new LiveCard2DRenderer class with the following code:
    public class LiveCard2DRenderer implements DirectRenderingCallback {
private static final String TAG = "LiveCardRenderer";

private static final long FRAME_TIME_MILLIS = 33; // about 30 FPS

private SurfaceHolder mHolder;
private boolean mPaused;
private RenderThread mRenderThread;
```

```java
private int canvasWidth;
private int canvasHeight;
private int diffX = 25;
private int incY = 1;

private float bouncingX;
private float bouncingY;
private double angle;
private Paint paint;
private Path path;

@Override
public void surfaceChanged(SurfaceHolder holder, int format, int width, int height) {
    canvasWidth = width;
    canvasHeight = height;
    bouncingX = canvasWidth / 2;
    bouncingY = canvasHeight / 2;
    angle = - Math.PI/4.0; //(2.0 * Math.PI) * (double) (Math.random() * 360) / 360.0;

    paint = new Paint(Paint.ANTI_ALIAS_FLAG);
    paint.setColor(Color.BLUE);
    paint.setStyle(Style.FILL);
    paint.setStyle(Style.STROKE);

    path = new Path();

    mHolder = holder;
    updateRendering();
}

@Override
public void surfaceCreated(SurfaceHolder holder) {
}

@Override
public void surfaceDestroyed(SurfaceHolder holder) {
    mHolder = null;
    updateRendering();
}

@Override
public void renderingPaused(SurfaceHolder holder, boolean paused) {
    mPaused = paused;
    updateRendering();
}

/**
 * Start or stop rendering according to the timeline state.
 */
private synchronized void updateRendering() {
    boolean shouldRender = (mHolder != null) && !mPaused;
    boolean rendering = mRenderThread != null;
```

```java
        if (shouldRender != rendering) {
            if (shouldRender) {
                mRenderThread = new RenderThread(this);
                mRenderThread.start();
            } else {
                mRenderThread.quit();
                mRenderThread = null;
            }
        }
    }
}

/**
 * Draws the view in the SurfaceHolder's canvas.
 */
public void drawInCanvas(View view) {
    Canvas canvas;

    try {
        canvas = mHolder.lockCanvas();
    } catch (Exception e) {
        return;
    }
    if (canvas != null) {
        // just a little math to calculate the new position of the bouncing ball
        bouncingX += diffX;
        bouncingY += diffX * Math.tan(angle);
        bouncingY *= incY;

        canvas.drawColor(Color.BLACK);
        canvas.drawCircle(bouncingX, bouncingY, 20, paint);

        // change the direction and/or angle if out of bounds
        if (bouncingX > canvasWidth || bouncingX < 0) {
            diffX = -diffX;
            angle = -angle;
        }
        else if (bouncingY > canvasHeight || bouncingY < 0) {
            angle = -angle;
        }

        float mid = canvasWidth / 2;
        float min = canvasHeight;
        float half = min / 2;
        mid -= half;

        paint.setStrokeWidth(min / 10);
        paint.setStyle(Paint.Style.STROKE);
        path.reset();
        paint.setStyle(Paint.Style.FILL);

        path.moveTo(mid + half * 0.5f, half * 0.84f);
        path.lineTo(mid + half * 1.5f, half * 0.84f);
```

```
            path.lineTo(mid + half * 0.68f, half * 1.45f);
            path.lineTo(mid + half * 1.0f, half * 0.5f);
            path.lineTo(mid + half * 1.32f, half * 1.45f);
            path.lineTo(mid + half * 0.5f, half * 0.84f);

            path.close();
            canvas.drawPath(path, paint);

            mHolder.unlockCanvasAndPost(canvas);

        }
    }

    /**
     * Redraws in the background.
     */
    private class RenderThread extends Thread {
        private boolean mShouldRun;
        LiveCard2DRenderer mRenderer;

        /**
         * Initializes the background rendering thread.
         */
        public RenderThread(LiveCard2DRenderer renderer) {
            mShouldRun = true;
            mRenderer = renderer;
        }

        /**
         * Returns true if the rendering thread should continue to run.
         *
         * @return true if the rendering thread should continue to run
         */
        private synchronized boolean shouldRun() {
            return mShouldRun;
        }

        /**
         * Requests that the rendering thread exit at the next opportunity.
         */
        public synchronized void quit() {
            mShouldRun = false;
        }

        @Override
        public void run() {
            while (shouldRun()) {
                mRenderer.drawInCanvas(null);
                SystemClock.sleep(FRAME_TIME_MILLIS);
            }
        }
    }
}
```

Run the app, and you'll see a bouncing blue ball on a screen with a centered blue star, as shown in Figure 3-4.

Figure 3-4. *Canvas drawing on a live card*

> **Note**   According to Google's documentation at `https://developers.google.com/glass/design/ui/live-cards`, high-frequency live cards can also show "rich 3D content." I'll show you how to render 3D content in the "Immersion" section, but I'll leave how to do it in a live card as an exercise for you.

Menu

A menu with at least one Stop menu item to remove the live card from the timeline is required for live card, or Glass won't even show the live card. To display a menu, you create an activity, set it as the live card's action, and handle user menu selection in the activity. GlasswareTemplate already has a menu implemented for the live card. To recap, here's what it takes to add a menu to a live card, whether low-frequency or high-frequency:

1. Create a menu XML file in the res/menu folder (for example, `main.xml` in the GlasswareTemplate app).

2. Create an activity (`MenuActivity.java` in the sample) that inflates the menu layout file `main.xml` in the `onCreateOptionsMenu` method and handles user selection—this is where you can launch an immersion if desired—in the `onOptionsItemSelected` method.

3. In the service file (AppService.java) that creates a live card, call the live
    card's setAction method with the menu activity.

```
Intent menuIntent = new Intent(this, MenuActivity.class);
mLiveCard.setAction(PendingIntent.getActivity(this, 0, menuIntent, 0));
```

Immersion

You create immersions using standard Android activities, meaning they're both simple and powerful.
In the activity, you should use GestureDetector to detect the gestures that your app needs to
support user interaction. Remember that for immersions, you cannot swipe forward and backward
to navigate the timeline because an immersion replaces the timeline. You have to swipe down or
use a Stop-like menu item to close the immersion to go back to the timeline. It is the capability of
capturing all kinds of user gestures that gives immersions the unique power to accomplish more
advanced features than live cards.

2D Canvas Drawing

The following is a working sample to create an immersion with canvas drawing that shows a new
star; it's not that beautiful but is colorful whenever you tap Glass. Gesture capture is used here
but will be discussed in detail in a later section. A menu is also used with a single Stop menu item,
although unlike in live cards, it's not required in immersions.

```
// add in AppService.java:
private void createImmersionFor2DDrawing() {
    Intent intent = new Intent(this, Immersion2DActivity.class);
    intent.addFlags(Intent.FLAG_ACTIVITY_NEW_TASK);
    startActivity(intent);
}


// change the onStartCommand calling code
public int onStartCommand(Intent intent, int flags, int startId) {
        createImmersionFor2DDrawing();
        return START_STICKY;
}
```

> **Note**   Without the second line of intent.addFlags(Intent.FLAG_ACTIVITY_NEW_TASK); in
> createImmersionFor2DDrawing(), the app would crash because the activity starts outside any activity.
> To fix the crash, the FLAG_ACTIVITY_NEW_TASK flag has to be set on the intent. If, however, you start the
> immersion from a menu activity, you don't need the addFlags line.

Listing 3-9 shows how to create an immersion that does 2D canvas drawing when you tap Glass.
Also, a menu appears when you long press the touchpad of Glass.

Listing 3-9. Creating an Immersion with Canvas Drawing

```
// create a new menu file juststop.xml with a single Stop menu item
<?xml version="1.0" encoding="utf-8"?>

<menu xmlns:android="http://schemas.android.com/apk/res/android">
    <item
        android:id="@+id/stop"
        android:title="@string/stop"
        android:icon="@drawable/ic_stop" />
</menu>

// create a View subclass to do the actual Canvas drawing
public class DrawView extends View {
    List<Point> points = new ArrayList<Point>();
    List<Paint> paints = new ArrayList<Paint>();

    public DrawView(Context context) {
        super(context);
        setFocusable(true);
        setFocusableInTouchMode(true);
        invalidate();
    }

    public void onDraw(Canvas canvas) {
        int i=0;
        for (Point point : points) {
            canvas.drawCircle(point.x, point.y, 5, paints.get(i++));
        }
    }
}

class Point {
    float x, y;
}

// create a new activity named Immersion2DActivity
public class Immersion2DActivity extends Activity {
    private static final String TAG = "Immersion2DActivity";

    TextView mTextView;
    DrawView mDrawView; // 2D
    private GestureDetector mGestureDetector;

    /** Called when the activity is first created. */
    @Override
    public void onCreate(Bundle savedInstanceState) {
        super.onCreate(savedInstanceState);

        // 2D Canvas-based drawing
        mDrawView = new DrawView(this);
        setContentView(mDrawView);
```

```
mDrawView.requestFocus();
mGestureDetector = new GestureDetector(this);

// Called when the following gestures happen: TAP, LONG_PRESS SWIPE_UP,
// SWIPE_LEFT, SWIPE_RIGHT, SWIPE_DOWN
// see the subsection "Gestures and Listeners" for more explanation
mGestureDetector.setBaseListener(new GestureDetector.BaseListener() {
    @Override
    public boolean onGesture(Gesture gesture) {
        if (gesture == Gesture.TAP) {
            // do something on tap
            Log.v(TAG, "TAP");
            Point point = new Point();
            point.x = (int )(Math.random() * 640 + 1);
            point.y = (int )(Math.random() * 360 + 1);
            Paint paint = new Paint();
            paint.setARGB(255, (int )(Math.random() * 255), (int )(Math.random() * 255), (int )
            (Math.random() * 255));
            paint.setAntiAlias(true);
            mDrawView.points.add(point);
            mDrawView.paints.add(paint);
            mDrawView.invalidate();
            return true;
        } else if (gesture == Gesture.TWO_TAP) {
            Log.v(TAG, "TWO_TAP");
            return true;
        } else if (gesture == Gesture.SWIPE_RIGHT) {
            Log.v(TAG, "SWIPE_RIGHT");
            return true;
        } else if (gesture == Gesture.SWIPE_LEFT) {
            return true;
        } else if (gesture == Gesture.LONG_PRESS) {
            Log.v(TAG, "LONG_PRESS");
            openOptionsMenu();
            return true;
        } else if (gesture == Gesture.SWIPE_DOWN) {
            Log.v(TAG, "SWIPE_DOWN");
            return false;
        } else if (gesture == Gesture.SWIPE_UP) {
            Log.v(TAG, "SWIPE_UP");
            return true;
        } else if (gesture == Gesture.THREE_LONG_PRESS) {
            Log.v(TAG, "THREE_LONG_PRESS");
            return true;
        } else if (gesture == Gesture.THREE_TAP) {
            Log.v(TAG, "THREE_TAP");
            return true;
        } else if (gesture == Gesture.TWO_LONG_PRESS) {
            Log.v(TAG, "TWO_LONG_PRESS");
            return true;
```

```java
            } else if (gesture == Gesture.TWO_SWIPE_DOWN) {
                Log.v(TAG, "TWO_SWIPE_DOWN");
                return false;
            } else if (gesture == Gesture.TWO_SWIPE_LEFT) {
                Log.v(TAG, "TWO_SWIPE_LEFT");
                return true;
            } else if (gesture == Gesture.TWO_SWIPE_RIGHT) {
                Log.v(TAG, "TWO_SWIPE_RIGHT");
                return true;
            } else if (gesture == Gesture.TWO_SWIPE_UP) {
                Log.v(TAG, "TWO_SWIPE_UP");
                return true;
            }

            return false;
        }
    });

    // Called when the finger count changes on the touch pad
    mGestureDetector.setFingerListener(new GestureDetector.FingerListener() {
        @Override
        public void onFingerCountChanged (int previousCount, int currentCount) {

            Log.v(TAG, "onFingerCountChanged:" + previousCount + "," + currentCount);
        }
    });

    // Called while the user is scrolling after initial horizontal scroll with one finger
    mGestureDetector.setScrollListener(new GestureDetector.ScrollListener() {
        @Override
        public boolean onScroll(float displacement, float delta,
                float velocity) {
            // do something on scrolling
            Log.v(TAG, "onScroll");
            return true;
        }
    });

    // Called while the user is scrolling with two fingers
    mGestureDetector.setTwoFingerScrollListener(new GestureDetector.TwoFingerScrollListener() {

        @Override
        // displacement: average distance between scroll state entering x value
        // delta: average delta between two consecutive x motion events
        // velocity: sverage velocity of current x motion event
        // return: true if the events were handled
        public boolean onTwoFingerScroll(float displacement, float delta, float velocity) {
            Log.v(TAG, "onTwoFingerScroll");
            return false;
        }
    });
}
```

```java
// Send generic motion events to the gesture detector
@Override
public boolean onGenericMotionEvent(MotionEvent event) {
    if (mGestureDetector != null) {
        return mGestureDetector.onMotionEvent(event);
    }
    return false;
}

@Override
public boolean onCreateOptionsMenu(Menu menu) {
    MenuInflater inflater = getMenuInflater();
    inflater.inflate(R.menu.juststop, menu);

    MenuItem item2 = menu.add(0, R.id.stop+1, 0, R.string.headoff);
    MenuItem item3 = menu.add(0, R.id.stop+2, 0, R.string.headon);

    MenuUtils.setDescription(item2, R.string.headoffDesc);
    MenuUtils.setDescription(item3, R.string.headonDesc);
    MenuUtils.setInitialMenuItem(menu, item2);

    getWindow().addFlags(WindowUtils.FLAG_DISABLE_HEAD_GESTURES);
    return true;
}

@Override
public boolean onOptionsItemSelected(MenuItem item) {
    switch (item.getItemId()) {
    case R.id.stop:
        finish();
        return true;

    // see the the subection "Menu and Head Gesture" for further explanation
    case R.id.stop+1:
        getWindow().addFlags(WindowUtils.FLAG_DISABLE_HEAD_GESTURES);
        return true;

    case R.id.stop+2:
        getWindow().clearFlags(WindowUtils.FLAG_DISABLE_HEAD_GESTURES);
        return true;

    default:
        return super.onOptionsItemSelected(item);
    }
}
}
```

Run the app and keep tapping Glass, and you'll see some nice stars in a night sky—or at least to some kids, as shown in Figure 3-5.

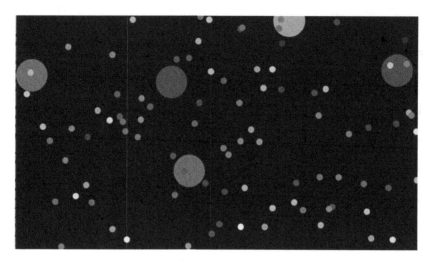

Figure 3-5. Immersion drawing canvas graphics

Long press Glass, and you'll see a menu with the options Stop, HeadOff, and HeadOn (more on the latter two in the next section). A menu in an immersion is created just like in a typical Android activity. Tap Stop to call finish() to stop the immersion activity. A more detailed discussion of menus in immersions is available at Glass's developer site at https://developers.google.com/glass/develop/gdk/ui/immersion-menus, but by looking at the integrated code here and trying it in your own app, you'll understand how to use it in no time.

Gestures and Listeners

If you just need to detect simple Glass gestures such as tapping the touchpad or swiping down, you can use Android's KeyEvent.Callback interface's onKeyDown and onKeyUp methods on immersion activities and check for their keycode values. For example, tapping the touchpad sets the keycode to KeyEvent.KEYCODE_DPAD_CENTER, and swiping down sets the keycode to KeyEvent.KEYCODE_BACK.

A better and more readable way for any nontrivial app to capture all possible Glass gestures is to use GestureDetector in the GDK. In the Immersion2DActivity class implementation shown earlier, a GestureDetector variable called mGestureDetector is instantiated, and the generic motion event is sent to it from the onGenericMotionEvent method. The four available gesture listeners (BaseListener, FingerListener, ScrollListener, and TwoFingerScrollListener) are added to mGestureDetector. Gestures that can be captured for each listener are self-explanatory in the code and comments.

Launch the app again, and this time pay close attention to ADT's LogCat's verbose output (LogCat is an Android feature that allows you to view logs output by your Android apps. See http://developer.android.com/tools/debugging/debugging-projects.html for more information.). Enter **tag:Imm** in the LogCat "Search for message" filter box and then tap once on Glass's touchpad. You'll see three lines as follows:

```
onFingerCountChanged:0,1
TAP
onFingerCountChanged:1,0
```

Two-finger tap, and you'll see five lines of output.

```
onFingerCountChanged:0,1
onFingerCountChanged:1,2
onFingerCountChanged:2,1
TWO_TAP
onFingerCountChanged:1,0
```

It's interesting to note that onFingerCountChanged logs all the discrete changes from the beginning to the end of the gesture.

One-finger swipe right will output several onScroll messages followed by SWIPE_RIGHT, enclosed by onFingerCountChanged:0,1 and onFingerCountChanged:1,0. Similarly, two-finger swipe left will print a bunch of onTwoFingerScroll followed by TWO_SWIPE_LEFT, enclosed between a few onFingerCountChanged messages. Figure 3-6 shows the logs for the four gestures. You may want to try other gestures listed in BaseListener to see what and how many events are invoked for each gesture.

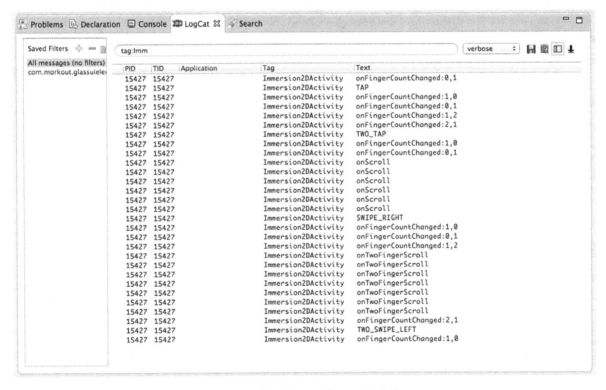

Figure 3-6. Gesture event logs: tap, two-finger tap, swipe right, two-finger swipe left

Menu and Head Gesture

A menu in immersion is created using the standard Android Menu API and/or menu inflating. In the onCreateOptionsMenu method in Listing 3-7, both methods are used: A Stop menu item is inflated from the menu resource, and then two other menu items, HeadOff and HeadOn, are created using the menu's add method. GDK also offers a setDescription method to let you set, of course, the description of a menu item; in this code, this is Turn Off Head Gesture for HeadOff, and Turn On Head Gesture for HeadOn. Another GDK menu-related API is setInitialMenuItem, which shows the specified item when the menu appears, instead of the default first item. Long press the touchpad, and you'll see the menu item HeadOff first; swipe left and right to see the other two items, as shown in Figure 3-7.

Figure 3-7. Menu description and initial menu item

Tap HeadOff or HeadOn uses another GDK feature called WindowUtils.FLAG_DISABLE_HEAD_GESTURES:

getWindow().addFlags(WindowUtils.FLAG_DISABLE_HEAD_GESTURES) disables head gesture, and getWindow().clearFlags(WindowUtils.FLAG_DISABLE_HEAD_GESTURES) reenables head gesture. Head gesture, meaning quickly nodding your head up, is used to turn your Glass display off. In an immersion, you may need to turn off head gesture so the Glass display won't be accidentally turned off. This is what the word *immersion* is meant to be: You are fully immersed in an activity with no distractions; your Glass screen suddenly going off would certainly be one extreme distraction.

3D OpenGL ES Drawing

If you have developed some OpenGL 3D app, especially on the Android platform, or if you wonder how well Glass supports OpenGL rendering, you'll be glad to know Glass has full support of OpenGL rendering—both OpenGL ES 1.0 and 2.0. I won't cover in detail how to develop OpenGL ES for Android; there are plenty of books on the topic. But I'll show you quickly some working sample code so you can get the idea. You have the app template to use when deciding to develop your own 3D app for Glass.

OpenGL ES 1.0

Listing 3-10 shows how to create an immersion that renders a shaking 3D tetrahedron in OpenGL ES 1.0.

Listing 3-10. Creating an Immersion with OpenGL ES 1.0 Rendering

```
// add in AppService.java:
private void createImmersionFor3DDrawing1() {
    Intent intent = new Intent(this, Immersion3DActivity.class);
    intent.addFlags(Intent.FLAG_ACTIVITY_NEW_TASK);
    startActivity(intent);
}

// change the onStartCommand calling code
public int onStartCommand(Intent intent, int flags, int startId) {
    createImmersionFor3DDrawing1();
        return START_STICKY;
}

// create an activity called Immersion3DActivity, and make its onCreate look like this:
public void onCreate(Bundle savedInstanceState) {
        super.onCreate(savedInstanceState);

    GLSurfaceView view = new GLSurfaceView(this);
        view.setRenderer(new TetrahedronRenderer(true));
        setContentView(view);
}
// create a class Tetrahedron as follows
class Tetrahedron {
    private FloatBuffer mFVertexBuffer;
    private ByteBuffer  mColorBuffer;
    private ByteBuffer  mIndexBuffer;

    public Tetrahedron() {
        byte ff = (byte)255;

        // four unique vertices for the tetrahedron
        float vertices[] = {
                -1.0f, 0.0f, 0.0f,
                1.0f, 0.0f, 0.0f,
                0.0f,  2.0f, 0.0f,
                0.0f, 0.6f, 0.5f
        };

        // color for each vertex
        byte colors[] = {
                ff, ff, 0, ff,
                0, ff, ff, ff,
                ff, 0, ff, ff,
                0, 0, ff, ff
        };
```

```java
        // how to draw triangles based on the four unique vertices - 0 means the first 3 values in
        vertices array
        byte indices[] = {
                0, 2, 1,
                0, 2, 3,
                0, 3, 1,
                3, 2, 1
        };

        ByteBuffer vbb = ByteBuffer.allocateDirect(vertices.length * 4);
        vbb.order(ByteOrder.nativeOrder());
        mFVertexBuffer = vbb.asFloatBuffer();
        mFVertexBuffer.put(vertices);
        mFVertexBuffer.position(0);

        mColorBuffer = ByteBuffer.allocateDirect(colors.length);
        mColorBuffer.put(colors);
        mColorBuffer.position(0);

        mIndexBuffer = ByteBuffer.allocateDirect(indices.length);
        mIndexBuffer.put(indices);
        mIndexBuffer.position(0);
    }

    public void draw(GL10 gl) {
        gl.glFrontFace(GL11.GL_CW);
        // 3 is for 3D, meaning each vertex consists of 3 values
        gl.glVertexPointer(3, GL11.GL_FLOAT, 0, mFVertexBuffer);
        gl.glColorPointer(4, GL11.GL_UNSIGNED_BYTE, 0, mColorBuffer);
        // 12 means there're 4 vertices, as each vertex has 3 values
        gl.glDrawElements(GL11.GL_TRIANGLES, 12, GL11.GL_UNSIGNED_BYTE, mIndexBuffer);

        gl.glFrontFace(GL11.GL_CCW);
    }
}
    // create one more class TetrahedronRenderer
    class TetrahedronRenderer implements GLSurfaceView.Renderer {
    private boolean mTranslucentBackground;
    private Tetrahedron mTetrahedron;
    private float mTransX;

    public TetrahedronRenderer(boolean useTranslucentBackground) {
        mTranslucentBackground = useTranslucentBackground;
        mTetrahedron = new Tetrahedron();
    }

    public void onSurfaceCreated(GL10 gl, EGLConfig config) {
        gl.glDisable(GL11.GL_DITHER);
        gl.glHint(GL11.GL_PERSPECTIVE_CORRECTION_HINT,GL11.GL_FASTEST);
```

```
    if (mTranslucentBackground)
        gl.glClearColor(0,0,0,0);
    else
        gl.glClearColor(1,1,1,1);

    gl.glEnable(GL11.GL_CULL_FACE);
    gl.glShadeModel(GL11.GL_SMOOTH);
    gl.glEnable(GL11.GL_DEPTH_TEST);
    }

    public void onSurfaceChanged(GL10 gl, int width, int height) {
        gl.glViewport(0, 0, width, height);

        float ratio = (float) width / height;
        gl.glMatrixMode(GL11.GL_PROJECTION);
        gl.glLoadIdentity();
        gl.glFrustumf(-ratio, ratio, -1, 1, 1, 10);
    }

    public void onDrawFrame(GL10 gl) {
        gl.glClear(GL10.GL_COLOR_BUFFER_BIT | GL10.GL_DEPTH_BUFFER_BIT);

        gl.glMatrixMode(GL10.GL_MODELVIEW);
        gl.glLoadIdentity();
        gl.glTranslatef((float)Math.sin(mTransX), -1.0f, -3.0f);

        gl.glEnableClientState(GL10.GL_VERTEX_ARRAY);
        gl.glEnableClientState(GL10.GL_COLOR_ARRAY);

        mTetrahedron.draw(gl);

        mTransX += .075f;
    }
}
```

Basically, the Android class GLSurfaceView and interface GLSurfaceView.Renderer are the building blocks you use to create OpenGL ES graphics. Here you are creating an instance of GLSurfaceView directly, but if you need to enable UI and capture Glass gestures, you should create a subclass of GLSurfaceView. The GLSurfaceView instance sets as its renderer a render object that implements the GLSurfaceView.Renderer interface, which has three required methods to be implemented: onSurfaceCreated, onSurfaceChanged, and onDrawFrame. The primary content rendering happens in the onDrawFrame method, which is called to draw the current frame.

Run the app, and you'll see a 3D tetrahedron shaking left and right in the center of Glass, as shown in Figure 3-8. Remember, you use the swipe-down gesture to exit the immersion.

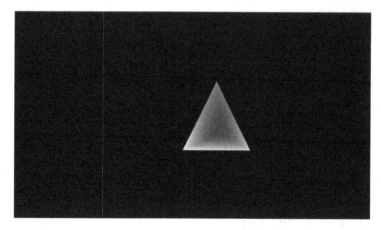

Figure 3-8. Immersion drawing OpenGL ES 1.0 graphics

OpenGL ES 2.0

There are some good OpenGLES Android samples at Android's developer web site that you should try: http://developer.android.com/training/graphics/opengl/index.html. Download and unzip OpenGLES.zip there, and you'll see two sample projects called HelloOpenGLES10 and HelloOpenGLES20. You can run them directly on your Android devices such as Nexus 7 tablet, and you should be able to port the HelloOpenGLES20 project to Glass with some minor changes. But there's a simpler tutorial at www.learnopengles.com/android-lesson-one-getting-started/, and you can get the renderer class source code at https://github.com/learnopengles/Learn-OpenGLES-Tutorials/blob/master/android/AndroidOpenGLESLessons/src/com/learnopengles/android/lesson1/LessonOneRenderer.java. Follow the next simple step to see it running on your Glass. Replace the onCreate method implementation in Immersion3DActivity of Listing 3-10 with the following code:

```
public void onCreate(Bundle savedInstanceState) {
    super.onCreate(savedInstanceState);

    // Check if the system supports OpenGL ES 2.0.
    final ActivityManager activityManager =
    (ActivityManager) getSystemService(Context.ACTIVITY_SERVICE);
    final ConfigurationInfo configurationInfo = activityManager.getDeviceConfigurationInfo();

    if (configurationInfo.reqGlEsVersion >=0x20000)
    {
        view3D = new MyGLView(this);
        setContentView(view3D);
    }
    else // because Glass supports OpenGL ES 2.0, this won't run, unless you remove the test above
    and just want to write or port some OpenGL ES 1.0 code
    {
        GLSurfaceView view = new GLSurfaceView(this);
        view.setRenderer(new TetrahedronRenderer(true));
        setContentView(view);
    }
}
```

```
// create a GLSurfaceView subclass MyGLView
public class MyGLView extends GLSurfaceView {
   private final MyGL20Renderer renderer2;
   Context mContext;

   MyGLView(Context context) {
      super(context);

      setEGLContextClientVersion(2);
      renderer2 = new MyGL20Renderer();
      setRenderer(renderer2);

   }
}

// save LessonOneRenderer.java file above and rename it as well as the class name to MyGL20Renderer
// then add the file to your project
```

> **Note**   The line setEGLContextClientVersion(2) in the MyGLView constructor is important. Without
> it, your app will crash with several error messages such as "Called unimplemented OpenGL ES API" when it
> calls shader-related APIs such as GLES20.glShaderSource and GLES20.glCompileShader.

That's all it takes to see an OpenGL ES 2.0 sample running in your Glass! Run the app, and say OK Glass" and then "Chapter 3" (yes, we're still in Chapter 3!), and you'll see, as shown in Figure 3-9, three triangles rotating nicely in 3D space.

Figure 3-9. *Immersion drawing OpenGL ES 2.0 graphics*

When to Use Which

So, you've seen working samples of how Glass-styled cards, live cards, and immersions are created and what kind of content can be rendered on them. You may have some intuition about when to use which. While I'll show you later in the book some real-world projects that are mainly based on live cards and immersions because they offer more user interaction and richer content, it's helpful to present a summary on the three main UI elements.

- Live cards are always on the left side of the OK Glass home screen. Swiping forward or backward on a live card navigates the timeline. An immersion, however, replaces the timeline completely. You cannot swipe forward or backward on an immersion to navigate the timeline; you have to swipe down to exit the immersion first before you can navigate the timeline again.

- Strictly speaking, static cards created by the Mirror API can typically accept user input (tapping) to show the menu, but this feature is not available yet in the GDK as of June 2014. Live cards are required to have a menu, and tapping a live card will show the menu. Swiping left or right on a live card, while the menu is not showing, will go to the previous or next card in the timeline, but other gestures won't be processed. Immersions can access a rich set of user gestures: tap, long press, swipe left and right, and multiple-finger versions of them. But both live cards and immersions can accept interesting sensor or location updates.

- You can use the Card API only to render a card's content in a predefined way: You set the main body text, images in full or layout mode, and a footnote. But you can render any layout, including 2D and 3D content, on live cards and immersions.

- Because of the characteristics of Glass-styled cards, live cards, and immersions discussed earlier, the major uses for each type are self-explanatory. However, a hybrid app that uses all three types of UIs can make sense in some cases; for example, you want to display a summary or preview in a live card and let users launch an immersion activity from a menu option if they want to have more interaction with the app. It's also easy to create cards from both live cards and immersions.

While developing real apps, you'll also find that some features are available only for immersions but not live cards. Disabling head gesture using `WindowUtils.FLAG_DISABLE_HEAD_GESTURES`, for example, is available only for an immersion.

Theme and UI Widgets

Glass developer's site has a well-documented guide and samples at `https://developers.google.com/glass/develop/gdk/ui/theme-widgets` on how to create consistent and great Glass themes and cards and how to create scrolling or swipeable cards in an activity, which can offer great Glass user experiences because the scrolling simulates the Glass timeline and should make users feel right at home about it. A typical use case is to launch the detailed scrollable view of cards for more information after the user chooses to see details on a summary live card. You can test CardScrollView by following these steps:

1. Create a new activity named CardScrollActivity and copy the sample code of CardScrollActivity from the previous Google URL; you can even add OpenGL views to the scrollable card view.

```
protected void onCreate(Bundle savedInstanceState) {
    super.onCreate(savedInstanceState);

    createCards();

    mCardScrollView = new CardScrollView(this);
    ExampleCardScrollAdapter adapter = new ExampleCardScrollAdapter();
    mCardScrollView.setAdapter(adapter);
    mCardScrollView.activate();
    setContentView(mCardScrollView);
}

private void createCards() {
    mCards = new ArrayList<View>();

    Card card;

    card = new Card(this);
    card.setText("This card has a footer.");
    card.setFootnote("I'm the footer!");
    mCards.add(card.getView());

    card = new Card(this);
    card.setText("This card has a puppy background image.");
    card.setFootnote("How can you resist?");
    card.setImageLayout(Card.ImageLayout.FULL);
    card.addImage(R.drawable.frown);
    mCards.add(card.getView());

    card = new Card(this);
    card.setText("This card has a mosaic of puppies.");
    card.setFootnote("Aren't they precious?");
    card.addImage(R.drawable.laugh);
    card.addImage(R.drawable.smile);
    card.addImage(R.drawable.surprise);
    mCards.add(card.getView());

    MyGLView v = new MyGLView(this);
    mCards.add(v);
    GLSurfaceView v2 = new GLSurfaceView(this);
    v2.setRenderer(new TetrahedronRenderer(true));
    mCards.add(v2);
    DrawView v3 = new DrawView(this);
    mCards.add(v3);

}
```

```
private class ExampleCardScrollAdapter extends CardScrollAdapter {
    @Override
    public int getPosition(Object item) {
        return mCards.indexOf(item);
    }

    @Override
    public int getCount() {
        return mCards.size();
    }

        @Override
    public Object getItem(int position) {
        return mCards.get(position);
    }

    @Override
    public View getView(int position, View convertView, ViewGroup parent) {
        return mCards.get(position);
    }
}
```

2. Add a new menu item in the `main.xml` in `res/menu` folder.

3. Add to the `onOptionsItemSelected` method of `MenuActivity.java` a new case for the ID defined in step 2.

```
Intent intent = new Intent(this, CardScrollActivity.class);
startActivity(intent);
```

4. Either copy some of your drawable images and rename them to those used in `CardScrollActivity` or rename them in `CardScrollActivity` to use your existing images.

5. Don't forget to add an activity element in your `AndroidManifest.xml` file.

```
<activity
    android:name="com.morkout.glassuielements.CardScrollActivity "
    android:label="@string/app_name"
    android:enabled="true" >
</activity>
```

6. Define your `AppService.java`'s `onStartCommand` to use any of the three live card calling methods (they all have the menu attached).

```
createLowFrequencyLiveCard();
createHighFrequencyLiveCardForLayoutInflating();
createHighFrequencyLiveCardForCanvasDrawing();
```

Run the app, tap the live card, and choose the new menu item. You'll see a scrolling view with three cards; they are created using the Card class, but because they're added to the CardScrollView instead of the timeline (starting XE 16, you actually can't add a card to the timeline), you won't see them in the timeline. The activity that holds the scrollview behaves just like an immersion: You cannot navigate to the timeline; the scrollview replaces the timeline. Swipe down on it, and it will exit the activity and take you back to the live card, where you can navigate to the timeline or tap to see the menu (with a Stop menu option to exit the live card) again.

> **Note**   If you have created quite a few test apps, which you should do, and need to uninstall any app from your Glass, simply run the command adb uninstall <your_app_package_name>. If needed, you can see the whole list of installed app package names with the command adb shell 'pm list packages -f'.

Summary

In this chapter, you entered the exciting world of Glass and learned what kinds of UI elements can be built with GDK for a Glass app. The main Glass UI elements—the timeline, Glass-styled cards, live cards, immersions, menu items, and gestures—were discussed in detail with fully tested sample code that showed you how to render standard UI content, content from an XML layout, and content created using Android's Canvas 2D and OpenGL ES 1.0 and 2.0. By now you should have a basic understanding of what kinds of apps you can build with GDK and when to use which or a combination of them. The journey has just started. In the following three chapters, I'll first cover camera and image processing and then discuss video processing before moving on to voice and audio processing, among other exciting topics.

Chapter 4

Camera and Image Processing

The camera is one of the essential features of Glass and also a perfect fit for it. Two of the most frequently used commands offered on Glass are "Take a picture" and "Record a video," both using the Glass camera. After a picture or video is taken, sharing is one typical task, but further processing of the image or video to achieve goals such as image recognition, barcode or character recognition, and image or video editing can all be desirable in many use cases. Also, in the latest GDK mini-game samples (`https://developers.google.com/glass/samples/mini-games`), a cool Fruit Ninja–like game called Shape Splitter detects slices when users move their hands in front of the camera.

In this chapter, I'll focus on how to use the GDK and Android SDK to develop camera and image-processing apps on Glass. There will be a lot to cover, so I'll discuss video-related topics in the next chapter. Problems you'll solve include the following:

- How to add preview and zoom features for your Glass camera. Preview is essential for many advanced image-processing techniques.

- How to share pictures taken by uploading to Google Drive and by e-mailing them to yourself.

- How to scroll over pictures saved on your Glass.

- How to do barcode and QR code recognition.

- How to do OCR.

- How to do image search via Google.

- How to do more image processing with OpenCV.

I hope this list excites you as it did me while I started writing the chapter. By the end of the chapter, you'll have a solid sense of what techniques can be used for building your next amazing camera-based image apps on Glass.

Taking Pictures

The first task when using the camera is, of course, to take a picture. You can do this in your code in two ways: the easy way and the custom way.

The Easy Way

You use the built-in camera activity and the ACTION_IMAGE_CAPTURE intent to take a picture that is saved by default in your Glass's external storage directory: DCIM/Camera.

```
Intent i = new Intent(android.provider.MediaStore.ACTION_IMAGE_CAPTURE);
startActivityForResult(i, CAPTURE_IMAGE_ACTIVITY_REQUEST_CODE);
```

Then in your activity's onActivityResult, you can get the path of the saved picture and do further processing.

```
protected void onActivityResult(int requestCode, int resultCode, Intent data) {
    if (requestCode == CAPTURE_IMAGE_ACTIVITY_REQUEST_CODE && resultCode == RESULT_OK) {
        String picturePath = data.getStringExtra(CameraManager.EXTRA_PICTURE_FILE_PATH);
        String thumbnailPath = data.getStringExtra(CameraManager.EXTRA_THUMBNAIL_FILE_PATH);
        // processPictureWhenReady(picturePath);
    }

    super.onActivityResult(requestCode, resultCode, data);
}
```

When onActivityResult gets called, the image file may not exist yet. So, you need to check whether it exists and, if not, start a file observer that can notify you when the file is ready so you can continue the processing. For a detailed code sample, you can check out Google's Glass developer site at https://developers.google.com/glass/develop/gdk/media-camera/camera.

This easy way of taking a picture does not require you to click the Camera button on Glass, so it's like the OK Glass voice command "Take a picture." But it doesn't automatically save the picture taken to the Glass timeline for you to make a vignette, share, or delete it. Furthermore, preview and zoom, two important features, are possible only with the custom method. Also, you can't use this method directly from a service, which implies that you can't use it from a live card. It's time to enter a more sophisticated world.

The Custom Method

You use the Android Camera API to have more control of your Glass camera. If you have used the Camera API for Android development, the following code will look quite familiar, but because of the Glass display size, there are some Glass-specific settings you should be aware of. Let's first see how to use the Camera API to add the preview feature to your Glass camera.

Preview

Follow these steps to create and run a new sample project for this chapter with the preview feature:

1. Create a new Android app called SmartCameraBasic and use GlasswareTemplate, as documented in Chapters 2 and 3, to set up your new project.

2. Change your app's voice command in values/strings.xml by changing the value for name say_glasswaretemplate to Smart Camera. You may also want to change the name say_glasswaretemplate referred to in strings.xml and xml/voice_trigger_start.xml to say_smartcamera.

3. Delete the tts and asr menu items in menu/main.xml and add a new entry as follows:

```
<item
        android:id="@+id/preview"
        android:title="@string/preview"/>
```

4. Create the new string value Preview for the name "preview" in strings.xml.

```
<string name="preview">Preview</string>
```

5. In onOptionsItemSelected of MenuActivity.java, create a new case for preview.

```
case R.id.preview:
    Intent intent = new Intent(this, PreviewActivity.class);
    startActivity(intent);
    return true;
```

6. Create a layout/preview.xml file.

```
<RelativeLayout xmlns:android="http://schemas.android.com/apk/res/android"
    xmlns:tools="http://schemas.android.com/tools"
    android:layout_width="match_parent"
    android:layout_height="match_parent"
    tools:context=".MainActivity" >

    <SurfaceView
        android:id="@+id/preview"
        android:layout_width="match_parent"
        android:layout_height="match_parent" >
    </SurfaceView>
</RelativeLayout>
```

7. Create a new activity called PreviewActivity, as shown in Listing 4-1.

Listing 4-1. Implementing Camera Preview

```java
public class PreviewActivity extends Activity
{
    private SurfaceView mPreview;
    private SurfaceHolder mPreviewHolder;
    private android.hardware.Camera mCamera;
    private boolean mInPreview = false;
    private boolean mCameraConfigured = false;

    // code copied from http://developer.android.com/guide/topics/media/camera.html
    /** A safe way to get an instance of the Camera object. */
    public static Camera getCameraInstance(){
        Camera c = null;
        try {
            c = Camera.open(); // attempt to get a Camera instance
        }
        catch (Exception e){
            // Camera is not available (in use or does not exist)
            System.out.println("Camera is not available");
        }
        return c; // returns null if camera is unavailable
    }

    @Override
    public void onCreate(Bundle savedInstanceState) {
        super.onCreate(savedInstanceState);

        setContentView(R.layout.preview);
        getWindow().addFlags(WindowManager.LayoutParams.FLAG_KEEP_SCREEN_ON);
        mPreview = (SurfaceView)findViewById(R.id.preview);
        mPreviewHolder = mPreview.getHolder();
        mPreviewHolder.addCallback(surfaceCallback);

        mCamera = Camera.open();
        if (mCamera != null)
            startPreview();
    }

    private void configPreview(int width, int height) {
        if ( mCamera != null && mPreviewHolder.getSurface() != null) {
            try {
                mCamera.setPreviewDisplay(mPreviewHolder);
            }
            catch (IOException e) {
                Toast.makeText(PreviewActivity.this, e.getMessage(), Toast.LENGTH_LONG).show();
            }

            if ( !mCameraConfigured ) {
                Camera.Parameters parameters = mCamera.getParameters();
                parameters.setPreviewFpsRange(30000, 30000);
                parameters.setPreviewSize(640, 360);
```

```
                mCamera.setParameters(parameters);
                mCameraConfigured = true;
            }
        }
    }

    private void startPreview() {
        if ( mCameraConfigured && mCamera != null ) {
            mCamera.startPreview();
            mInPreview = true;
        }
    }

    SurfaceHolder.Callback surfaceCallback = new SurfaceHolder.Callback() {
        public void surfaceCreated( SurfaceHolder holder ) {
        }

        public void surfaceChanged( SurfaceHolder holder, int format, int width, int height ) {
            configPreview(width, height);
            startPreview();
        }

        public void surfaceDestroyed( SurfaceHolder holder ) {
            if (mCamera != null) {
                mCamera.release();
                mCamera = null;
            }
        }
    };

    @Override
    public void onResume() {
        super.onResume();

        // Re-acquire the camera and start the preview.
        if (mCamera == null) {
            mCamera = getCameraInstance();
            if (mCamera != null) {
                configPreview(640, 360);
                startPreview();
            }
        }
    }

    @Override
    public void onPause() {
        if ( mInPreview ) {
            mCamera.stopPreview();
            mCamera.release();
            mCamera = null;
            mInPreview = false;
        }
        super.onPause();
    }
```

```
    @Override
    public boolean onKeyDown(int keyCode, KeyEvent event) {
        // see note 2 after the code for explanation
        if (keyCode == KeyEvent.KEYCODE_CAMERA) {
            if ( mInPreview ) {
                mCamera.stopPreview();
                mCamera.release();
                mCamera = null;
                mInPreview = false;
            }
            return false;
        } else return super.onKeyDown(keyCode, event);
    }
}
```

8. Add the activity to AndroidManifest.xml.

```
    <activity
                android:name="com.morkout.smartcamerabasic.PreviewActivity"
                android:label="@string/app_name"
                android:enabled="true" >
    </activity>
```

You also need to add camera-related permission and feature lines in the AndroidManifest.xml file.

```
    <uses-permission android:name="android.permission.CAMERA" />
    <uses-feature android:name="android.hardware.camera" />
```

Run the app and say "OK Glass" and then "Smart Camera." You'll see the big two-line text "Smart Camera" on your Glass. Tap the touchpad to reveal the menu, tap Preview to see things in front of your camera (unlike the default Glass "Take picture" command, which does not allow you to see a preview before taking a picture), and then turn around your head until the preview in your Glass looks good and click the Camera button to take a picture. After the click, you'll hear the standard "Take picture" sound and see the picture taken. Tapping it will show the standard menu items "Make vignette," "Share," and "Delete." The picture is also saved to your Glass timeline. As with other immersion (activity), you can swipe down to exit the Preview screen and return to the main Smart Camera screen, which you should remember is a live card.

There are two important things to note about the previous code.

■ In initPreview, two Camera.Parameters are set specifically for Glass:

```
    parameters.setPreviewFpsRange(30000, 30000);
    parameters.setPreviewSize(640, 360);
```

Without the two settings, the preview picture will be distorted.

■ Inside onKeyDown, there is a test to see whether the Camera button is clicked and, if so, another test to see whether the app is in preview mode. If it is, you need to stop the preview, release mCamera (because this app does not handle taking pictures, you have to let the system handle it by releasing the camera), and reset the two variables mCamera and mInPreview. If you don't do these tests, the app will crash when the Camera button is clicked.

> **Note** The `if (keyCode == KeyEvent.KEYCODE_CAMERA)` test in onKeyDown will return true even if you long press the Camera button to capture a video. You can use `event.isLongPress()` to check whether it's a long press (for video capture) or not (for picture taking). So, this preview actually works for video too.

If this is the first time you see the preview working on your Glass, you should feel pretty good. But it's easy to want more; the next thing naturally is to zoom while doing the preview, isn't it?

Zoom

The steps to add the zoom feature to your app are as follows:

1. Create a new layout XML file called zoom.xml as follows (a new TextView is added to the preview.xml):

```xml
<RelativeLayout xmlns:android="http://schemas.android.com/apk/res/android"
    xmlns:tools="http://schemas.android.com/tools"
    android:layout_width="match_parent"
    android:layout_height="match_parent"
    tools:context=".MainActivity" >

    <SurfaceView  android:id="@+id/preview"
        android:layout_width="match_parent"
        android:layout_height="match_parent">
    </SurfaceView>

    <TextView
        android:id="@+id/zoomLevel"
        android:layout_width="wrap_content"
        android:layout_height="wrap_content"
        android:layout_alignParentBottom="true"
        android:layout_alignParentRight="true"
        android:layout_marginBottom="16dp"
        android:layout_marginRight="16dp"
        android:shadowColor="#000000"
        android:shadowDx="1"
        android:shadowDy="1"
        android:shadowRadius="1"
        android:text="ZOOM: 0">
    </TextView>
</RelativeLayout>
```

2. Create a new activity called ZoomActivity with the code snippet shown in Listing 4-2 (the complete code listing is quite long, so you should download it from the book's source code).

Listing 4-2. Implementing Camera Zoom

```
public void onCreate(Bundle savedInstanceState) {
        ... // same as PreviewActivity.java

        mZoomLevelView = (TextView)findViewById(R.id.zoomLevel);
        mGestureDetector = new GestureDetector(this, this);

        mCamera = getCameraInstance();
        if (mCamera != null)
            startPreview();
    }

    private void initPreview(int width, int height) {
        if ( mCamera != null && mPreviewHolder.getSurface() != null) {
            try {
                mCamera.setPreviewDisplay(mPreviewHolder);
            }
            catch (Throwable t) {
                Toast.makeText(ZoomActivity.this, t.getMessage(), Toast.LENGTH_LONG).show();
            }

            if ( !mCameraConfigured ) {
                Camera.Parameters parameters = mCamera.getParameters();
                parameters.setPreviewFpsRange(30000, 30000);
                parameters.setPreviewSize(640, 360);
                mCamera.setParameters(parameters);
                mCamera.setZoomChangeListener(this);
                mCameraConfigured = true;
            }
        }
    }

    @Override
    public boolean onGenericMotionEvent(MotionEvent event) {
        mGestureDetector.onTouchEvent(event);
        return true;
    }

    @Override
    public boolean onFling( MotionEvent e1, MotionEvent e2, float velocityX, float velocityY ) {
        if (mCamera==null || mPreviewHolder.getSurface() == null) return true;

        Camera.Parameters parameters = mCamera.getParameters();
```

```java
        int zoom = parameters.getZoom();
        if ( velocityX < 0.0f ) {
            zoom -= 5;
            if ( zoom < 0 )
                zoom = 0;
        }
        else if ( velocityX > 0.0f ) {
            zoom += 5;
            if ( zoom > parameters.getMaxZoom() )
                zoom = parameters.getMaxZoom();
        }

        mCamera.stopSmoothZoom();
        mCamera.startSmoothZoom(zoom);

        return false;
    }

    public void onLongPress(MotionEvent e) {
        mCamera.takePicture(null, null, mPictureCallback);
    }

    @Override
    public void onZoomChange(int zoomValue, boolean stopped, Camera camera) {
        mZoomLevelView.setText("ZOOM: " + zoomValue);
    }

    Camera.PictureCallback mPictureCallback = new Camera.PictureCallback() {
        public void onPictureTaken(byte[] data, Camera camera) {
            // copied from http://developer.android.com/guide/topics/media/camera.html#custom-camera
            File pictureFile = getOutputMediaFile(MEDIA_TYPE_IMAGE);
            if (pictureFile == null){
                Log.v(TAG, "Error creating media file, check storage permissions: ");
                return;
            }

            try {
                FileOutputStream fos = new FileOutputStream(pictureFile);
                fos.write(data);
                fos.close();

                finish();

            } catch (FileNotFoundException e) {
                Log.d(TAG, "File not found: " + e.getMessage());
            } catch (IOException e) {
            }
        }

    };
```

```
    @Override
    public boolean onKeyDown(int keyCode, KeyEvent event) {
        if (keyCode == KeyEvent.KEYCODE_CAMERA) {
            if (event.isLongPress()) // video capture
                return true; // If you return true from onKeyDown(), your activity consumes
the event and the Glass camera doesn't handle it

            if ( mInPreview ) {
                mCamera.stopPreview();

                mCamera.release();
                mCamera = null;
                mInPreview = false;
            }
            return false;
        } else return super.onKeyDown(keyCode, event);
    }
}
```

Basically, a new TextView that shows the current zoom level at the bottom-right corner is created as mZoomLevelView. In addition, a GestureDetector is created (see Chapter 3 for details) to capture long press (used to take the zoomed picture), and the camera's setZoomChangeListener is called so onZoomChange gets called when the camera's startSmoothZoom is called inside the onFling method, meaning swiping forward and backward will zoom in and out on the picture being previewed. Glass's max zoom level is 60, so you'll see the zoom value between 0 and 60 at the bottom right.

Because the default Camera button click will take the picture only as its original size, you need to disable the default behavior, done in onKeyDown, and also manually call the camera's takePicture method inside the onLongPress method. The third argument of the takePicture method defines a Camera.PictureCallback with a callback method onPictureTaken, which mainly saves the zoomed image to Glass for later processing.

3. Create a new menu item <item android:id="@+id/zoom" android:title="@ string/zoom"/>in main.xml, a new string item <string name="zoom">Zoom</ string> in strings.xml, and a new case for the zoom menu option in MenuActivity.java.

```
case R.id.zoom:
    Intent intent2 = new Intent(this, ZoomActivity.class);
    startActivity(intent2);
    return true;
```

4. Don't forget to declare the ZoomActivity in AndroidManifest.xml.

```
<activity
    android:name="com.morkout.smartcamerabasic.ZoomActivity"
    android:enabled="true"
    android:label="@string/app_name" >
</activity>
```

Run the app and say "OK Glass" and then "Smart Camera." Tap and select Zoom on the menu, swipe to zoom in or out, and long press the touchpad to take and save the zoomed picture.

Again, only pressing the Camera button automatically saves the picture taken to the timeline with menu options, and the Camera button cannot take a zoomed picture by default; that's why you need to write your own code to enable the previewing, sharing, and deleting functions.

Upload and E-mail

If you tap a picture that was taken and saved to the timeline, you'll see a menu with at least Share and Delete. Tapping Share will show a list of options, including Google Plus, Evernote, Path, Facebook, and Twitter—if you have chosen to install those apps. Maybe you already have a web site of your own and want to share the zoomed picture taken in the previous section to your site or develop an app to share it on a third-party web site. I'll discuss in detail in a later chapter how to implement such a sharing solution because it is quite a big topic. But here at least you should be able to view and send the picture to yourself so you can share it with more people if necessary. Here's what it takes to view the picture, upload it to your Google Drive, or e-mail to yourself:

1. Create a new activity called ImageViewActivity (don't forget to specify it in AndroidManifest.xml), as shown in Listing 4-3.

Listing 4-3. Uploading to Google Drive and E-mailing It to Yourself

```
public class ImageViewActivity extends Activity implements Runnable {
    ImageView mImageview;
    private GestureDetector mGestureDetector;
    File mPictureFilePath;
    String mEmail;

    @Override
    protected void onCreate(Bundle savedInstanceState) {
        super.onCreate(savedInstanceState);

        setContentView(R.layout.imageview);
        Bundle extras = getIntent().getExtras();
        mPictureFilePath = (File)extras.get("picturefilepath");
        mImageview = (ImageView) findViewById(R.id.picture);

        // need to scale down the image to avoid the error of loading a bitmap too big
        Bitmap myBitmap = BitmapFactory.decodeFile(mPictureFilePath.getAbsolutePath());
        int h = (int) ( myBitmap.getHeight() * (640.0 / myBitmap.getWidth()) );

        Bitmap scaled = Bitmap.createScaledBitmap(myBitmap, 640, h, true);
        mImageview.setImageBitmap(scaled);

        mGestureDetector = new GestureDetector(this);
```

```
        mGestureDetector.setBaseListener(new GestureDetector.BaseListener() {
            @Override
            public boolean onGesture(Gesture gesture) {
                if (gesture == Gesture.TAP)
                    openOptionsMenu();
                }
                return true;
            }
        });
    }

    public boolean onGenericMotionEvent(MotionEvent event) {
        if (mGestureDetector != null) {
            return mGestureDetector.onMotionEvent(event);
        }
        return false;
    }

    Handler mHandler = new Handler() {
        @Override
        public void handleMessage(Message msg) {
            String text = (String)msg.obj;
            Toast.makeText(ImageViewActivity.this, text, Toast.LENGTH_SHORT).show();
        }
    };

    public void run() {
        Mail m = new Mail("<yourown@gmail.com>", "<yourpassword>");

        Pattern emailPattern = Patterns.EMAIL_ADDRESS;
        Account[] accounts = AccountManager.get(AppService.appService()).getAccounts();
        for (Account account : accounts) {
            if (emailPattern.matcher(account.name).matches()) {
                mEmail = account.name;
            }
        }

        String[] toArr = {mEmail};
        m.setTo(toArr);
        m.setFrom("<yourown@gmail.com>");
        m.setSubject("Picture taken with Smart Camera");
        m.setBody("To get the app for your Glass, go to https://github.com/xjefftang/smartcamera");

        try {
            m.addAttachment(mPictureFilePath.getAbsolutePath());
            if(m.send()) {
                Message msg = new Message();
                msg.obj = "Email sent successfully.";
                mHandler.sendMessage(msg);
            } else {
                Message msg = new Message();
                msg.obj = "Email not sent.";
```

```java
                    mHandler.sendMessage(msg);
            }
        } catch(Exception e) {
            Log.e("MailApp", "Could not send email", e);
        }
    }


    @Override
    public boolean onCreateOptionsMenu(Menu menu) {
        MenuInflater inflater = getMenuInflater();
        inflater.inflate(R.menu.imageview, menu);
        return true;
    }


    @Override
    public boolean onOptionsItemSelected(MenuItem item) {
        switch (item.getItemId()) {
        case R.id.upload:
            Uri imgUri = Uri.parse("file://" + mPictureFilePath.getAbsolutePath());
            Intent shareIntent = ShareCompat.IntentBuilder.from(this)
                    .setText("Share image taken by Glass")
                    .setType("image/jpeg")
                    .setStream(imgUri )
                    .getIntent()
                    .setPackage("com.google.android.apps.docs");
            startActivity(shareIntent);

            return true;

        case R.id.email:
            Toast.makeText(ImageViewActivity.this, "Sending email...", Toast.LENGTH_LONG).show();
            // send network activity in the background, not the main thread, to avoid app exception
            Thread thread = new Thread(ImageViewActivity.this);
            thread.start();
            return true;

        case R.id.delete:
            mPictureFilePath.delete();
            Toast.makeText(ImageViewActivity.this, "Deleted", Toast.LENGTH_SHORT).show();
            finish();
            return true;

        default:
            return super.onOptionsItemSelected(item);
        }
    }

}
```

2. Add the following lines in onPictureTaken in Listing 4-2, after
    FileOutputStream fos = new FileOutputStream(pictureFile);
    fos.write(data); fos.close();:

    ```
    Intent intent = new Intent(AppService.appService(),ImageViewActivity.class);
        intent.putExtra("picturefilepath", pictureFile);
        startActivity(intent);
    ```

3. Download the Google Drive app APK file from the book's source code,
    named com.google.android.apps.docs-1.2.461.14.apk, and use the
    following command to install it to your Glass:

    ```
    adb install com.google.android.apps.docs-1.2.461.14.apk
    ```

4. Download the three JavaMail for Android library files at
    https://code.google.com/p/javamail-android/downloads/list and
    add them to your project's libs folder.

5. Add these lines to your AndroidManifest.xml so you can send e-mail or
    upload photos to Google Drive:

    ```
    <uses-permission android:name="android.permission.INTERNET" />
    <uses-permission android:name="android.permission.GET_ACCOUNTS" />
    <uses-permission android:name="android.permission.READ_PROFILE" />
    <uses-permission android:name="android.permission.READ_CONTACTS" />
    ```

6. Create a layout imageview.xml file.

    ```
    <FrameLayout
        xmlns:android="http://schemas.android.com/apk/res/android"
        android:layout_width="match_parent"
        android:layout_height="match_parent"
        android:background="@color/black" >
        <ImageView
            android:id="@+id/picture"
            android:layout_width="match_parent"
            android:layout_height="match_parent"
        />
    </FrameLayout>
    ```

7. Create a menu imageview.xml file.

    ```
    <?xml version="1.0" encoding="utf-8"?>
    <menu xmlns:android="http://schemas.android.com/apk/res/android" >

        <item
            android:id="@+id/upload"
            android:title="@string/upload"/>
        <item
            android:id="@+id/email"
    ```

```
                    android:title="@string/email"/>
            <item
                    android:id="@+id/delete"
                    android:title="@string/delete"/>
        </menu>
```

8. Create upload, e-mail, and delete entries in `strings.xml`.

```
<string name="upload">Upload to GDrive</string>
<string name="email">Email to Self</string>
<string name="delete">Delete from Glass</string>
```

Run the app, zoom, and take a new picture. This time you'll see the picture taken after zooming. Tapping the picture will show a menu with options. Tap Upload to GDrive, and you'll see your Glass Gmail address, your picture name, a thumbnail, and Cancel and OK buttons. Swipe forward and backward to navigate to different UI elements, and tap the Glass touchpad will send the picture to your Google Drive, as shown in Figure 4-1.

Figure 4-1. *Uploading a picture to Google Drive*

Tapping Email to Self will simply send an e-mail in a background thread with the picture just taken as an attachment to your Glass Gmail account. After the e-mail is sent, you'll see this message on Glass: "Email sent successfully." If you import the project from the book's source code, don't forget to change `ImageViewActivity.java` to use your own Gmail and password to test this Email to Self feature.

Finally, selecting Delete from the Glass menu option simply deletes the image file.

Before entering the more advanced image-processing world, I'll show you quickly how to view the photos in Glass's external storage directory, `DCIM/Camera`.

Photo View

From now on, I won't repeat the steps to create a new menu item to launch a new immersion activity. Just remember that you need to update the menu XML file, the strings.xml file, the `AndroidManifest.xml` file, and the `MenuActivity.java` file, and if necessary, you need to add a new layout XML file. I'll just show you a code snippet or the whole listing of each new activity file. The complete code is in the `PhotoViewActivity.java` file in the source code for Chapter 4.

In Listing 4-4, CardScrollView is used to show a list of photos in a directory defined by mAppPicDir. First you iterate the directory recursively to get a list of JPEG files. Then you use GDK's Card class to create Card objects; before you call Card's addImage file, you scale down the image file to prevent the large-sized bitmap from causing an error.

Listing 4-4. Showing Photos in a Folder

```
private List<View> mCards;
private CardScrollView mCardScrollView;
ArrayList<FilenameDir> mPicInfo = new ArrayList<FilenameDir>();
final private String mAppPicDir = Environment.getExternalStorageDirectory()+"/"+Environment.
DIRECTORY_PICTURES + "/SmartCamera";

private void createCards() {
    mCards = new ArrayList<View>();
    getPictureLists(mAppPicDir);

    for (FilenameDir fDir : mPicInfo) {
        Card card = new Card(this);
        card.setFootnote(fDir.mDirname + "/" + fDir.mFilename);
        card.setImageLayout(Card.ImageLayout.FULL);

        // without scale down, you'll get "Bitmap too large to be uploaded into a texture" error
        Bitmap myBitmap = BitmapFactory.decodeFile(fDir.mDirname + "/" + fDir.mFilename);
        int h = (int) ( myBitmap.getHeight() * (640.0 / myBitmap.getWidth()) );
        Bitmap scaled = Bitmap.createScaledBitmap(myBitmap, 640, h, true);

        try {
            File file = new File(mAppPicDir + "/scaled-" + fDir.mFilename);
            FileOutputStream fOut = new FileOutputStream(file);
            scaled.compress(Bitmap.CompressFormat.JPEG, 85, fOut);
            fOut.close();
        }
        catch (Exception e) {
        }

        card.addImage(BitmapFactory.decodeFile(mAppPicDir + "/scaled-" + fDir.mFilename));
        mCards.add(card.getView());
    }
}

private void getPictureLists(String directory) {
    File dir = new File(directory);
    File[] files = dir.listFiles();
    int count = 1; // used to limit the number of photos to add to CardScrollView at one time
    for (File file : files) {
        if (file.isDirectory()) {
            if (file.getAbsolutePath().indexOf("/Pictures/cache") == -1)
                getPictureLists(file.getAbsolutePath());
        }
```

```
        else {
            if (file.getName().indexOf(".jpg") == -1) continue;

            if (count++ == 10) break; // likely out of memory if more than 20
            mPicInfo.add(new FilenameDir(file.getName(), directory));
        }
    }
}

private class FilenameDir {
    private String mFilename;
    private String mDirname;

    public FilenameDir(String filename, String dirname)
    {
        mFilename = filename;
        mDirname = dirname;
    }
}
```

To test this, launch the app and select the Photo View menu, and after the pictures in your camera folder are loaded and processed, you can swipe left and right to browse them.

You can improve the code in a few ways to make it more useful.

1. Present an easy-to-navigate way to browse all the picture folders and let the user choose the picture folder.

2. Remove the limit of how many photo cards can be added to CardScrollView. A possible solution is to show only three cards, and when the user navigates the photos, you dynamically update the cards in the scroll view.

3. Improve the performance by caching scaled-down bitmaps so you don't repeat the same photo's bitmap scaling.

The source code project that includes the previewing, zooming, photo viewing, sharing with Google Drive, and e-mailing features is named SmartCameraBasic. Let's move on to more advanced image-processing topics. To follow along with the upcoming sections, you can either refactor the SmartCameraBasic project by renaming both the project name and package name to SmartCamera or import the completed project named SmartCamera from the source code of this chapter.

Barcode Recognition

Have you ever wondered how Glass scans and recognizes the QR code (for an explanation of QR code and barcode, check out http://en.wikipedia.org/wiki/QR_code) when you set up your Glass's wi-fi network? Or how do you let your app figure out what the QR code in Figure 4-2 means? Soon you'll find that it's my home network's name and password; you're welcome to use them when you pay me a visit.

Figure 4-2. My Glass setup showing QR code

I know you'd be more interested in recognizing any barcode or QR code in your app. Can't wait to get started? Follow these tested steps to add the barcode support to your Glass app in a few minutes:

1. Download the open source Android barcode library ZBarScanner at `https://github.com/DushyanthMaguluru/ZBarScanner` and import it to your Eclipse workspace.

2. Change the `minSdkVersion` in `AndroidManifest.xml` to 19.

3. In the `surfaceChanged` method of `CameraPreview.java` of the ZBarScanner project, replace the following:

```
parameters.setPreviewSize(mPreviewSize.width, mPreviewSize.height);
```

with the following:

```
parameters.setPreviewFpsRange(30000, 30000);
parameters.setPreviewSize(640, 360);
```

so the preview picture on Glass won't be distorted.

4. Change your SmartCamera app's property to add the ZBarScanner library, as shown in Figure 4-3.

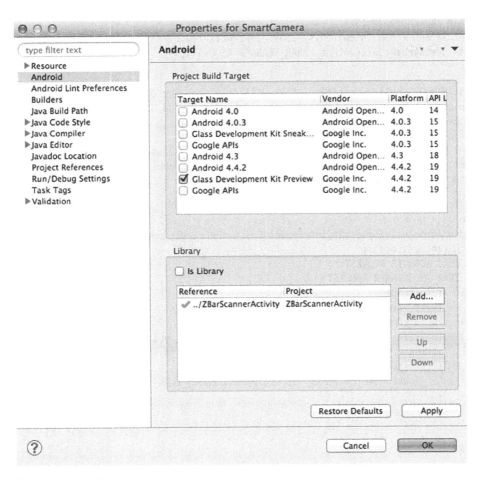

Figure 4-3. Adding the barcode library

5. Create a new activity ScannerActivity (and menu, strings, and so on), as shown in Listing 4-5.

Listing 4-5. Recognizing Barcodes

```java
public class ScannerActivity extends Activity {

    private static final int ZBAR_SCANNER_REQUEST = 0;
    private static final int ZBAR_QR_SCANNER_REQUEST = 1;

    @Override
    public void onCreate(Bundle savedInstanceState) {
        super.onCreate(savedInstanceState);
        launchQRScanner();
    }

    // this will scan for any type of barcodes - see https://github.com/dm77/ZBarScanner under
Advanced Options for a complete list
```

```
    public void launchScanner() {
        Intent intent = new Intent(this, ZBarScannerActivity.class);
        startActivityForResult(intent, ZBAR_SCANNER_REQUEST);
    }

    // with SCAN_MODES option specified, this will only scan for QR code. other supported scan modes
are listed in the URL above, also under Advanced Options. If you only need to scan for QR code,
calling this method is faster than calling launchScanner above.
    public void launchQRScanner() {
        Intent intent = new Intent(this, ZBarScannerActivity.class);
        intent.putExtra(ZBarConstants.SCAN_MODES, new int[]{Symbol.QRCODE});
        startActivityForResult(intent, ZBAR_SCANNER_REQUEST);
    }

    @Override
    protected void onActivityResult(int requestCode, int resultCode, Intent data) {
        switch (requestCode) {
        case ZBAR_SCANNER_REQUEST:
        case ZBAR_QR_SCANNER_REQUEST:
            if (resultCode == RESULT_OK) {
                Toast.makeText(this, "Scan Result = " + data.getStringExtra(ZBarConstants.SCAN_
RESULT), Toast.LENGTH_LONG).show();
            } else if(resultCode == RESULT_CANCELED && data != null) {
                String error = data.getStringExtra(ZBarConstants.ERROR_INFO);
                if(!TextUtils.isEmpty(error)) {
                    Toast.makeText(this, error, Toast.LENGTH_LONG).show();
                }
            }
        }
    }
}
```

That's all there is to add barcode support to your app! Now if you run the app, select the Scanner menu option, and move your Glass to the QR code in Figure 4-2, you'll see the recognized code in Figure 4-4. Or you can open http://en.wikipedia.org/wiki/QR_code and move your Glass close to the sample QR code there, and you'll see the recognized code "http://en.m.wikipedia.org" on your Glass screen.

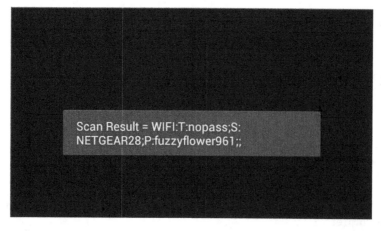

Figure 4-4. Recognized wi-fi name and password

Note If you wonder how I figured out these steps and how this compares to the other popular open source barcode project ZXing, I can honestly say that it took me many nights of testing on Glass as well as looking into how those Android barcode apps work on an Android tablet like Nexus 7. You can use a tool called dex2jar, which converts an APK file to a JAR file, and the `jar tvf <jar_file>` command to get some insight into what library those apps use and how well they run on Nexus before selecting a library to port to Glass. A ZXing library open source port to Glass called BarcodeEye also works by itself, but the integration of it is much more complicated than the ZBarScanner library. You could also try another newer library by the same author of ZBarScanner and see whether you can port it to Glass: `https://github.com/dm77/barcodescanner`.

OCR

What's next after barcode recognition? Character recognition sounds reasonable. The best open source OCR library is Tesseract, and many OCR apps (for example, OCR Instantly) in Google Play use it. With Tesseract, you can do OCR offline, meaning you don't need network connectivity to upload an image to a web service such as Google Drive to get OCR results. It takes more time to integrate the Tesseract library to your Glass app, but the following steps should still be straightforward:

1. Get the open source Tesseract Android library at
   `https://github.com/rmtheis/tess-two`.

2. Build the library from source code by entering the `tess-two` directory first and
   then running the Android NDK (`http://developer.android.com/tools/sdk/ndk/index.html`) build command `ndk-build` (a total of more than 1,700 C files
   will be built, so it can take quite a while to complete).

3. Run `android update project --target android-19 --path .` because the
   Glass GDK Preview uses API level 19. You may need to change the API level
   if there's an Android update for Glass by the time you read the book.

4. Import the `tess-two` directory as a library in Eclipse, right-click the project,
   and select Android Tools ➤ Fix Project Properties. You should see something
   like Figure 4-5.

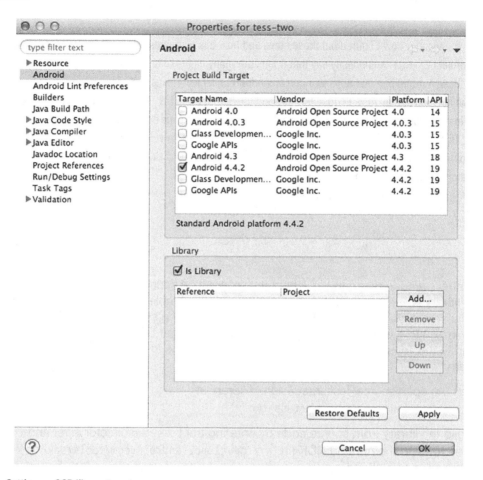

Figure 4-5. Setting up OCR library tess-two

5. Select the SmartCamera's Properties and add `tess-two` as a library, as shown in Figure 4-6 (depending on where you save the `tess-two` library, your paths in Reference could be different).

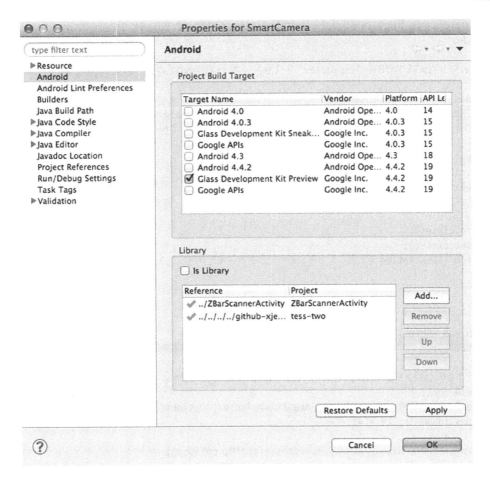

Figure 4-6. Adding the OCR library to app

6. Download the Tesseract English trained data (Tesseract can be trained to recognize characters of any language. The training result is called the trained data.) `tesseract-ocr-3.02.eng.tar.gz` at `https://code.google.com/p/tesseract-ocr/downloads/list` and unzip and copy the file `eng.traineddata` to SmartCamera's `assets/tessdata` folder. Note that if you use the sample project SmartCamera that comes with the book, you can skip this step because the project already contains the file.

7. Create a new menu item OCR and a new activity called `OCRActivity` (based on `ZoomActivity`). First add this line before `onCreate`:

```
public static final String DATA_PATH = Environment.getExternalStorageDirectory().toString() + "/
SmartCamera/";
```

Then in onCreate, copy the trained data from the assets directory to external storage with the following code:

```
if (!(new File(DATA_PATH + "tessdata/" + lang + ".traineddata")).exists()) {
try {
        AssetManager assetManager = getAssets();
        InputStream in = assetManager.open("tessdata/" + lang + ".traineddata");
        OutputStream out = new FileOutputStream(DATA_PATH + "tessdata/" + lang + ".traineddata");

        byte[] buf = new byte[1024];
        int len;
        while ((len = in.read(buf)) > 0) {
            out.write(buf, 0, len);
        }
        in.close();
        out.close();
    } catch (IOException e) {
    }
}

// add at the end of onPictureTaken of Listing 4-2:
Thread thread = new Thread(OCRActivity.this);
thread.start();

// thread that calls the Tess API with the captured image bitmap and sends the recognized text to UI
public void run() {
    BitmapFactory.Options options = new BitmapFactory.Options();
    options.inSampleSize = 4;

    Bitmap bitmap = BitmapFactory.decodeFile(mPath, options);
    try {
        // use the Android ExifInterface class to read the Exif orientation tag (one of the meta
        data) of the captured image and rotate it if necessary
        ExifInterface exif = new ExifInterface(mPath);
        int exifOrientation = exif.getAttributeInt(ExifInterface.TAG_ORIENTATION,
                ExifInterface.ORIENTATION_NORMAL);
        int rotate = 0;

        switch (exifOrientation) {
        case ExifInterface.ORIENTATION_ROTATE_90:
            rotate = 90;
            break;
        case ExifInterface.ORIENTATION_ROTATE_180:
            rotate = 180;
            break;
        case ExifInterface.ORIENTATION_ROTATE_270:
            rotate = 270;
            break;
        }
        if (rotate != 0) {
            int w = bitmap.getWidth();
            int h = bitmap.getHeight();
```

```
            Matrix mtx = new Matrix();
            mtx.preRotate(rotate);
            bitmap = Bitmap.createBitmap(bitmap, 0, 0, w, h, mtx, false);
        }

        bitmap = bitmap.copy(Bitmap.Config.ARGB_8888, true);
    } catch (IOException e) {
        Log.e(TAG, "Couldn't correct orientation: " + e.toString());
    }

    TessBaseAPI baseApi = new TessBaseAPI();
    baseApi.setDebug(true);
    baseApi.init(DATA_PATH, lang);
    baseApi.setImage(bitmap);

    String recognizedText = baseApi.getUTF8Text();
    baseApi.end();

    if ( lang.equalsIgnoreCase("eng") ) {
        recognizedText = recognizedText.replaceAll("[^a-zA-Z0-9]+", " ");
    }
    recognizedText = recognizedText.trim();

    if ( recognizedText.length() != 0 ) {
        Message msg = new Message();
        msg.obj = recognizedText;
        mHandler.sendMessage(msg);
    }
}

Handler mHandler = new Handler() {
    @Override
    public void handleMessage(Message msg) {
        String text = (String)msg.obj;
        finish();
        Toast.makeText(OCRActivity.this, text, Toast.LENGTH_LONG).show();
    }
};
```

Run the app, select OCR from the menu, move your Glass closer or zoom in to a large piece of text (preferably printed text), and long press the Glass touchpad. After a few seconds, you'll see the recognized text on your Glass! One of the tests I did was with the Bank of America checkbook cover; the text "Simple Ways to Save Time" is printed as white text on the red background. I moved Glass closer to the text to make sure only the line is in the Glass view and then long pressed the touchpad, and the OCR did a perfect recognition.

It's likely you won't get all the text recognized 100 percent accurately; this is the nature of almost all OCR applications. But this integration with the most popular open source OCR library should give you a good foundation on which to build many OCR-based Glass apps. The language download list in step 6 shown previously has most languages' trained data, and by integrating with other web services such as Google Translate, lots of exciting Glass apps can be built. Speaking of web services, how about uploading a picture taken to Google Image search and seeing whether there are any matching results?

Image Web Search

This idea was inspired by an open source Glass project called WhatIsThat, available at https://github.com/quiteconfused/GlassWhatIsThat. I've removed the unnecessary integration with OpenCV to create many images. Listing 4-6 shows the code snippet in a new activity called SearchActivity, which is based on PreviewActivity (no need for OnZoomChangeListener) and ZoomActivity.

Listing 4-6. Code Snippet for Image Search

```
Camera.PictureCallback mjpeg = new Camera.PictureCallback() {
    public void onPictureTaken(byte[] data, Camera camera) {

        .

        .

        .

        mCapturedFilePath = new File(mDataPath + "captured.jpg");
            if (mCapturedFilePath.exists()) {
                Thread thread = new Thread(SearchActivity.this);
                thread.start();

                Card card = new Card(AppService.appService());
                card.setImageLayout(Card.ImageLayout.FULL);
                card.addImage(BitmapFactory.decodeFile(mCapturedFilePath.getAbsolutePath()));
                card.setFootnote("processing image...");
                setContentView(card.getView());
            }
    }
};

public void run() {
    String new_result="";
    try {
        new_result = getResult(mCapturedFilePath);
    } finally {
        Message msg = new Message();
        msg.obj = new Result(new_result, mCapturedFilePath);
        mHandler.sendMessage(msg);
    }
}

static Handler mHandler = new Handler() {
    @Override
    public void handleMessage(Message msg) {
        Result result = (Result)msg.obj;
        Toast.makeText(AppService.appService(), result.mText, Toast.LENGTH_LONG).show();
        updateResultsInUi(AppService.appService(), result.mText, result.mImage);
    }
};

private class Result {
    private String mText;
    private File mImage;
```

```
public Result(String text, File image)
{
    mText = text;
    mImage = image;
}
}
```

You can see the implementation of the methods getResult and updateResultsInUifrom and the HTTP post request from the GitHub URL listed previously or, better yet, from the book's source code, where the necessary changes have been made to integrate with the app. Run the app and select Search from the menu, adjust what you see in the preview mode, and then long press to upload the image to Google for possible image search results. If you use the cover of one of those bestsellers, you'll have a better chance of getting results.

The sample shown here can be extended for many uses. For example, you could upload an image taken to a server for all kinds of processing such as emotion detection, facial recognition (but be aware of Google's privacy policy), or shopping recommendations. OpenCV is one of the most popular open source libraries for common image and video processing, and it can run on a server or on your Glass.

OpenCV

OpenCV is a big topic about which a whole book could be written. My goal here is to show you how to use OpenCV in your own Glass GDK app so you can get started quickly. I'll discuss how to integrate the OpenCV library on your Glass and perform a specific cool image manipulation technique called *Canny edge detector* using the OpenCV APIs. Figure 4-7 is a sample image before and after being processed.

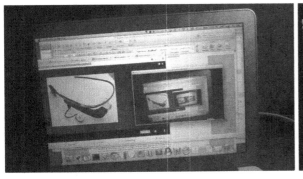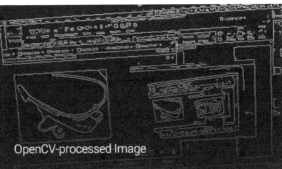

Figure 4-7. Canny edge detector: before and after

For more information about the canny edge detector, you can go to
http://en.wikipedia.org/wiki/Canny_edge_detector or
http://docs.opencv.org/doc/tutorials/imgproc/imgtrans/canny_detector/canny_detector.html.

Follow these steps to add and use OpenCV library in your app:

1. Go to the OpenCV Android download page at `http://sourceforge.net/projects/opencvlibrary/files/opencv-android/` to download the latest version. The version I have used and tested is 2.4.7.1 released on 2013-12-05 in the `2.4.7` folder of the previous link, but it should work with newer versions.

2. Unzip the downloaded file, which will generate a directory with the OpenCV SDK library as well as samples.

3. In Eclipse, select File ➤ Import and then Android ➤ Existing Android Code Into Workspace. Browse to the unzipped folder mentioned earlier. You can check only the OpenCV Library entry to import, but you can also import some OpenCV samples. If you have another Android device (not Glass) or you want to use an emulator, you can check out how the samples work there first.

> **Note**   In your Glass GDK development, you'll experience many occasions of porting some existing Android libraries or code to Glass. It's definitely beneficial to see how they run on other Android devices first.

4. Drag the `OpenCV-2.4.7.1-android-sdk/sdk/native/libs/armeabi-v7a` folder to the SmartCamera project's `libs` folder and select "Copy files and folder." Figure 4-8 shows what you should see in Eclipse after that.

Figure 4-8. Adding the OpenCV native library files

5. In the SmartCamera project's Properties window, add the OpenCV library.
    You should see something like Figure 4-9.

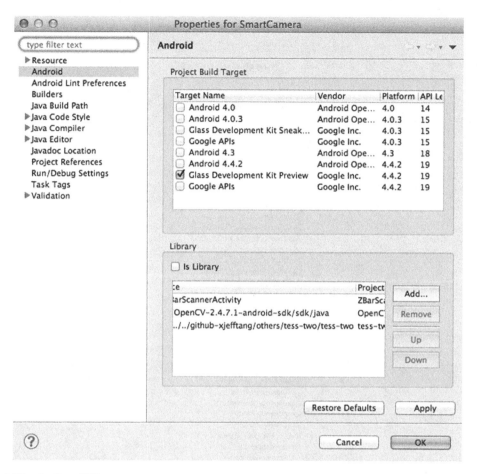

Figure 4-9. Adding the OpenCV library

6. Create a new menu item called OpenCV and create a new activity
    OpenCVActivity based, again, on PreviewActivity and ZoomActivity, as
    shown in Listing 4-7.

Listing 4-7. Code Snippet for Using OpenCV APIs for the Canny Effect

```
// in onCreate, after setContentView(R.layout.preview);
OpenCVLoader.initDebug();

// add the following method to convert captured image data to bitmap
public static Bitmap decodeSampledBitmapFromData(byte[] data, int reqWidth, int reqHeight) {
    final BitmapFactory.Options options = new BitmapFactory.Options();
    options.inJustDecodeBounds = true;
    BitmapFactory.decodeByteArray(data, 0, data.length,options);
    options.inSampleSize = 2;
    options.inJustDecodeBounds = false;
    return BitmapFactory.decodeByteArray(data, 0, data.length,options);
}
```

```
// add the following code in onPictureTaken after
//decode the data obtained by the camera into a Bitmap
Bitmap bmp =  itmapFromData(data,640,360);

try {
    FileOutputStream fos = new FileOutputStream(mDataPath + "captured.jpg");
    final BufferedOutputStream bos = new BufferedOutputStream(fos, 1024 * 8);
    bmp.compress(CompressFormat.JPEG, 100, bos);
    bos.flush();
    bos.close();
    fos.close();
} catch (FileNotFoundException e){
    Log.e(TAG, e.getMessage());
} catch (IOException e){
    Log.e(TAG, e.getMessage());
}

mCapturedFilePath = new File(mDataPath + "captured.jpg");
if (mCapturedFilePath.exists()) {
    // OpenCV Canny Image Processing
    Mat matFrom = Highgui.imread(mCapturedFilePath.getAbsolutePath());

    Size sizeRgba = matFrom.size();
    Mat matFinal;
    Mat matIntermediate = new Mat();

    int rows = (int) sizeRgba.height;
    int cols = (int) sizeRgba.width;
    int left = cols / 8;
    int top = rows / 8;
    int width = cols * 3 / 4;
    int height = rows * 3 / 4;

    matFinal = matFrom.submat(top, top + height, left, left + width);

    Imgproc.Canny(matFinal, matIntermediate, 80, 90);
    Imgproc.cvtColor(matIntermediate, matFinal, Imgproc.COLOR_GRAY2BGRA, 4);
    Highgui.imwrite(mDataPath + "captured-canny.jpg", matFinal);

    matFinal.release();

    Card card = new Card(AppService.appService());
    card.setImageLayout(Card.ImageLayout.FULL);
    card.addImage( Uri.fromFile(new File(mDataPath + "captured-canny.jpg")));
    card.setFootnote("OpenCV-processed Image");
    setContentView(card.toView());
}
}
```

Here the OpenCV API calls `Highgui.imread`, `Imgproc.Canny`, `Imgproc.cvtColor`, `Highgui.imwrite`, and `Mat`. With just a few lines of code, you can see amazing image manipulation effects. After the Canny processing is done, the generated image is saved to a file and then displayed as a card in the activity's content area.

Run the app, choose the OpenCV menu item, preview and frame a picture, and then long press your touchpad. You'll see something like Figure 4-7. Congratulations! You just made one of the most advanced image-processing and computer vision libraries work on your Glass.

The Complete App

The whole SmartCamera project's source code, along with the libraries it uses (barcode scanner, OCR, image search, and OpenCV), can be downloaded at the book's web site and imported into Eclipse. In a few minutes, you can see a lot of cool image-processing features working on your Glass.

Summary

In this chapter, you started with how to use the Glass camera to take pictures, both in the easy way and in the custom way, which allows you to preview and zoom before taking a picture. Then I briefly covered how to browse the photos in any directory of your Glass. After that, I discussed step by step many common practical image-processing tasks, including barcode and QR code recognition, OCR, image web search, and OpenCV. I covered how to integrate the best open source libraries out there, if needed, to your own app and how to call their APIs from within your app. I hope by now you're well prepared for exploring your own great app ideas using all kinds of image-processing techniques.

In the next chapter, you'll enter the video world of Glass with interesting topics such as taking, playing, and processing videos. OpenCV will be further used for video processing. And it's about time to give yourself a nice treat; a Glass karaoke app will be expecting you.

Video: Basics and Applications

In the previous chapter, I covered the Glass camera and image processing, so naturally the next step is video. One of the most important features of Glass is recording video. Hands-free video recording, initiated by your voice with the commands "OK Glass" and then "Record a video," is a major selling point of Glass. Obviously, as a developer, you want to integrate video in your apps, expecting to record a video, play it, process it, and maybe do some other fun stuff with the videos out there in the world. By the end of this chapter, you'll know exactly how to achieve all these goals.

The solutions you'll see covered in detail here, along with tested working code, include the following:

- How to capture a video quickly, using the standard way

- How to capture a video in a custom way, with a preview feature

- How to play video, in a general Android way and in a Glass-specific way

- How to extract frames from a video and use OpenCV to process the frames with effects such as canny, sepia, pixelize, posterize, and color conversions

- How to use the powerful FFmpeg library and accomplish video processing tasks including offering rotation; applying effects such as canny, sepia, and vintage; and extracting sound and images

- How to search YouTube videos and play your favorite song like in karaoke

After learning these techniques, you should be ready to integrate video into your own apps and build some great tools and fun apps.

Capturing Video

The Android Camera developer guide (http://developer.android.com/guide/topics/media/camera.html) summarizes two ways to capture videos: the quick way that uses a camera intent and the custom way that may be more appropriate if you want to have a more customized look and special features. In the following sections, I'll introduce the detailed steps to capture videos in both ways, and I'll note what's unique on Glass. Before starting, I assume you have built a new app called MyVideoApps based on the GlasswareTemplate app used in previous chapters. You can also check out the complete app in the book's source code; if you import the project and see any errors, you can fix the errors by opening its Properties window, selecting Android, and then changing the Target Name under Project Build Target to Glass Development Kit Preview.

The Quick Way

The camera intent `ACTION_VIDEO_CAPTURE` lets you record a video from your app in a few lines of code. Follow these steps to test this:

1. Change your res/menu/main.xml to have the following two menu items:

    ```
    <item
        android:id="@+id/basicvideocapture"
        android:title="@string/basicvideocapture"/>
    <item
        android:id="@+id/stop"
        android:icon="@drawable/ic_stop"
        android:title="@string/stop"/>
    ```

2. In res/values/strings.xml, add these lines:

    ```
    <string name="app_name">My Video Apps</string>
    <string name="say_videoapps">Chapter Five</string>
    <string name="basicvideocapture">Basic Capture</string>
    ```

3. In MenuActivity.java's onOptionsItemSelected method, add this case statement:

    ```
    case R.id.basicvideocapture:
        Intent intent = new Intent(this, BasicVideoCaptureActivity.class);
        startActivity(intent);
        return true;
    ```

4. Create a new class called BasicVideoCaptureActivity and add the code in Listing 5-1.

Listing 5-1. Capturing Video Using the Camera Intent

```
private static final int CAPTURE_VIDEO_ACTIVITY_REQUEST_CODE = 100;
    private static final int VIDEO_PLAY_REQUEST_CODE = 200;
    private Uri mFileUri;

private static File getOutputMediaFile(int type){
        File mediaStorageDir = new File(Environment.getExternalStoragePublicDirectory(
                Environment.DIRECTORY_MOVIES), "MyVideoApps");

        // Create the storage directory if it does not exist
        if (! mediaStorageDir.exists()){
            if (! mediaStorageDir.mkdirs()){
```

```java
            Log.d("MyCameraApp", "failed to create directory");
            return null;
        }
    }

    // Create a media file name
    String timeStamp = new SimpleDateFormat("yyyyMMdd_HHmmss").format(new Date());
    File mediaFile;
    if (type == MEDIA_TYPE_IMAGE){
        mediaFile = new File(mediaStorageDir.getPath(), "IMG_"+ timeStamp + ".jpg");
    }
    else if (type == MEDIA_TYPE_VIDEO) {
        mediaFile = new File(mediaStorageDir.getPath, "VID_"+ timeStamp + ".mp4");
    }
    else return null;

    return mediaFile;
}

public void onCreate(Bundle savedInstanceState) {
    super.onCreate(savedInstanceState);
    setContentView(R.layout.start);

    Intent intent = new Intent(MediaStore.ACTION_VIDEO_CAPTURE);
    mFileUri = getOutputMediaFileUri(MEDIA_TYPE_VIDEO);
    intent.putExtra(MediaStore.EXTRA_OUTPUT, mFileUri);
    intent.putExtra(MediaStore.EXTRA_VIDEO_QUALITY, 1); // set the video image quality to high
    startActivityForResult(intent, CAPTURE_VIDEO_ACTIVITY_REQUEST_CODE);
}


@Override
protected void onActivityResult(int requestCode, int resultCode, Intent data) {
    if (requestCode == VIDEO_PLAY_REQUEST_CODE) {
        finish();
        return;
    }

    if (requestCode == CAPTURE_VIDEO_ACTIVITY_REQUEST_CODE) {
        if (resultCode == RESULT_OK) {
            Intent i = new Intent();
            i.setAction("com.google.glass.action.VIDEOPLAYER");
            i.putExtra("video_url", ""+data.getExtras().get
                (CameraManager.EXTRA_VIDEO_FILE_PATH));
            startActivityForResult(i, VIDEO_PLAY_REQUEST_CODE);
        }
        else if (resultCode == RESULT_CANCELED) {
            Toast.makeText(this, "Video capture cancelled", Toast.LENGTH_LONG).show();
        }
    }
}
```

5.   Add `BasicVideoCaptureActivity` to your `AndroidManifest.xml`.

```
<activity
    android:name="com.morkout.myvideoapps.BasicVideoCaptureActivity"
    android:enabled="true"
    android:label="@string/app_name" >
</activity>
```

Run the app on Glass and say "OK Glass" and then "Chapter 5." You'll see a live card with the message "My Video Apps." Tap the touchpad to see the first item in the menu, which is Basic Capture. Tap again to start the video capture, which is the same UI of the default Glass video capture. After "Stop recording" is selected and you tap to accept the video, you'll see the recorded video playing, using the Glass's video player intent `com.google.glass.action.VIDEOPLAYER`. I'll discuss video play in more detail soon.

Here are a few things to note in Listing 5-1:

1.   `intent.putExtra(MediaStore.EXTRA_OUTPUT, mFileUri);` is called for the `ACTION_VIDEO_CAPTURE` intent. In the "Video capture intent" section of the Android Camera developer guide mentioned earlier, it states that the `EXTRA_OUTPUT` setting is optional but strongly recommended. It also says, "If you do not specify this value, the Camera application saves the requested video in the default location with a default name, specified in the returned intent's `Intent.getData()` field." However, this is not the case: `date.getData()` in `onActivityResult` always returns `null` on Glass whether you have the `putExtra` call or not. On other Android devices such as Nexus 7, the behavior is as documented.

2.   In addition to that, even if you call `putExtra`, the video doesn't get saved to the location specified in `putExtra`; it's still saved in the default `DCIM/Camera` directory. Fortunately, you can retrieve the saved path using `data.getExtras().get(CameraManager.EXTRA_VIDEO_FILE_PATH)`.

Video captured this way (or in the custom way discussed next), unlike video captured using the Glass camera button, doesn't show in the Glass timeline. But you can implement your own share features, such as the ability to upload to Google Drive shown in Chapter 4.

The Custom Way

What if you want to preview the scene before you start recording a video or set the recorded video format or frame rate? Or what if you want to add a custom UI such as showing the recorded frames while capturing a video? Then you have to implement video capture in the custom way, using the

Android MediaRecorder class; see its API documentation page for all the customization you can do, at http://developer.android.com/reference/android/media/MediaRecorder.html. Now follow these steps to capture video using MediaRecorder on Glass:

1. Add a new menu item in menu.xml and a new string entry in strings.xml.

```xml
<item
        android:id="@+id/customvideocapture"
        android:title="@string/customvideocapture"/>

<string name="customvideocapture">Custom Capture</string>
```

2. Add a new case statement in MenuActivity.java.

```java
case R.id.customvideocapture:
    Intent intent2 = new Intent(this, CustomVideoCaptureActivity.class);
    startActivity(intent2);
    return true;
```

3. Create a preview.xml file in layout.

```xml
<FrameLayout xmlns:android="http://schemas.android.com/apk/res/android"
    xmlns:tools="http://schemas.android.com/tools"
    android:layout_width="match_parent"
    android:layout_height="match_parent"
    tools:context=".MainActivity" >

    <SurfaceView
        android:id="@+id/preview"
        android:layout_width="match_parent"
        android:layout_height="match_parent" >
    </SurfaceView>

    <TextView
        android:id="@+id/timer"
        android:layout_width="wrap_content"
        android:layout_height="wrap_content"
        android:layout_marginTop="95dp"
        android:layout_gravity="center"
        android:text="" />
</FrameLayout>
```

4. Create a new class called CustomVideoCaptureActivity.java, as shown in Listing 5-2.

Listing 5-2. Capturing Video Using the Custom Method

```java
public void onCreate(Bundle savedInstanceState) {
    super.onCreate(savedInstanceState);
    setContentView(R.layout.preview);
    getWindow().addFlags(WindowManager.LayoutParams.FLAG_KEEP_SCREEN_ON);
    mTimerInfo = (TextView)findViewById(R.id.timer);
    mTimerInfo.setText("Long Press to Record");
    mPreview = (SurfaceView)findViewById(R.id.preview);
    mPreviewHolder = mPreview.getHolder();
    mPreviewHolder.addCallback(surfaceCallback);
    mCamera = getCameraInstance();

    mGestureDetector = new GestureDetector(this, this);
}

private void initPreview() {
    if ( mCamera != null && mPreviewHolder.getSurface() != null) {
        try {
            mCamera.setPreviewDisplay(mPreviewHolder);
        }
        catch (IOException e) {
            Toast.makeText(CustomVideoCaptureActivity.this, e.getMessage(),
Toast.LENGTH_LONG).show();
        }

        if ( !mCameraConfigured ) {
            Camera.Parameters parameters = mCamera.getParameters();
            parameters.setPreviewFpsRange(30000, 30000);
            parameters.setPreviewSize(640, 360);
            mCamera.setParameters(parameters);
            mCameraConfigured = true;
        }
    }
}

private void startPreview() {
    if ( mCameraConfigured && mCamera != null ) {
        mCamera.startPreview();
        mInPreview = true;
    }
}

SurfaceHolder.Callback surfaceCallback = new SurfaceHolder.Callback() {
    public void surfaceCreated( SurfaceHolder holder ) {
        initPreview();
    }

    public void surfaceChanged( SurfaceHolder holder, int format, int width, int height ) {
        startPreview();
    }
```

```java
    public void surfaceDestroyed( SurfaceHolder holder ) {
        releaseCamera();
    }
};

private final Handler mHandler = new Handler();
private final Runnable mUpdateTextRunnable = new Runnable() {
    @Override
    public void run() {
        if (mRecording) {
            mTimerInfo.setText(String.format("%02d:%02d:%02d",
                    TimeUnit.MILLISECONDS.toHours(second*1000),
                    TimeUnit.MILLISECONDS.toMinutes(second*1000) -
                    TimeUnit.HOURS.toMinutes(TimeUnit.MILLISECONDS.toHours(second*1000)),
                    TimeUnit.MILLISECONDS.toSeconds(second*1000) -
                    TimeUnit.MINUTES.toSeconds(TimeUnit.MILLISECONDS.toMinutes(second*1000))));
            second++;
        }
        mHandler.postDelayed(mUpdateTextRunnable, 1000);
    }
};

@Override
public void onLongPress(MotionEvent e)
{
    if (mRecording)
        return;

    if (prepareVideoRecorder()) {
        mrec.start();
        mRecording = true;
        second = 0;
        mHandler.post(mUpdateTextRunnable);

    } else {
        releaseMediaRecorder();
    }
}

@Override
public boolean onCreateOptionsMenu(Menu menu) {
    MenuInflater inflater = getMenuInflater();
    inflater.inflate(R.menu.videocapture, menu);
    return true;
}

@Override
public boolean onOptionsItemSelected(MenuItem item) {
    switch (item.getItemId()) {
    case R.id.stoprecording:
        stopAndPlayVideo();
    }
```

```
        return true;
}

void stopAndPlayVideo() {
    stopRecording();
    mTimerInfo.setText("Recording Done");
    Toast.makeText(CustomVideoCaptureActivity.this, "Video saved to " + mOutputFile.
getAbsolutePath(), Toast.LENGTH_SHORT).show();

    Intent i = new Intent();
    i.setAction("com.google.glass.action.VIDEOPLAYER");
    i.putExtra("video_url", mOutputFile.getAbsolutePath());
    startActivity(i);
}

public static Camera getCameraInstance(){
    Camera c = null;
    try {
        c = Camera.open();
    }
    catch (Exception e){
        Log.e(TAG, e.getMessage());
    }
    return c;
}

private boolean prepareVideoRecorder(){

    if (mCamera != null){
        mCamera.release(); // release the camera for other applications
    }
    mCamera = getCameraInstance();
    if (mCamera == null) return false;

    mrec = new MediaRecorder();

    mCamera.unlock();
    mrec.setCamera(mCamera);
    mrec.setAudioSource(MediaRecorder.AudioSource.CAMCORDER);
    mrec.setVideoSource(MediaRecorder.VideoSource.CAMERA);
    mrec.setProfile(CamcorderProfile.get(CamcorderProfile.QUALITY_HIGH));
    mrec.setPreviewDisplay(mPreviewHolder.getSurface());

    mOutputFile = getOutputMediaFile(MEDIA_TYPE_VIDEO);
    mrec.setOutputFile(mOutputFile.toString());

    try {
        mrec.prepare();
    }
```

```java
    catch (Exception e) {
        Log.e(TAG, e.getMessage());
        return false;
    }

    return true;
}

@Override
protected void onPause() {
    super.onPause();
    releaseMediaRecorder(); // if you are using MediaRecorder, release it first
    releaseCamera();        // release the camera immediately on pause event
}

@Override
protected void onDestroy() {
    if (mRecording)
        stopAndPlayVideo();
    mRecording = false;
    super.onDestroy();
}
private void releaseMediaRecorder(){
    if (mrec != null) {
        mrec.reset();
        mrec.release();
        mrec = null;
    }
}

private void releaseCamera(){
    if (mCamera != null){
        mCamera.release();
        mCamera = null;
    }
}

protected void stopRecording() {
    if(mrec!=null)
    {
        mrec.stop();
        mrec.release();
        mrec = null;
        releaseCamera();
        mRecording = false;
    }
}
```

5. As always, don't forget to add `CustomVideoCaptureActivity` in `AndroidManifest.xml`.

```
<activity
    android:name="com.morkout.myvideoapps.CustomVideoCaptureActivity"
    android:enabled="true"
    android:label="@string/app_name" >
</activity>
```

6. Create a new `videocapture.xml` file in res/menu with the following content to show a Stop Recording menu option while recording a video:

```
<?xml version="1.0" encoding="utf-8"?>
<menu xmlns:android="http://schemas.android.com/apk/res/android" >
    <item
        android:id="@+id/stoprecording"
        android:title="@string/stoprecording"/>
</menu>
```

7. Add `<string name="stoprecording">Stop Recording</string>` in `strings.xml`.

Run the app, and now you'll see another menu option, Custom Capture, after Basic Capture. Tap it, and you'll see the camera preview; long press the Glass touchpad to start recording. A `TextView` indicating the time passed would also show. Tapping the touchpad while recording shows a single menu item, Stop Recording. Swipe down on it to exit the menu and continue recording, and tap it to stop recording and start playing the recorded video.

Listing 5-2 looks a little long, but it consists of three main, easier-to-understand parts.

1. Here's the preview part: You should be familiar with the preview-related code in `onCreate`, `initPreview`, `startPreview`, `surfaceCreated`, `surfaceChanged`, and `surfaceDestroyed`. The code is basically the same as the preview code in the previous chapter.

2. Here's the new `prepareVideoRecorder` and the UI during recording part: The order of setting `mrec`, a `MediaRecorder` instance, is important, although the order doesn't have to be 100 percent like the one in the listing. For example, the order of `setAudioSource` and `setVideoSource` can be changed. But the code here has been tested and runs well on Glass, so unless you have a good reason to change it, I recommend you use the time saved to do something more interesting. While recording, a thread keeps updating the time information on the UI thread.

3. Here's the stop, play, and cleanup part: After a video is stopped via the menu selection or the swipe-down gesture, `MediaRecorder` and `Camera` need to be released, and the saved video, set with `mrec.setOutputFile`, is played with the `com.google.glass.action.VIDEOPLAYER` intent.

Before exploring how to apply powerful video-processing techniques to the video captured, let's give video play a more detailed treatment.

Playing Video

You saw in the previous two sections how the `com.google.glass.action.VIDEOPLAYER` intent is used to play video. This should be the preferred way to play video on Glass because it provides the consistent Glass UI for video play. However, if you're an experienced Android developer, you're probably already familiar with using `VideoView` to play video. In this section, I'll discuss what works for Glass and what doesn't when you apply your previous Android knowledge of `VideoView`.

Follow the similar steps you've done in this chapter and previous two chapters to create a new menu item called Play and a new class called VideoPlayerActivity and tie together all the pieces (which means you need to update the `menu.xml`, `strings.xml`, `MenuActivity.java`, and `AndroidManifest.xml` files).

Create a new layout file called `videoview.xml`.

```xml
<?xml version="1.0" encoding="utf-8"?>
<RelativeLayout xmlns:android="http://schemas.android.com/apk/res/android"
    android:layout_width="match_parent"
    android:layout_height="match_parent"
    android:layout_gravity="center_horizontal"
    android:background="@color/black" >

    <VideoView
        android:id="@+id/video_player_view"
        android:layout_width="match_parent"
        android:layout_height="match_parent"
        android:layout_centerInParent="true" />

</RelativeLayout>
```

Add the code in Listing 5-3 to `VideoPlayerActivity.java`.

Listing 5-3. Two Ways to Play Video

```java
public void onCreate(Bundle savedInstanceState) {
        super.onCreate(savedInstanceState);

        String filepath;
        Bundle extras = getIntent().getExtras();
        if (extras != null)
            filepath = extras.getString("filepath");
        else {
            filepath = copyAsset("in.mp4");
        }

        // play video using VideoView
        Uri uri = Uri.parse(filepath);
        setContentView(R.layout.videoview);
        VideoView videoView = (VideoView) findViewById(R.id.video_player_view);
        MediaController mediaController = new MediaController(this);
        mediaController.setAnchorView(videoView);
```

```
        videoView.setMediaController(mediaController);
        videoView.setVideoURI(uri);
        videoView.start();

        // play video using the Glass video player
        // Intent i = new Intent();
        // i.setAction("com.google.glass.action.VIDEOPLAYER");
        // i.putExtra("video_url", filepath);
        // startActivityForResult(i, VIDEO_PLAY_REQUEST_CODE);
    }

    protected void onActivityResult(int requestCode, int resultCode, Intent data) {
        if (requestCode == VIDEO_PLAY_REQUEST_CODE)
            finish();
    }

    String copyAsset(String filename) {
        final String PATH = Environment.getExternalStorageDirectory().toString() + "/myvideoapps/";
        File dir = new File(PATH);
        if (!dir.exists()) {
            if (!dir.mkdirs()) {
                Log.v(TAG, "ERROR: Creation of directory " + PATH + " on sdcard failed");
                return null;
            } else {
                Log.v(TAG, "Created directory " + PATH + " on sdcard");
            }
        }

        if (!(new File( PATH + filename).exists())) {
            try {
                AssetManager assetManager = getAssets();
                InputStream in = assetManager.open(filename);
                OutputStream out = new FileOutputStream(PATH + filename);

                byte[] buf = new byte[1024];
                int len;
                while ((len = in.read(buf)) > 0) {
                    out.write(buf, 0, len);
                }
                in.close();
                out.close();

            } catch (IOException e) {
                Log.e(TAG, "Was unable to copy " + filename + e.toString());
                return null;
            }
        }
        return PATH + filename;
    }
```

Run the app again and select the third menu item, Play. You'll see a sample video file in.mp4, being played with the VideoView class. The in.mp4 file will be copied from the app's asset directory to the external storage's myvideoapps subdirectory.

VideoView basically is a wrapper of MediaPlayer, the primary API for playing sound and video on Android. VideoView makes it much easier to add video play in your app. Its setMediaController can easily add a nice video control to your app, including play, pause, fast-forward, reverse, and time information, as shown in Figure 5-1.

Figure 5-1. *Video play using the Android VideoView API*

However, there's some glitch with the media controller on Glass, as least as of the XE 16 update: Only the play and pause functions work fine, and you cannot drag the circle to move the video play position. It's likely that by the time you read the book, the glitch will have been fixed and you can continue to use VideoView like it's supposed to do. But as a general principle, when you apply your Android knowledge and port your Android code to Glass, always watch out for subtle differences. Although MediaPlayer, on which VideoView is based, offers a more powerful way to play video than VideoView and may fix the issue with VideoView, I won't discuss it further because the native Glass intent com.google.glass.action.VIDEOPLAYER provides the simplest and best solution for video play on Glass. You can pause and replay the video and easily move to any position of the video. In Listing 5-3, comment out the eight lines of code after the comment play video using VideoView and uncomment the four lines of code after the comment play video using the Glass video player. Then run the app to see again how the native Glass video player works, as shown in Figure 5-2.

Figure 5-2. Video play using the Glass com.google.glass.action.VIDEOPLAYER intent

Now that you have the basics of video capture and play covered, it's time to move on to something more powerful and fun.

OpenCV Video Processing

In the previous chapter, you saw an example of OpenCV being used to create a Canny edge detector effect on an image. In this section, I'll show you more examples of using OpenCV APIs to process frames of a video. First, you need to use the Android `MediaMetadataRetriever` class's `getFrameAtTime` method to get a `Bitmap` object of a specific frame. Then you call OpenCV's `core` and `imgproc` modules to process the bitmap for different effects. The sample code in Listing 5-3 retrieves frames from the first three seconds of video, at an interval of 0.5 second, and applies OpenCV functions to each frame before displaying it in an `ImageView`. To build and test this, simply follow these steps:

1. Create a new menu item called OpenCV Frame in `menu.xml` and update `strings.xml` and `MenuActivity.java`.

2. Add a new layout file called `videoframe.xml`.

```
<RelativeLayout xmlns:android="http://schemas.android.com/apk/res/android"
    xmlns:tools="http://schemas.android.com/tools"
    android:layout_width="match_parent"
    android:layout_height="match_parent"
    tools:context=".VideoFrameActivity" >

    <ImageView
        android:id="@+id/frame"
        android:layout_width="wrap_content"
        android:layout_height="wrap_content"
        android:layout_alignParentTop="true"
        android:layout_centerHorizontal="true" />

</RelativeLayout>
```

3. Create a new class called VideoFramesActivity.java with the code in
    Listing 5-4.

Listing 5-4. Retrieving and Processing Video Frames Using OpenCV

```java
public class VideoFramesActivity extends Activity {
    ImageView mFrame;
    MediaMetadataRetriever mRetriever;
    int sec = 0;
    public final static String TAG = "VideoFramesActivity";

    @Override
    public void onCreate(Bundle savedInstanceState) {
        super.onCreate(savedInstanceState);
        setContentView(R.layout.videoframe);

        mFrame = (ImageView) findViewById(R.id.frame);

        // load and initialize OpenCV library - see http://docs.opencv.org/java/org/opencv/android/
OpenCVLoader.html#initDebug()
        if (!OpenCVLoader.initDebug()) {
            finish();
        }
        showFrame();
    }

    private final Handler mHandler = new Handler();
    private final Runnable mUpdateFrameRunnable = new Runnable() {
        @Override
        public void run() {
            mRetriever = new MediaMetadataRetriever();
            try {
                mRetriever.setDataSource(copyAsset("in.mp4"));
                mFrame.setImageBitmap(processBitmap(mRetriever.getFrameAtTime(sec,
                MediaMetadataRetriever.OPTION_CLOSEST)));

                mFrame.invalidate();
                sec+=500000;
                if (sec>3000000) return;

                mHandler.post(mUpdateFrameRunnable);
            } catch (Exception e) {
                e.printStackTrace();
            } finally {
                try {
                    mRetriever.release();
                } catch (RuntimeException e) {
                }
            }
        }
    };
```

```
String copyAsset(String filename) {
    ... // same as Listing 5-3
}

public Bitmap processBitmap(Bitmap bitmap) {
    Bitmap newBitmap;
    Mat matFrom = new Mat();
    Utils.bitmapToMat(bitmap, matFrom);

    Mat matIntermediate = new Mat();
    Mat matFinal = new Mat();

    Imgproc.resize(matFrom, matIntermediate, new Size(), 2.0, 2.0, Imgproc.INTER_NEAREST);

    // canny
    Mat matIntermediate2 = new Mat();
    Imgproc.Canny(matIntermediate, matIntermediate2, 80, 90);
    Imgproc.cvtColor(matIntermediate2, matFinal, Imgproc.COLOR_GRAY2BGRA, 4);

    // sepia
    // Mat mSepiaKernel;
    // mSepiaKernel = new Mat(4, 4, CvType.CV_32F);
    // mSepiaKernel.put(0, 0, /* R */0.189f, 0.769f, 0.393f, 0f);
    // mSepiaKernel.put(1, 0, /* G */0.168f, 0.686f, 0.349f, 0f);
    // mSepiaKernel.put(2, 0, /* B */0.131f, 0.534f, 0.272f, 0f);
    // mSepiaKernel.put(3, 0, /* A */0.000f, 0.000f, 0.000f, 1f);
    // Core.transform(matIntermediate, matFinal, mSepiaKernel);

    // pixelize
    // Size size = new Size();
    // Mat matIntermediate2 = new Mat();
    // Imgproc.resize(matIntermediate, matIntermediate2, size, 0.1, 0.1, Imgproc.INTER_NEAREST);
    // Imgproc.resize(matIntermediate2, matFinal, matIntermediate.size(), 0., 0.,
    Imgproc.INTER_NEAREST);

    // posterize
    // Mat matIntermediate2 = new Mat();
    // Imgproc.Canny(matIntermediate, matIntermediate2, 80, 90);
    // matIntermediate.setTo(new Scalar(0, 0, 0, 255), matIntermediate2);
    // Core.convertScaleAbs(matIntermediate, matIntermediate2, 1./16, 0);
    // Core.convertScaleAbs(matIntermediate2, matFinal, 16, 0);

    // http://docs.opencv.org/java/org/opencv/imgproc/Imgproc.html#COLOR_BayerGB2RGB
    //Imgproc.cvtColor(matIntermediate, matFinal, Imgproc.COLOR_BGR2GRAY); // black and white
    //Imgproc.cvtColor(matIntermediate, matFinal, Imgproc.COLOR_BGR2RGB);  // blue
    //Imgproc.cvtColor(matIntermediate, matFinal, Imgproc.COLOR_BGR2Luv);
    //Imgproc.cvtColor(matIntermediate, matFinal, Imgproc.COLOR_BGR2HLS);
    //Imgproc.cvtColor(matIntermediate, matFinal, Imgproc.COLOR_BGR2HSV);

    newBitmap = Bitmap.createBitmap(matFinal.cols(), matFinal.rows(), Bitmap.Config.ARGB_8888);
    Utils.matToBitmap(matFinal, newBitmap);
```

```
        matFinal.release();
        return newBitmap;
    }

    public void showFrame() {
        mHandler.post(mUpdateFrameRunnable);
    }
}
```

4. Add `VideoFramesActivity` to `AndroidManifest.xml`.

5. Add the OpenCV library to your project, as shown in the "OpenCV"
    section of the previous chapter, by selecting the properties of your project
    MyVideoApps. Then select Android and click Add in the Library section
    of the Properties window. Then copy `libs`'s `armeabi-v7a` folder from
    the SmartCamera project in Chapter 4 (see Figure 4-8 of Chapter 4) to
    MyVideoApps's `libs` folder.

Run the app on Glass and select OpenCV Frame. You'll see six images, two of which shown in
Figure 5-3, with the Canny effects on Glass.

Figure 5-3. Applying the OpenCV Canny effect to video frames

Note   Retrieving frame function `getFrameAtTime` takes 0.6 to 1.2 seconds on Glass to return, but the OpenCV call returns almost immediately. Also, the first parameter of `getFrameAtTime` is for microseconds, 1/1000,000 second, and a typical frame rate is 30 per second.

To see different OpenCV effects, comment out the code after `// canny`, uncomment the code after `// sepia, pixelize, posterize, or color change`, and run the app. For example, Figure 5-4 shows a frame with the sepia effect, and Figure 5-5 shows the posterize effect.

Figure 5-4. Applying the OpenCV sepia effect to a frame

Figure 5-5. Applying the OpenCV posterize effect to a frame

See `http://docs.opencv.org/java/org/opencv/imgproc/Imgproc.html` for complete documentation of OpenCV image processing, which you can apply to your video frames.

What if you want to process and apply some special effect to an entire video, instead of just some frames of it? Obviously, it'd be infeasible to process each frame of a video. A 5-second video with 30 frames per second would have 150 frames, and on average each frame would take about 1 second to be retrieved and processed, meaning it'd take 2.5 minutes to process the short video. There has to be a better way.

> **Note**   If you're interested in how to process the camera preview frames in real time, you should check out the `ZBarScannerActivity.java` file of the ZBarScannerActivity project I discussed in Chapter 4, where `onPreviewFrame` is used to scan barcode image in real time.

FFmpeg Video Processing

FFmpeg is the best open source library to record, convert, and stream video (and audio too). There are several FFmpeg libraries for Android, but unfortunately none of them is easy to build and integrate with your own app. The easiest way to add FFmpeg to your Glass app is to use a library called FFmpeg4Android, which has an Android app in Google Play that, if you have a non-Glass Android device such as Nexus 7, you can install and try the FFmpeg commands.

Test the Library Client on Glass

To test the library on your Glass in order to integrate it into your app, follow the steps at `http://androidwarzone.blogspot.com/2011/12/ffmpeg4android.html` to download the FFmpeg4Android project library source and the demo client source. Import both projects into your Eclipse workspace. You should see something like Figure 5-6.

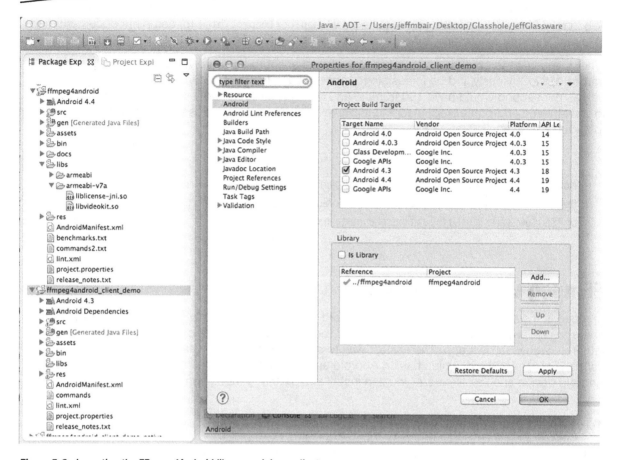

Figure 5-6. Importing the FFmpeg4Android library and demo client

To test the demo client on your Glass, you need to download launchy, an app to launch native Android apps, at `https://github.com/kaze0/launchy`.

> **Note** Native Glass apps can be launched via voice commands or the touchpad after speaking or selecting OK Glass. Native Android apps are not started by voice command or shown in the OK Glass menu, so the app appears to run only once right after installation, but with launchy, you can run a native Android app as many times as you want.

After downloading and importing launchy into Eclipse, install it to Glass. Then you can say "OK Glass" followed by "Run an app," or you can select "Run an app" from the OK Glass menu to launch it. After it's launched, you'll see a list of apps you can start. Simply swipe forward or backward to navigate the list and tap to select the highlighted app. Figure 5-7 shows the two screens.

Figure 5-7. Launching and selecting a native Android app

Select the demo client app, and you'll see the FFmpeg demo client UI as shown in Figure 5-8; swipe forward to reveal the Invoke button. Tap the Glass touchpad when Invoke is highlighted. You'll see a message box saying "Exporting As MP4 Video." After the exporting is done, the video is saved as /sdcard/videokit/out.mp4. You do remember how to use the adb shell command to explore your Glass folders, right? If not, you should review Chapter 2 or check out a great blog article, written by Andres Calvo, the technical reviewer of this book, about the adb tool (http://ocddevelopers.com/2014/installing-native-android-apps-on-glass-adb-101/).

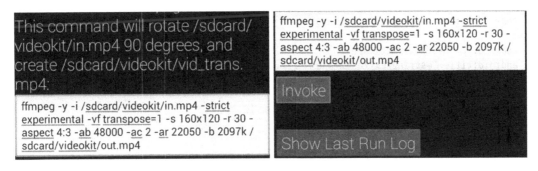

Figure 5-8. Testing the FFmpeg library demo client

Installing the FFmpeg4Android demo client and using launchy to test the client are optional. But I found using launchy and testing a native Android app on Glass to be helpful in Glass app development.

Integrating the FFmpeg Library

Follow these steps to integrate and use the library in the app MyVideosApp:

1. Add the FFmpeg4Android library to the project (similar to Figure 5-6).

2. Add a new menu entry called FFmpeg Processing to menu.xml, strings.xml, and MenuActivity.java.

3. Add a new menu XML file called videoprocessing.xml.

```xml
<?xml version="1.0" encoding="utf-8"?>
<menu xmlns:android="http://schemas.android.com/apk/res/android" >

    <item
        android:id="@+id/original"
        android:title="@string/original"/>
    <item
        android:id="@+id/processed"
        android:title="@string/processed"/>
    <item
        android:id="@+id/sepia"
        android:title="@string/sepia"/>
    <item
        android:id="@+id/vintage"
        android:title="@string/vintage"/>
    <item
        android:id="@+id/canny"
        android:title="@string/canny"/>
    <item
        android:id="@+id/rotate"
        android:title="@string/rotate"/>
    <item
        android:id="@+id/extractsound"
        android:title="@string/extractsound"/>
    <item
        android:id="@+id/extractimages"
        android:title="@string/extractimages"/>
</menu>
```

4. Add to strings.xml the menu items in step 3.

```xml
<string name="original">Original Video</string>
<string name="processed">Processed Result</string>
<string name="sepia">Sepia Effect</string>
<string name="vintage">Vintage Effect</string>
<string name="canny">Canny Effect</string>
<string name="rotate">Rotate Video</string>
<string name="extractsound">Extract Sound</string>
<string name="extractimages">Extract Images</string>
```

5. Copy and paste the PhotoViewActivity.java file from the SmartCamera app of the previous chapter; this is to show the images extracted from video.

6. Create a new class called VideoProcessingActivity.java with the code in Listing 5-5.

Listing 5-5. Video Processing Using FFmpeg

```java
public void onCreate(Bundle savedInstanceState) {
        super.onCreate(savedInstanceState);
        setContentView(R.layout.start);
        mTextView = (TextView) findViewById(R.id.hello_view);
        mTextView.setText("Tap for Menu");
```

```
    copyAsset(mOriginal);

    setWorkingFolder(PATH);
    copyLicenseAndDemoFilesFromAssetsToSDIfNeeded();

    mGestureDetector = new GestureDetector(this);

    mGestureDetector.setBaseListener(new GestureDetector.BaseListener() {
        @Override
        public boolean onGesture(Gesture gesture) {
            if (gesture == Gesture.TAP) {
                openOptionsMenu();
            }
            return true;
        }
    });
}

public boolean onGenericMotionEvent(MotionEvent event) {
    if (mGestureDetector != null) {
        return mGestureDetector.onMotionEvent(event);
    }
    return false;
}

@Override
public boolean onCreateOptionsMenu(Menu menu) {
    MenuInflater inflater = getMenuInflater();
    inflater.inflate(R.menu.videoprocessing, menu);
    return true;
}

@Override
public boolean onOptionsItemSelected(MenuItem item) {
    switch (item.getItemId()) {
    case R.id.original:
        Intent i = new Intent();
        i.setAction("com.google.glass.action.VIDEOPLAYER");
        i.putExtra("video_url", PATH + mOriginal);
        startActivity(i);
        return true;

    case R.id.processed:
        if (mProcessed == null)
            Toast.makeText(VideoProcessingActivity.this,
                    "No video or image just processed yet", Toast.LENGTH_LONG)
                    .show();
        else if (mProcessed.equalsIgnoreCase("image_extracted")) {
            mTextView.setText("");
            Intent intent = new Intent(this, PhotoViewActivity.class);
            startActivity(intent);
            finish();
        }
```

```
            else {
                Intent i2 = new Intent();
                i2.setAction("com.google.glass.action.VIDEOPLAYER");
                i2.putExtra("video_url", PATH + mProcessed);
                startActivity(i2);
            }
            return true;

    case R.id.sepia:
        mProcessed = "m-sepia.mp4";
        setCommand("ffmpeg -y -i /sdcard/myvideoapps/in.mp4 -strict experimental -vf
colorchannelmixer=.393:.769:.189:0:.349:.686:.168:0:.272:.534:.131 -s 640x480 -r 30 -aspect 4:3 -ab
48000 -ac 2 -ar 22050 -b 2097k -vcodec mpeg4 /sdcard/myvideoapps/m-sepia.mp4");
        setProgressDialogTitle("Adding Sepia Effect...");
        setProgressDialogMessage("After completed, tap to see more options");
        runTranscoing();
        return true;


    case R.id.vintage:
        mProcessed = "m-vintage.mp4";
        setCommand("ffmpeg -y -i /sdcard/myvideoapps/in.mp4 -strict experimental -vf
curves=vintage -s 640x480 -r 30 -aspect 4:3 -ab 48000 -ac 2 -ar 22050 -b 2097k -vcodec mpeg4 /
sdcard/myvideoapps/m-vintage.mp4");
        setProgressDialogTitle("Adding Vintage Effect...");
        setProgressDialogMessage("After completed, tap to see more options");
        runTranscoing();
        return true;


    case R.id.canny:
        mProcessed = "m-canny.mp4";
        setCommand("ffmpeg -y -i /sdcard/myvideoapps/in.mp4 -strict experimental -vf
edgedetect=low=0.1:high=0.2 -s 640x480 -r 30 -aspect 4:3 -ab 48000 -ac 2 -ar 22050 -b 2097k -vcodec
mpeg4 /sdcard/myvideoapps/m-canny.mp4");
        setProgressDialogTitle("Adding Canny Effect...");
        setProgressDialogMessage("After completed, tap to see more options");
        runTranscoing();
        return true;


    case R.id.rotate:
        mProcessed = "m-rotate.mp4";
        setCommand("ffmpeg -y -i /sdcard/myvideoapps/in.mp4 -strict experimental -vf transpose=1
-s 160x120 -r 30 -aspect 4:3 -ab 48000 -ac 2 -ar 22050 -b 2097k /sdcard/myvideoapps/m-rotate.mp4");
        setProgressDialogTitle("Rotating Video...");
        setProgressDialogMessage("After completed, tap to see more options");
        runTranscoing();
        return true;


    case R.id.extractsound:
        mProcessed = "m-sound.mp3";
        setCommand("ffmpeg -i /sdcard/myvideoapps/in.mp4 -vn -ar 44100 -ac 2 -ab 192 -f mp3 /
        sdcard/myvideoapps/m-sound.mp3");
        setProgressDialogTitle("Sound Extracting...");
```

```
                setProgressDialogMessage("After completed, tap to see more options");
                runTranscoing();
                return true;

        case R.id.extractimages:
            mProcessed = "image_extracted";
            setCommand("ffmpeg -i /sdcard/myvideoapps/in.mp4 /sdcard/myvideoapps/in-image%d.jpg");
            setProgressDialogTitle("Image Extracting...");
            setProgressDialogMessage("After completed, tap to see more options");
            runTranscoing();
            return true;

        default:
            return super.onOptionsItemSelected(item);
        }
}
```

Add `VideoProcessingActivity` and `PhotoViewActivity` to `AndroidManifest.xml`, and run the app. Select the FFmpeg Processing menu option; you'll see a Tap for Menu option. Tap and swipe on Glass, and you'll see the options Original Video, Processed Result, Sepia Effect, Vintage Effect, Canny Effect, Rotate Video, Extract Sound, and Extract Images. Select one of the effects, wait about 20 seconds to see the "Transcoding Finished" message, and then choose Processed Result. You'll see the whole video has been processed and applied with the effect. Extracting sound or images takes about three seconds. You can see selected images in a `CardScrollView`.

The code in Listing 5-5 is pretty self-explanatory. If you need to write your own FFmpeg commands to achieve your desired video processing result, you should check out the FFmpeg documentation at `www.ffmpeg.org/ffmpeg-filters.html` and download and test with a command-line FFmpeg tool for your OS platform at `www.ffmpeg.org/download.html`. The previous commands in Listing 5-5 have been tested first on Mac using the binary download at `http://ffmpegmac.net`.

YouTube Integration

It's hard to imagine the Internet without YouTube these days, and it's easy to think of a video search app using YouTube. In the Fireside Chat with the Glass team at Google I/O 2013 (available at `https://developers.google.com/events/io/sessions/332695704`), when asked what Glass app each person expects developers to build, Isabelle Olsson, the industrial designer behind Glass, said she'd love to see a karaoke app because she loves karaoke and thinks it'd be awesome to sing karaoke facing your friends, with Glass, "instead of staring into a screen with words on it." While it's not possible to build a full-fledged Glass karaoke app in this section of this chapter, YouTube integration gives you the best chance for an app pretty close to that.

Calling Data API

First you need to figure out how to query YouTube and get the results. YouTube offers an easy-to-use API at `https://developers.google.com/youtube/2.0/developers_guide_protocol_api_query_parameters`. A sample query that returns videos, in the JSON data format, of the *Godfather* movie theme song "Speak Softly Love" with, yes, lyrics (now this sounds like karaoke, doesn't it?) is this: https://gdata.youtube.com/feeds/api/videos?q=speak+softly+love+lyrics&orderby=viewCount&v= 2&alt=json.

Listing 5-6 shows the code that makes a simple HTTP get call. In Chapter 7, I'll cover network programming and HTTP requests in detail, implemented in AsyncTask with JSON parsing.

Listing 5-6. Using the YouTube API to Query Data

```java
private class GetVideos extends AsyncTask<Void, Void, Void> {
    @Override
    protected void onPreExecute() {
        super.onPreExecute();
    }

    @Override
    protected Void doInBackground(Void... arg0) {
        try {
            DefaultHttpClient httpClient = new DefaultHttpClient();
            HttpGet httpGet = new HttpGet(url);
            HttpResponse httpResponse = httpClient.execute(httpGet);
            HttpEntity httpEntity = httpResponse.getEntity();

            String jsonStr = EntityUtils.toString(httpEntity);
            if (jsonStr != null) {
                JSONObject jsonObj = new JSONObject(jsonStr);
                entries = jsonObj.getJSONObject("feed").getJSONArray("entry");
            } else {
                Log.e(TAG, "Couldn't get any data from the url");
            }

        } catch (Exception e) {
            Log.e(TAG, e.getMessage());
        }
        return null;
    }

    @Override
    protected void onPostExecute(Void result) {
        super.onPostExecute(result);

        try {
            for (int i = 0; i < entries.length(); i++) {
                JSONObject entry = entries.getJSONObject(i);
                String title = entry.getJSONObject("title").getString("$t");
                String viewCount = entry.getJSONObject("yt$statistics").getString("viewCount");
                String thumbnail = entry.getJSONObject("media$group").
                getJSONArray("media$thumbnail").getJSONObject(0).getString("url");
                JSONObject link = entry.getJSONArray("link").getJSONObject(0);
                mVideos.add(new Video(title, link.getString("href"), viewCount, thumbnail));
            }
        }

    }
```

```
        catch (Exception e) {
        }
    }
}
```

Video is a simple class that encapsulates the video's attributes that you're interested in.

```
class Video {
    String mtitle;
    String murl;
    String mviewCount;
    String mThumbnail;
    ImageView mImageView;
    Bitmap mBitmap;
    Boolean mDrawn;
    ...
}
```

Displaying Query Result

Follow these steps to use a ListView to display the query result mVideos:

1. Add a new layout file called videolist.xml.

    ```xml
    <?xml version="1.0" encoding="utf-8"?>
    <FrameLayout xmlns:android="http://schemas.android.com/apk/res/android"
            xmlns:tools="http://schemas.android.com/tools"
            android:layout_width="match_parent"
            android:layout_height="match_parent"
            android:keepScreenOn="true"
            android:background="@color/black"
            tools:context=".MainActivity">

        <ListView
                android:layout_width="wrap_content"
                android:layout_height="wrap_content"
                android:id="@+id/listView"
                android:layout_gravity="left|top"
                android:paddingLeft="18dp"
                android:listSelector="#0000FF"/>

    </FrameLayout>
    ```

2. In the new VideoSearchActivity.java's onCreate method, call
    setContentView(R.layout.videolist);.

3. At the end of onPostExecute in Listing 5-6, right after the for loop that builds the query result mVideos, add the following lines of code:

```
mListView = (ListView) findViewById(R.id.listView);
mMovieList = new VideoAdapter(mActivity, R.layout.listitem, mVideos);
mListView.setAdapter(mMovieList);
mListView.setOnItemClickListener(new VideoLauncher());
```

4. Add a new layout file called listitem.xml for each video result entry.

```
<?xml version="1.0" encoding="utf-8"?>
<LinearLayout xmlns:android="http://schemas.android.com/apk/res/android"
    android:layout_width="fill_parent"
    android:layout_height="?android:attr/listPreferredItemHeight"
    android:orientation="horizontal"
    android:padding="3dip" >

    <ImageView
        android:id="@+id/thumbnail"
        android:layout_width="30dp"
        android:layout_height="30dp"
        android:layout_marginRight="3dp"
        android:layout_marginTop="5dp"
        android:adjustViewBounds="true"
        android:maxHeight="50dp"
        android:maxWidth="50dp"
        android:scaleType="center" />

    <LinearLayout
        android:layout_width="wrap_content"
        android:layout_height="wrap_content"
        android:layout_marginLeft="10dip"
        android:orientation="vertical" >

        <TextView
            android:id="@+id/title"
            android:layout_width="wrap_content"
            android:layout_height="wrap_content"
            android:ellipsize="marquee"
            android:singleLine="true"
            android:textStyle="bold" />

        <TextView
            android:id="@+id/viewcount"
            android:layout_width="wrap_content"
            android:layout_height="wrap_content" />
    </LinearLayout>

</LinearLayout>
```

5. Add the VideoAdapter class implementation with the getView method, which defines how to show each video item. Because you use the thumbnail URL for each result to make the list look nicer, you need to load those URLs asynchronously so the main UI thread doesn't get blocked. This is what the SetImageTask AsyncTask is for in Listing 5-7.

Listing 5-7. Loading Thumbnail URLs Asynchronously

```
class VideoAdapter extends ArrayAdapter<Video> {
private ArrayList<Video> videos;

public VideoAdapter(Context context, int resource, ArrayList<Video> videos) {
    super(context, resource, videos);
    this.videos = videos;
}

// for each list item
public View getView(int position, View convertView, ViewGroup parent){
    View v = convertView;

    if (v == null) {
        LayoutInflater inflater = (LayoutInflater) getContext().getSystemService(Context.LAYOUT_
        INFLATER_SERVICE);
        v = inflater.inflate(R.layout.listitem, null);
    }

    Video video = videos.get(position);

    if (video != null) {
        TextView title = (TextView) v.findViewById(R.id.title);
        TextView viewCount = (TextView) v.findViewById(R.id.viewcount);
        ImageView thumbnail = (ImageView) v.findViewById(R.id.thumbnail);
        video.mImageView = thumbnail;
        if (!(VideoSearchActivity.thumbnailMaps.containsKey(video.getThumbnail()))) {
            // set image asynchronously
            new SetImageTask().execute(video);
        }

        if (title != null){
            title.setText(video.getTitle());
        }
        if (viewCount != null) {
            viewCount.setText("Views: " + video.getViewCount());
        }

        if (VideoSearchActivity.thumbnailMaps.containsKey(video.getThumbnail()))
            thumbnail.setImageBitmap(VideoSearchActivity.thumbnailMaps.get(video.getThumbnail()));
    }
```

```
        // the view must be returned to our activity
        return v;
}

private class SetImageTask extends AsyncTask<Video,Void,Void> {
    @Override
    protected void onPreExecute() {
        super.onPreExecute();
    }

    @Override
    protected Void doInBackground(Video... params) {
        try {
            Video video = params[0];
            VideoSearchActivity.thumbnailMaps.put(video.getThumbnail(),
            downloadBitmap(video.getThumbnail()));
        }
        catch(Exception e) {
            e.printStackTrace();
        }
        return null;
    }

    @Override
    protected void onPostExecute(Void result) {
        super.onPostExecute(result);
        for (int i = 0; i < videos.size(); i++) {
            Video v = videos.get(i);
            if(v.mBitmap!=null && !v.mDrawn) {
                v.mImageView.setImageBitmap(v.mBitmap);
                v.mDrawn = true;
            }
            if (VideoSearchActivity.thumbnailMaps.containsKey(v.getThumbnail()))
                v.mImageView.setImageBitmap(VideoSearchActivity.thumbnailMaps.get
                (v.getThumbnail()));
        }
    }
}

private Bitmap downloadBitmap(String url) {
    final DefaultHttpClient client = new DefaultHttpClient();
    Bitmap image = null;
    final HttpGet getRequest = new HttpGet(url);
    try {
        HttpResponse response = client.execute(getRequest);
        final int statusCode = response.getStatusLine().getStatusCode();
        if (statusCode != HttpStatus.SC_OK) {
            return null;
        }

        final HttpEntity entity = response.getEntity();
        if (entity != null) {
```

```
            InputStream inputStream = null;
            try {
                inputStream = entity.getContent();
                image = BitmapFactory.decodeStream(inputStream);
            } finally {
                if (inputStream != null) {
                    inputStream.close();
                }
                entity.consumeContent();
            }
        }
    } catch (Exception e) {
        Log.e(TAG, e.getMessage());
    }

    return image;
    }
}
```

Making the Voice Query

You're working in the Glass world and no keyboard entry is available, so you have to use voice input for query. This may sound a bad thing if you're used to other smartphone keyboard input, but after you get used to Glass's hands-free voice input, you'll find Glass's speech recongnition engine powerful and easy to use. So, just add the following three lines of code at the end of onCreate to launch the speech recognition intent:

```
Intent i = new Intent(RecognizerIntent.ACTION_RECOGNIZE_SPEECH);
i.putExtra(RecognizerIntent.EXTRA_PROMPT, "Speak a song title:");
startActivityForResult(i, VOICE_RECOGNIZER_REQUEST_CODE);
```

Then add a new method and call the AsyncTask GetVideos().execute method, shown here:

```
protected void onActivityResult(int RequestCode, int ResultCode, Intent data) {
        switch(RequestCode) {
        case VOICE_RECOGNIZER_REQUEST_CODE:
            if(RequestCode == VOICE_RECOGNIZER_REQUEST_CODE && ResultCode == RESULT_OK) {
                    ArrayList<String> results = data.getStringArrayListExtra(RecognizerIntent.EXTRA_
                    RESULTS);

                    if (results.size() > 0) {
                            mTitle = results.get(0);
                            mTitle = mTitle.replace(' ', '+');
                            url = url.replaceAll("<title>", mTitle);
                            new GetVideos().execute();
                    }
            }
            break;
        }
        super.onActivityResult(RequestCode, ResultCode, data);
}
```

Playing the Video and Let's Karaoke

This part is easy, especially on Glass. With the `com.google.glass.action.VIDEOPLAYER` intent on Glass, you can simply pass a regular YouTube URL, and the video will play with the built-in media controls. Unlike on other Android devices, other play solutions like `VideoView` or `WebView` won't work.

```
public void launchVideo(String youtubeurl) {
    Intent i = new Intent();
    i.setAction("com.google.glass.action.VIDEOPLAYER");
    i.putExtra("video_url", youtubeurl);
    startActivity(i);
}

private class VideoLauncher implements AdapterView.OnItemClickListener {
    public void onItemClick(AdapterView parent, View v, int position, long id) {
        Video video = (Video)parent.getSelectedItem();
        mActivity.launchVideo(video.murl);
    }
}
```

Keeping Code Updated

In XE 12, the previous code works perfectly. But with the XE 16 update, you can't scroll the `ListView` implemented earlier. This little annoyance won't scare away us developers, though. Just replace the last line of the code in step 3 earlier, shown here:

```
mListView.setOnItemClickListener(new VideoLauncher());
```

with the following:

```
mListView.setChoiceMode(ListView.CHOICE_MODE_SINGLE);
mListView.setClickable(true);
```

Remove the class `VideoLauncher` implementation in the previous section, add `GestureDetector mGestureDetector;` before `onCreate`, add `mGestureDetector = createGestureDetector(this);` at the end of `onCreate`, and add the following code to make the `ListView` scrollable and selectable:

```
private GestureDetector createGestureDetector(Context context) {
    GestureDetector gestureDetector = new GestureDetector(context);
    gestureDetector.setBaseListener( new GestureDetector.BaseListener() {
        @Override
        public boolean onGesture(Gesture gesture) {
            if (gesture == Gesture.TAP) { // On Tap, generate a new number
                Video video = (Video)mListView.getSelectedItem();
                mActivity.launchVideo(video.murl);
                return true;
            } else if (gesture == Gesture.SWIPE_RIGHT) {
                mListView.setSelection(mListView.getSelectedItemPosition()+1);
                return true;
            } else if (gesture == Gesture.SWIPE_LEFT) {
```

```
                // do something on left (backwards) swipe
                mListView.setSelection(mListView.getSelectedItemPosition()-1);
                return true;
            }
            return false;
        }
    });

    return gestureDetector;
}

// this method is required for tap on touchpad to work!
public boolean onGenericMotionEvent(MotionEvent event) {
    if (mGestureDetector != null) {
        return mGestureDetector.onMotionEvent(event);
    }
    return false;
}
```

Running the App

Finally, just add a new menu item called YouTube Search, update `MenuActivity.java`, and add `VideoProcessingActivity` to `AndroidManifest.xml`. Run the app and say "OK Glass" and then "Chapter 5." Then select YouTube Search and say your favorite song title. You'll see a list of matched results, as shown in Figure 5-9. Swipe forward and backward and select the highlighted one; then start singing facing your friends! Enjoy yourself because you deserve it!

Figure 5-9. YouTube video search results

Summary

In this chapter, you started with the basic video capture and custom video capture with preview and then looked at how video can play on Glass. Then I discussed how to use OpenCV to add image effects on frames extracted from video. A more powerful video-processing library, FFmpeg, was introduced with detailed instructions of how to integrate it with your own app. Commands for various video filtering effects were presented. Finally, a YouTube video search and play app was covered in detail, which can be used as the foundation of a full-fleged karaoke app.

You probably have noticed more than once the inconvenience, at least under certain circumstances, of having to use the touchpad to make a selection after the voice commands "OK Glass," "Smart camera," "Chapter 5," or "Speak softly, love." Is it possible to go 100 percent hands-free? If not, what exactly can you do and cannot do? Also, how about some in-depth coverage of audio processing, such as recoding what you sing while you're doing the karaoke? Voice and audio will be the topic of next chapter.

Chapter 6

Voice and Audio

You have already seen voice commands in action in all the sample projects discussed so far in the book, and the template app uses voice to launch Glass apps from the OK Glass menu. You have also seen text to speech and speech recognition activities supported in Glass. In this chapter, I'll cover in detail the following solutions, which you can use as the foundation for your next amazing Glass voice apps:

- How to launch a service or activity in your Glassware using a voice trigger
- How to play specific Glass sound effects
- How to capture and play audio and how to further improve your karaoke app to record and play your voice when doing karaoke
- How to do pitch detection to recognize a musical note
- How to do touchtone detection to recognize each key you press on your phone
- How to identify music or a song you're listening to

Sound exciting? Let's dive in. To start, follow the same steps as in previous chapters to create a new project called VoiceAndAudio based on GlasswareTemplate. You can take a peek at the complete project source code for this chapter on the book's site, but you may understand the topics better by starting from scratch, so it would be beneficial to start a new project of your own.

Voice Input

Google has pretty good documentation on how to use voice input to start Glassware and start the speech recognition activity at https://developers.google.com/glass/develop/gdk/starting-glassware. The GDK's Sounds class, used to play Glass-specific sounds, is also described on the GDK's Reference page. I'll cover here how to apply, and modify when necessary, the code snippets in the documentation to launch both a service, which you have seen before, and an activity that plays different Glass sound effects.

But first, I will show you quickly how to use two voice triggers to launch two services in your app (you can copy AppService.java and rename it to AppServiceTwo.java). The content in AndroidManifest.xml, as shown in Listing 6-1, will create two entries in the OK Glass voice menu.

Listing 6-1. Adding Voice Commands to Multiple Services

```
<service
    android:name="com.morkout.smartcamera.AppService"
    android:enabled="true"
    android:exported="true"
    android:icon="@drawable/ic_app"
    android:label="@string/app_name" >
    <intent-filter>
        <action android:name="com.google.android.glass.action.VOICE_TRIGGER" />
    </intent-filter>

    <meta-data
        android:name="com.google.android.glass.VoiceTrigger"
        android:resource="@xml/voice_trigger_start" />
</service>
<service
    android:name="com.morkout.smartcamera.AppServiceTwo"
    android:enabled="true"
    android:exported="true"
    android:icon="@drawable/ic_app"
    android:label="@string/app_name_two" >
    <intent-filter>
        <action android:name="com.google.android.glass.action.VOICE_TRIGGER" />
    </intent-filter>

    <meta-data
        android:name="com.google.android.glass.VoiceTrigger"
        android:resource="@xml/voice_trigger_start2" />
</service>
```

The content for voice_trigger_start.xml, voice_trigger_start2.xml, and strings.xml is as follows:

```
<trigger keyword="@string/say_smartcamera" >
</trigger>

<trigger keyword="@string/say_smartcamera_two" >
</trigger>

<string name="say_smartcamera">Camera One</string>
<string name="say_smartcamera_two">Camera Two</string>
```

> **Note**   If you change the second service name, `AppServiceTwo`, in `AndroidManifest.xml` to
> `AppService`, hoping that both voice commands will trigger the service, you'll find that only one entry,
> "Camera two" for `voice_trigger_start2`, will appear and that only one voice command, "Camera 2," will
> launch the service.

You can also apply the `VOICE_TRIGGER` action to any activity declared in `AndroidManifest.xml`. For
example, if you change the `ZoomActivity` in the Chapter 4 SmartCamera project's `AndroidManifest.`
`xml` file to look like Listing 6-2, then a voice command will show in the Glass voice menu. After you
speak the command defined in the trigger keyword, the `ZoomActivity` will be launched directly,
which is different from what you have seen so far, which is that a service is started by a voice
command, then a live card gets created, and choosing a menu item associated with the live card
launches an activity.

Listing 6-2. Adding Voice Commands to an Activity

```
<activity
    android:name="com.morkout.smartcamera.ZoomActivity"
    android:enabled="true"
    android:label="@string/app_name" >
    <intent-filter>
        <action android:name="com.google.android.glass.action.VOICE_TRIGGER" />
    </intent-filter>
    <meta-data
        android:name="com.google.android.glass.VoiceTrigger"
        android:resource="@xml/voice_trigger_start2" />
</activity>
```

Sound Effects

In the project VoiceAndAudio you created earlier in this chapter, follow these steps to add voice
commands to both the service that launches the app and the activity that launches the Glass sound
effect test:

1. In the `res/menu/main.xml` file, add a new menu item.

    ```
    <item
            android:id="@+id/soundeffect"
            android:title="@string/soundeffect"/>
    ```

2. In `res/menu`, add a new XML file called `soundeffect.xml`.

    ```
    <?xml version="1.0" encoding="utf-8"?>
    <menu xmlns:android="http://schemas.android.com/apk/res/android" >

        <item
            android:id="@+id/disallowed"
            android:title="@string/disallowed"/>
    ```

```xml
        <item
            android:id="@+id/dismissed"
            android:title="@string/dismissed"/>
        <item
            android:id="@+id/error"
            android:title="@string/error"/>
        <item
            android:id="@+id/selected"
            android:title="@string/selected"/>
        <item
            android:id="@+id/success"
            android:title="@string/success"/>
        <item
            android:id="@+id/tap"
            android:title="@string/tap"/>
    </menu>
```

3. Add a new XML file called voice_trigger_start2.xml in res/xml:

```xml
<?xml version="1.0" encoding="utf-8"?>
<trigger keyword="@string/sound_effect" >
    <input prompt="@string/glass_voice_prompt" />
</trigger>
```

4. Make your res/values/strings.xml file look like this:

```xml
<resources>
    <string name="app_name">Voice And Audio</string>
    <string name="say_glasswaretemplate">Voice and Audio</string>
    <string name="glass_voice_prompt">Which sound to hear?</string>
    <string name="soundeffect">Sound Effect</string>
    <string name="stop">STOP</string>
    <string name="disallowed">Disallowed</string>
    <string name="dismissed">Dismissed</string>
    <string name="error">Error</string>
    <string name="selected">Selected</string>
    <string name="success">Success</string>
    <string name="tap">Tap</string>
</resources>
```

5. In AndroidManifest.xml, add the following content:

```xml
<activity
    android:name="com.morkout.voiceandaudio.GlassSoundActivity"
    android:enabled="true"
    android:label="@string/app_name" >
    <intent-filter>
        <action android:name="com.google.android.glass.action.VOICE_TRIGGER" />
    </intent-filter>
```

```
    <meta-data
        android:name="com.google.android.glass.VoiceTrigger"
        android:resource="@xml/voice_trigger_start2" />
</activity>
```

6. In MenuActivity.java, add the following statement in the
    onOptionsItemSelected method:

```
case R.id.soundeffect:
    Intent intent2 = new Intent(this, GlassSoundActivity.class);
    startActivity(intent2);
    return true;
```

7. Finally, create a new Activity subclass file called GlassSoundActivity.java,
    as shown in Listing 6-3.

    Listing 6-3. Activity Playing Glass Sound Effects and Processing a Voice Prompt

```java
public class GlassSoundActivity extends Activity {
    public final static String TAG = "GlassSoundActivity";

    @Override
    protected void onCreate(Bundle savedInstanceState) {
        super.onCreate(savedInstanceState);
        openOptionsMenu();
    }

    @Override
    public boolean onCreateOptionsMenu(Menu menu) {
        MenuInflater inflater = getMenuInflater();
        inflater.inflate(R.menu.soundeffect, menu);
        return true;
    }

    @Override
    public void onResume() {
        super.onResume();
        if (getIntent().getExtras() == null) return;
        ArrayList<String> voiceResults = getIntent().getExtras()
                .getStringArrayList(RecognizerIntent.EXTRA_RESULTS);
        if (voiceResults != null) {
            if (voiceResults.size() > 0) {
                AudioManager audio = (AudioManager) this.
                                getSystemService(Context.AUDIO_SERVICE);

                // loop through the recognition results to see if
                // any of them matches any Glass sound name
                for (String result: voiceResults) {
                    Toast.makeText(this, result,
                        Toast.LENGTH_SHORT).show();
```

```
            if (result.equalsIgnoreCase("disallowed")) {
                audio.playSoundEffect(Sounds.DISALLOWED);
                break;
            }
            else if (result.equalsIgnoreCase("dismissed")) {
                audio.playSoundEffect(Sounds.DISMISSED);
                break;
            }
            else if (result.equalsIgnoreCase("error")) {
                audio.playSoundEffect(Sounds.ERROR);
                break;
            }
            else if (result.equalsIgnoreCase("selected")) {
                audio.playSoundEffect(Sounds.SELECTED);
                break;
            }
            else if (result.equalsIgnoreCase("success")) {
                audio.playSoundEffect(Sounds.SUCCESS);
                break;
            }
            else if (result.equalsIgnoreCase("tap")) {
                audio.playSoundEffect(Sounds.TAP);
                break;
            }
    }}}}

@Override
public void onOptionsMenuClosed (Menu menu) {
    finish();
}

@Override
public boolean onOptionsItemSelected(MenuItem item) {
    AudioManager audio = (AudioManager) this.
                getSystemService(Context.AUDIO_SERVICE);

    switch (item.getItemId()) {
    case R.id.disallowed:
        audio.playSoundEffect(Sounds.DISALLOWED);
        Toast.makeText(this, "Disallowed",
                        Toast.LENGTH_SHORT).show();
        return true;

    case R.id.dismissed:
        audio.playSoundEffect(Sounds.DISMISSED);
        Toast.makeText(this, "Dismissed",
                        Toast.LENGTH_SHORT).show();
        return true;
```

```
            case R.id.error:
                audio.playSoundEffect(Sounds.ERROR);
                Toast.makeText(this, "Error", Toast.LENGTH_SHORT).show();
                return true;

            case R.id.selected:
                audio.playSoundEffect(Sounds.SELECTED);
                Toast.makeText(this, "Selected",
                    Toast.LENGTH_SHORT).show();
                return true;

            case R.id.success:
                audio.playSoundEffect(Sounds.SUCCESS);
                Toast.makeText(this, "Success", Toast.LENGTH_SHORT).show();
                return true;

            case R.id.tap:
                audio.playSoundEffect(Sounds.TAP);
                Toast.makeText(this, "Tap", Toast.LENGTH_SHORT).show();
                return true;

            default:
                return super.onOptionsItemSelected(item);
            }
        }
    }
```

Run the app and after saying "OK Glass," you can try two different voice commands. Saying "Voice and audio" will launch the app service you're used to, and tapping Glass will show the Glass sound effect menu. Saying "Sound effect" will launch the Glass sound effect activity directly, and because you have a voice prompt defined in step 3 in the previous exercise, you'll see the prompt shown in Figure 6-1. After your voice input is recognized, for example you say "Dismissed" (also shown in Figure 6-1), the GlassSoundActivity, because of the description in AndroidManifest.xml, will be launched. Then you use getIntent().getExtras().getStringArrayList in onResume to retrieve the recognized result. In the sample, you test to see whether there's a match between the result and one of Glass's sound effects and play the sound if so.

Figure 6-1. *Voice input with prompt to launch an activity*

For a voice prompt that launches a service, you can get the recognized test in the service's onStartCommand method. This and other voice input–related details are well documented at Google's Glass developer site (https://developers.google.com/glass/develop/gdk/starting-glassware), so I won't repeat them here.

If you're interested in a 100 percent hands-free app so you can still do karaoke while your hands are coding, debugging, or writing, you should check out the contextual voice command feature request discussion at https://code.google.com/p/google-glass-api/issues/detail?id=273. This is a commonly requested feature, and it's likely to be improved in a future Glass update. Therefore, I won't discuss it further since the text would probably be outdated by the time you read the book. Instead, let's see how you can improve the karaoke feature in the video app by capturing your beautiful voice and playing it back.

Audio Capture and Play

Basically, there are two ways of capturing audio and playing back the recorded audio. The first method is to use the same MediaRecorder class you saw in Chapter 5 for custom video capture.

Using MediaRecorder and MediaPlayer

The following code is based on the Android developer site, but it has some important changes to make it work for Google Glass, mainly in the settings of the MediaRecorder object and to simplify the record/play process:

1. Add a new menu entry in VoiceAndAudio's res/menu/main.xml.

```
<item
        android:id="@+id/audiocapture"
        android:title="@string/audiocapture"/>
```

2. Add the following in MenuActivity.java's onOptionsItemSelected:

```
case R.id.audiocapture:
    Intent intent3 = new Intent(this, AudioCaptureActivity.class);
    startActivity(intent3);
    return true;
```

3. Add `<string name="audiocapture">Audio Capture</string>` in strings.xml.

4. Add the following in AndroidManifest.xml:

```
<uses-permission android:name="android.permission.RECORD_AUDIO" />
<uses-permission android:name="android.permission.WRITE_EXTERNAL_STORAGE" />

<activity
    android:name="com.morkout.voiceandaudio.AudioCaptureActivity"
    android:enabled="true"
    android:label="@string/app_name" >
</activity>
```

5. Create a new AudioCaptureActivity.java file, as shown in Listing 6-4.

Listing 6-4. Capturing and Playing Audio Using MediaRecorder and MediaPlayer

```
public class AudioCaptureActivity extends Activity {
    private static final String TAG = "AudioCaptureActivity";
    private static String mFileName = null;

    private RecordButton mRecordButton = null;
    private MediaRecorder mRecorder = null;

    private MediaPlayer   mPlayer = null;

    private void onRecord(boolean start) {
        if (start) {
            startRecording();
        } else {
            stopRecording();
        }
    }

    private void startPlaying() {
        mPlayer = new MediaPlayer();

        mPlayer.setOnCompletionListener(new MediaPlayer.
                    OnCompletionListener() {
            public void onCompletion(MediaPlayer mp) {
                mRecordButton.setText("Start recording");
                mPlayer.release();
                mPlayer = null;
            }
        });
```

```
            try {
                mPlayer.setDataSource(mFileName);
                mPlayer.prepare();
                mPlayer.start();
            } catch (IOException e) {
                Log.e(TAG, "prepare() failed");
            }
        }

        private void startRecording() {
            mRecorder = new MediaRecorder();
            // the settings below are important for the capture
            // and playback to work in Glass
            mRecorder.setAudioSource(MediaRecorder.AudioSource.DEFAULT);
            mRecorder.setOutputFormat(MediaRecorder.OutputFormat.DEFAULT);
            mRecorder.setAudioEncoder(MediaRecorder.AudioEncoder.AAC);
            mRecorder.setOutputFile(mFileName);

            try {
                mRecorder.prepare();
            } catch (IOException e) {
                Log.e(TAG, "prepare() failed");
            }
            mRecorder.start();
        }

        private void stopRecording() {
            mRecorder.stop();
            mRecorder.release();
            mRecorder = null;
        }

        class RecordButton extends Button {
            boolean mStartRecording = true;

            OnClickListener clicker = new OnClickListener() {
                public void onClick(View v) {
                    onRecord(mStartRecording);
                    if (mStartRecording) {
                        setText("Stop recording");
                    } else {
                        setText("Playing...");
                        startPlaying();
                    }
                    mStartRecording = !mStartRecording;
                }
            };
```

```java
        public RecordButton(Context ctx) {
            super(ctx);
            setText("Start recording");
            setOnClickListener(clicker);
        }
    }

    @Override
    public void onCreate(Bundle icicle) {
        super.onCreate(icicle);

        mFileName = Environment.getExternalStorageDirectory().
                    getAbsolutePath();
        mFileName += "/audiorecordtest.3gp";

        LinearLayout ll = new LinearLayout(this);
        mRecordButton = new RecordButton(this);
        ll.addView(mRecordButton,
                new LinearLayout.LayoutParams(
                        ViewGroup.LayoutParams.WRAP_CONTENT,
                        ViewGroup.LayoutParams.WRAP_CONTENT,
                        0));
        setContentView(ll);
    }

    @Override
    public void onPause() {
        super.onPause();
        if (mRecorder != null) {
            mRecorder.release();
            mRecorder = null;
        }

        if (mPlayer != null) {
            mPlayer.release();
            mPlayer = null;
        }
    }
}
```

Run the app and say "OK Glass" and then "Voice and audio." Tap to show the menu, and swipe to select Audio Capture. You'll see a button titled "Start recording." Tap your Glass touchpad to start recording and then say something and tap again; you'll hear your recorded voice being played back. You can repeat the record-play process as many times as you want.

MediaRecorder and MediaPlayer are powerful high-level Android APIs for both video and audio capture and playback. There is another set of Android APIs, AudioRecord and AudioTrack, that can be used for audio-specific capture and playback. For audio play (no capture) only, SoundPool is yet another API, which I won't discuss here, but if you're interested in knowing when you should use which API, you can check out this article: www.wiseandroid.com/post/2010/07/13/Intro-to-the-three-Android-Audio-APIs.aspx.

Using AudioRecord and AudioTrack

AudioRecord and AudioTrack are low-level APIs that deal directly with the audio raw data. So, AudioRecord is appropriate for audio processing, which can lead to many interesting applications like those that will be introduced in the following sections of this chapter.

To see how to use AudioRecord and AudioTrack to capture and play audio, follow these steps:

1. Add another menu entry, audiocapture2, in `main.xml`. Add a new `case` statement in `MenuActivity.java`. Add `<string name="audiocapture2">Audio Capture2</string>` in `strings.xml`.

2. Create a new `audiorecorder.xml` file in the `layout` folder.

```xml
<?xml version="1.0" encoding="utf-8"?>
<LinearLayout xmlns:android="http://schemas.android.com/apk/res/android"
    android:layout_width="fill_parent"
    android:layout_height="fill_parent"
    android:orientation="vertical" >

    <TextView
        android:layout_width="fill_parent"
        android:layout_height="wrap_content"
        android:text="HB-Record Audio" />

    <Button
        android:id="@+id/startrec"
        android:layout_width="fill_parent"
        android:layout_height="wrap_content"
        android:text="Start Recording" />

    <Button
        android:id="@+id/stoprec"
        android:layout_width="fill_parent"
        android:layout_height="wrap_content"
        android:text="Stop Recording" />

    <Button
        android:id="@+id/playback"
        android:layout_width="fill_parent"
        android:layout_height="wrap_content"
        android:text="Play Back" />

</LinearLayout>
```

3. Declare a new activity called `AudioCapture2Activity` in `AndroidManifest.xml`.

4. Create a new class called `AudioCapture2Activity`, as in Listing 6-5.

Listing 6-5. Capturing and Playing Audio Using AudioRecord and AudioTrack

```java
public class AudioCapture2Activity extends Activity {
    Button startRec, stopRec, playBack;
    Boolean recording;
    GestureDetector mGestureDetector;

    @Override
    public void onCreate(Bundle savedInstanceState) {
        super.onCreate(savedInstanceState);
        setContentView(R.layout.audiorecorder);

        startRec = (Button)findViewById(R.id.startrec);
        stopRec = (Button)findViewById(R.id.stoprec);
        playBack = (Button)findViewById(R.id.playback);

        startRec.setOnClickListener(startRecOnClickListener);
        stopRec.setOnClickListener(stopRecOnClickListener);
        playBack.setOnClickListener(playBackOnClickListener);

        stopRec.setEnabled(false);
        playBack.setEnabled(false);

        mGestureDetector = createGestureDetector(this);
    }

    // GestureDetector needed since XE16 to swipe to next/prev button
    private GestureDetector createGestureDetector(Context context) {
        GestureDetector gestureDetector = new GestureDetector(context);
        //Create a base listener for generic gestures
        gestureDetector.setBaseListener(new GestureDetector.BaseListener() {
            @Override
            public boolean onGesture(Gesture gesture) {
                if (gesture == Gesture.SWIPE_RIGHT) {
                    if (startRec.isEnabled()) {
                        startRec.setEnabled(false);
                        stopRec.setEnabled(true);
                        stopRec.requestFocus();
                        playBack.setEnabled(false);
                    }
                    else if (stopRec.isEnabled()) {
                        stopRec.setEnabled(false);
                        playBack.setEnabled(true);
                        playBack.requestFocus();
                        startRec.setEnabled(false);
                    }
```

```
                          else if (playBack.isEnabled()) {
                              playBack.setEnabled(false);
                              startRec.setEnabled(true);
                              startRec.requestFocus();
                              stopRec.setEnabled(false);
                          }
                          return true;
                      } else if (gesture == Gesture.SWIPE_LEFT) {
                          if (startRec.isEnabled()) {
                              startRec.setEnabled(false);
                              playBack.setEnabled(true);
                              playBack.requestFocus();
                              stopRec.setEnabled(false);
                          }
                          else if (stopRec.isEnabled()) {
                              stopRec.setEnabled(false);
                              startRec.setEnabled(true);
                              startRec.requestFocus();
                              playBack.setEnabled(false);
                          }
                          else if (playBack.isEnabled()) {
                              playBack.setEnabled(false);
                              stopRec.setEnabled(true);
                              stopRec.requestFocus();
                              startRec.setEnabled(false);
                          }
                          return true;
                      }
                      return false;
                  }
              });

        return gestureDetector;
    }

    public boolean onGenericMotionEvent(MotionEvent event) {
        if (mGestureDetector != null) {
            return mGestureDetector.onMotionEvent(event);
        }
        return false;
    }

    OnClickListener startRecOnClickListener = new OnClickListener() {
        @Override
        public void onClick(View arg0) {
            startRec.setEnabled(false);
            stopRec.setEnabled(true);
            stopRec.requestFocus();
```

```java
        Thread recordThread = new Thread(new Runnable() {
            @Override
            public void run() {
                recording = true;
                startRecord();
            }
        });

        recordThread.start();
    }
};

OnClickListener stopRecOnClickListener = new OnClickListener() {
    @Override
    public void onClick(View arg0) {
        recording = false;
        startRec.setEnabled(false);
        stopRec.setEnabled(false);
        playBack.setEnabled(true);
        playBack.requestFocus();
    }
};

OnClickListener playBackOnClickListener   = new OnClickListener() {
    @Override
    public void onClick(View v) {
        startRec.setEnabled(true);
        stopRec.setEnabled(false);
        playBack.setEnabled(false);
        startRec.requestFocus();
        playRecord();
    }
};

private void startRecord() {
    File file = new File(Environment.getExternalStorageDirectory(),
                " audiorecordtest.pcm");
    try {
        file.createNewFile();
        OutputStream outputStream = new FileOutputStream(file);
        BufferedOutputStream bufferedOutputStream = new
                        BufferedOutputStream(outputStream);
        DataOutputStream dataOutputStream = new
                        DataOutputStream(bufferedOutputStream);

        int minBufferSize = AudioRecord.getMinBufferSize(11025,
            AudioFormat.CHANNEL_IN_MONO,
            AudioFormat.ENCODING_PCM_16BIT);

        short[] audioData = new short[minBufferSize];
```

```
                    AudioRecord audioRecord = new AudioRecord(
                        MediaRecorder.AudioSource.MIC,
                        11025,
                        AudioFormat.CHANNEL_IN_MONO,
                        AudioFormat.ENCODING_PCM_16BIT,
                        minBufferSize);

                    audioRecord.startRecording();

                    while(recording) {
                        int numberOfShort = audioRecord.read(audioData, 0,
                                            minBufferSize);
                        for(int i = 0; i < numberOfShort; i++)
                            dataOutputStream.writeShort(audioData[i]);
                    }
                    audioRecord.stop();
                    dataOutputStream.close();
                }
                catch (IOException e) {
                    e.printStackTrace();
                }
            }

            void playRecord() {
                File file = new File(Environment.getExternalStorageDirectory(),
                            " audiorecordtest.pcm");
                int shortSizeInBytes = Short.SIZE/Byte.SIZE;

                int bufferSizeInBytes = (int)(file.length()/shortSizeInBytes);
                short[] audioData = new short[bufferSizeInBytes];

                try {
                    InputStream inputStream = new FileInputStream(file);
                    BufferedInputStream bufferedInputStream = new
                                    BufferedInputStream(inputStream);
                    DataInputStream dataInputStream = new
                                    DataInputStream(bufferedInputStream);

                    int i = 0;
                    while(dataInputStream.available() > 0) {
                        audioData[i] = dataInputStream.readShort();
                        i++;
                    }

                    dataInputStream.close();

                    AudioTrack audioTrack = new AudioTrack(
                        AudioManager.STREAM_MUSIC,
                        11025,
                        AudioFormat.CHANNEL_CONFIGURATION_MONO,
                        AudioFormat.ENCODING_PCM_16BIT,
```

```
                bufferSizeInBytes,
                AudioTrack.MODE_STREAM);

            audioTrack.play();
            audioTrack.write(audioData, 0, bufferSizeInBytes);
        } catch (FileNotFoundException e) {
            e.printStackTrace();
        } catch (IOException e) {
            e.printStackTrace();
        }
    }
}
```

The two most important methods here are startRecord and playRecord. Also, notice that startRecord needs to run in a non-UI thread to avoid the blocking of the main thread. Now run the app and select the Audio Capture2 menu item, and you'll see three buttons (called Start Recording, Stop Recording, and Play Back) that allow you to test the audio capture and play.

If you use adb shell and look at the audio files recorded in the two methods, you may notice the file generated in the second method has a much larger size than the file generated in the first method, especially with longer recording. This is as expected because the raw audio data audiorecordtest.pcm takes more space than the compressed MediaRecorder-generated file audiorecordtest.3gp. Furthermore, if for test purposes you use adb pull to grab the two files, you can most likely play the audiorecordtest.3gp file but will probably need a tool such as open source Audacity (available for download at http://audacity.sourceforge.net/download/) to import the audiorecordtest.pcm file with the settings in Figure 6-2, which match the settings used in the new AudioRecord.

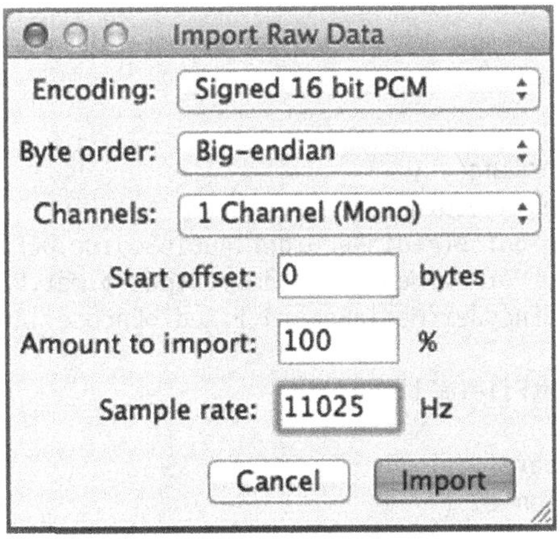

Figure 6-2. Using Audacity to import an audio file recorded using AudioRecord

Improving the Karaoke App

Now you're ready to further improve your karaoke app by capturing your singing while playing the selected video and playing back the recorded audio after the video play is done. Make the following changes in MyVideoApps' VideoSearchActivity.java file:

1. Add the following code after public void launchVideo(String youtubeurl):

```java
private static String mFileName = Environment.getExternalStorageDirectory().
    getAbsolutePath() + "/karaoke-recording.3gp";
private MediaRecorder mRecorder = null;
private MediaPlayer    mPlayer = null;
private Boolean mRecording;

private void startPlaying() {
    mPlayer = new MediaPlayer();
    try {
        mPlayer.setDataSource(mFileName);
        mPlayer.prepare();
        mPlayer.start();
    } catch (IOException e) {
        Log.e(TAG, "prepare() failed");
    }

}

private void stopPlaying() {
    if (mPlayer != null) {
        mPlayer.release();
        mPlayer = null;
    }
}

private void startRecording() {
    mRecorder = new MediaRecorder();
    mRecorder.setAudioSource(MediaRecorder.AudioSource.DEFAULT);
    mRecorder.setOutputFormat(MediaRecorder.OutputFormat.DEFAULT);
    mRecorder.setAudioEncoder(MediaRecorder.AudioEncoder.AAC);

    mRecorder.setOutputFile(mFileName);
    try {
        mRecorder.prepare();
    } catch (IOException e) {
        Log.e(TAG, "prepare() failed");
    }

    mRecorder.start();
}
```

```
    private void stopRecording() {
        if (mRecorder != null) {
            mRecorder.stop();
            mRecorder.release();
            mRecorder = null;
        }
    }
```

2. Add a new case statement in onActivityResult to handle the return from the video play activity. This will stop the audio recording and start playing the recorded audio.

```
protected void onActivityResult(int RequestCode,
            int ResultCode, Intent data) {
    switch(RequestCode) {
    case VIDEO_PLAY_ACTIVITY:
        stopRecording();
        startPlaying();
        break;
    case VOICE_RECOGNIZER_REQUEST_CODE:
```

3. Add the following code at the end of public void launchVideo(String youtubeurl):

```
new Thread(new Runnable() {
        @Override
    public void run() {
        mRecording = true;
        startRecording();
    }
}).start();
```

4. Add stopPlaying(); at the end of onPause.

You can also use the second method of capturing and playing audio here. Now you can sing all you can while listening to your favorite YouTube video and find out whether you should go to *American Idol* right away!

Pitch Detection

I just started learning how to play piano last year, and with months of effort, I'm now able to play, with both hands, only three songs. What I find even more challenging than playing with both hands is detecting whether I just played an incorrect note. Mark, my son, has been playing piano for years, and he can always easily tell me what note I just played, which simply amazes me. I'll probably never be able to do that, but, hey, I'm a developer, so how about letting Glass do that for me? Call it cheating? I guess I can live with that.

After some research, I found a couple of useful web sites talking about how to use Fast Fourier Transform for pitch detection (www.codeproject.com/Articles/32172/FFT-Guitar-Tuner) and how to map note names to frequencies (www.phys.unsw.edu.au/jw/notes.html). There's also an Android open source project called Android Tuner: https://code.google.com/p/androidtuner/source/brows e/?r=134743f47bfb0a0842f3dc73a75fed52923c8917. They should be enough for you to integrate into the app.

First, download the ZIP file of the open source Android project from https://code.google.com/p/ androidtuner/source/browse/?r=134743f47bfb0a0842f3dc73a75fed52923c8917. Unzip it, and you'll see a folder called androidtuner-134743f47bfb. Then, import the project to Eclipse; a project called GuitarTunerActivity will show up in Eclipse's Package Explorer. Run the app on an Android device such as Nexus 7 or Glass (with the help of the Launcher app) and play a note or make a sound. The message "frequency detected" will appear.

Now follow these steps to integrate the project and make the necessary changes:

1. Copy the four source files from GuitarTunerActivity's `src/com.example. AndroidTuner` to VoiceAndAudio's `src/com.morkout.voiceandaudio`, and rename `AndroidTunerActivity` to `PitchDetectionActivity`.

2. Create and initialize a new instance variable in `DrawableView.java`, after its constructor, with the frequency value for each key in a 88-key piano (the MIDI value starts as 21 for the first element in the array and then increases by 1 for each following element).

```
private double frequencies[] = new double[] {27.50, 29.14, 30.87, // A0, A0#, B0
    32.70, 34.65, 36.71, 38.89, 41.20, 43.65, 46.25, 49.00, 51.91, 55.00, 58.27,
61.74, // C1 - B1
        // C, C#, D, D#, E, F, F#, G, G#, A, A#, B
    65.51, 69.30, 73.42, 77.78, 82.41, 87.31, 92.50, 98.00, 103.83, 110.00, 116.54,
123.47, // C2 - B2
    130.81, 138.59, 146.83, 155.56, 164.81, 174.61, 185.00, 196.00, 207.65, 220.00,
233.08, 246.94, // C3 - B3
    261.63, 277.18, 293.67, 311.13, 329.63, 349.23, 369.99, 392.00, 415.30, 440.00,
466.16, 493.88, // C4 - B4
    523.25, 554.37, 587.33, 622.25, 659.26, 698.46, 739.99, 783.99, 830.61, 880.00,
932.33, 987.77, // C5 - B5
    1046.5, 1108.7, 1174.7, 1244.5, 1318.5, 1396.9, 1480.0, 1568.0, 1661.2, 1760.0,
1864.7, 1975.5, // C6 - B6
    2093.0, 2217.5, 2349.3, 2489.0, 2637.0, 2793.0, 2960.0, 3136.0, 3322.4, 3520.0,
3729.3, 3951.1, // C7 - B7
    4186.0}; // C8
```

3. Also in DrawableView.java, at the end of the DrawCurrentFrequency
    method implementation, replace the line canvas.drawText(Math.
    round(representation_.pitch * 10) / 10.0 + " Hz", 20, 40, paint);
    with the following code to find the number closest to a note frequency and
    show the right note:

```java
double freq = Math.round(representation_.pitch * 10) / 10.0;
int index = -1;
for (int i=0; i<frequencies.length-1; i++) {
    if (frequencies[i] <= freq && freq <= frequencies[i+1]) {
        if (freq-frequencies[i] <= frequencies[i+1]-freq)
            index = i;
        else
            index = i+1;
        break;
    }
}
if (index==-1) {
    if (freq<frequencies[0] && (frequencies[0]-freq<2.0))
        index = 0;
    else if (freq>frequencies[frequencies.length-1] && (freq-frequencies[frequencies.
length-1]<100.0))
        index = frequencies.length - 1;
}
if (index==-1)
    canvas.drawText(Math.round(representation_.pitch * 10) / 10.0 +
                " Hz", 20, 40, paint);
else {
    String noteString;
    if (index == 0) noteString = "A0";
    else if (index == 1) noteString = "A0 Sharp";
    else if (index == 2) noteString = "B0";
    else {
        int n = (int) ((index-3) / 12);
        int m = (int) ((index-3) % 12);
        String[] notes  = new String[] { "C", "C#", "D", "D#", "E", "F", "F#", "G", "G#",
        "A", "A#", "B"};
        noteString = notes[m];
        noteString = noteString.substring(0, 1) + (n+1) + (notes[m].length()==1?"":"#");
    }
    canvas.drawText(noteString + " - " + freq + " Hz", 20, 40, paint);
}
```

> **Note**   A slightly more accurate way to get the MIDI number from frequency, so you can find out which note is played, is to use the formula `midi = 12*log2(fm/440hz) + 69`. Or, in Java, use this:
>
> `Math.round((float)(12*Math.log(freq/440f)/Math.log(2))) + 69`
>
> Also, be aware that the AndroidTuner library used here may not reliably produce the correct frequencies for all notes and for all instruments, digital or not, but it works fine in most of these test cases. The example here is meant to be a good starting point for you to develop a full-blown pitch detection or tuner app on Glass.

4. Copy the `jni` directory from GuitarTunerActivity to VoiceAndAudio and change in `fft.cpp` the line `jniRegisterNativeMethods(env, "com/example/AndroidTuner/PitchDetector", gMethods, 1);` to `jniRegisterNativeMethods(env, "com/morkout/voiceandaudio/ PitchDetector", gMethods, 1);` then in your computer's Terminal window, cd to the location of the VoiceAndAudio project and run `ndk-build`. You should see something like the following (and in Eclipse you'll see a subfolder named armeabi with the file `libfft-jni.so` added under the `libs` folder):

```
$ ndk-build
[armeabi] Install : libfft-jni.so => libs/armeabi/libfft-jni.so
```

5. Finally, you know the drill—add a new menu option in menu's `main.xml`, add `Pitch Detection` in `strings.xml`, and update `MenuActivity.java` and `AndroidManifest.xml`.

Run the app and select Pitch Detection from the menu. You'll see a "Play a musical note" screen. Then, after playing, for example, the middle C note, you'll see the detected note with its frequency, as shown in Figure 6-3.

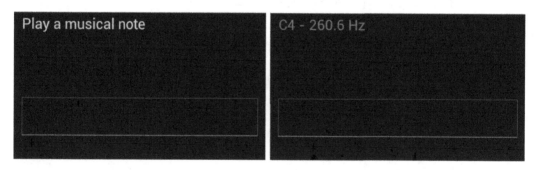

Figure 6-3. Detecting a musical note

I won't go into the details of the source code imported from the Android Tuner open source. You can look at it from either the integrated VoiceAndAudio project or the GuitarTunerActivity project to understand how Fast Fourier Transform and the math work, but you can see from the `PitchDetector.java` file how AudioRecord is used to record some audio to be processed later. This is similar to how touchtone is recorded for detection (which will be described in the next section) and most other audio-processing scenarios.

Touchtone Detection

Well, although Mark can recognize any musical note played, he cannot detect a touchtone sound entered on a phone. You may not know that each key, whether in a push-button telephone or a smartphone, generates two unique tones of specific frequencies (that's why it's called Dual-Tone Multi-Frequency, or DTMF) when pressed (see `http://searchnetworking.techtarget.com/definition/DTMF` for more information). But I have a friend who's been working in computer telephony for years, and he can easily detect any touchtone (so people had better not enter some secret phone numbers around him!). So, how do you implement the touchtone detection in Glass? This problem may also be interesting to those of you who want to impress your friends or are just curious to see how Glass can decode the numbers entered on a phone. You'll also see how AudioRecord is used to capture the raw audio data, which gets processed by the recognizer.

After some searching and testing, I found another open source project as a good candidate for being integrated to your project. The steps to add touchtone detection to the VoiceAndAudio project are as follows:

1. Download the open source project at `https://code.google.com/p/dtmf-decoder/source/browse/`.

2. Unzip the downloaded file and import it to Eclipse; you'll see a project called *recognizer* in Eclipse.

3. Comment the line `Apphance.start(this, APP_KEY);` in `src/pam.recognizer`'s `MainActivity.java` file to fix the project build error caused by the call to a testing service that is unrelated to the touchtone detection.

4. Run the app to test it on Glass and use your phone, smart or dumb, to enter any of the ten digits or * and # keys. You need to put your phone close to Glass to see the detected key.

5. Copy both the `match` and `wpam.recognizer` packages from recognizer to VocieAndAudio, and fix any possible errors in the copied files by importing `com.morkout.voiceandaudio.R`.

6. Add a Touchtone Detection menu option in `main.xml`, `strings.xml`, and `MenuActivity.java`.

```
case R.id.touchtone:
    Intent intent5 = new Intent(this, MainActivity.class);
    startActivity(intent5);
    return true;
```

7. In `AndroidManifest.xml`, add the following line:

```
<activity
    android:name="wpam.recognizer.MainActivity"
    android:enabled="true"
    android:label="@string/app_name" >
</activity>
```

8. Open the `Controller.java` file in the `wpam.recognizer` package and replace the following two lines (you should take a look at `RecordTask.java` and `RecognizerTask.java` to see how audio is captured and processed):

```
recordTask.execute();
recognizerTask.execute();
```

with the following:

```
recordTask.executeOnExecutor(AsyncTask.THREAD_POOL_EXECUTOR);
recognizerTask.executeOnExecutor(AsyncTask.THREAD_POOL_EXECUTOR);
```

This has to be done to make the app work on Glass because async tasks have been executed on a single thread since Android API Level 11, and if you want parallel execution of the two tasks (`recordTask` and `recognizerTask`), you need to call the `executeOnExecutor` method on the `async` tasks. Check out `http://developer.android.com/reference/android/os/AsyncTask.html` for more information.

Run the VoiceAndAudio app from Eclipse and say "OK Glass" and then "Voice and audio." Tap to see the app menu and select the Touchtone Detection menu item; you'll see the UI shown in Figure 6-4. Tap Start and enter the Glass support number **1800GLASSXE** on your phone. Your Glass will know the number you're calling, as shown in Figure 6-4.

Figure 6-4. *Detecting touchtone phone number*

There's some UI improvement that can be done for the app. The 12 tiny buttons in Figure 6-4 are supposed to show the 10 digits and * and #. I didn't bother changing the open source project code because I just wanted to show you how the touchtone detection can work on Glass, which I hope will save you time if you consider building a related commercial app.

Song Identification

A more challenging task than musical note and touchtone detection is song identification. You have probably heard of apps like Shazam and Soundhound that recognize millions of songs. Can you let Glass accomplish the same task? If so, a server-based solution is more likely because of the necessity of processing a large amount of data. And research shows that Echoprint (http://echoprint.me) is the best open source music identification system; it works by fingerprinting audio and sending the audio to a server for identification. I have spent several days and nights of intense work on finding the best open source project and figuring out how to integrate it with the example app. I hope this will again save you time when building your own app. So, without further ado, the steps to add the song identification feature to the VoiceAndAudio app are as follows:

1. Register at http://developer.echonest.com and get an API key. According to Echonest, each account is limited to 20 API calls per minute, and you need to contact Echonest if you need to increase the limit.

2. Get the Android port of Echoprint at https://github.com/gvsumasl/EchoprintForAndroid by running the command git clone https://github.com/gvsumasl/EchoprintForAndroid.git.

3. Import the two projects EchoprintLib and EchoprintTest in the EchoprintForAndroid folder to Eclipse.

4. Select VoiceAndAudio's properties, click Add in the Library section, and add EchoprintLib.

5. In the EchoprintLib project's AudioFingerprint.java file, replace <your server address here>/query?fp_code= in the line private final String SERVER_URL with "http://developer.echonest.com/api/v4/song/identify?api_key=AV6AWC8NL7IJPZ5QO&version=4.12&code=".

> **Note** The example GET URL in the Echonest identify API's documentation at http://developer.echonest.com/docs/v4/song.html#identify does not have an important version parameter, meaning it's not for open source, free use. You have to use version 4.12 in the URL to make the fingerprint code generated in the library work with the open source Echonest server.

6. Still in AudioFingerprint.java, after the line JSONObject jobj = new JSONObject(result);, use the correct parsing code:

```
if(jobj.has("songs")) {
    Hashtable<String, String> match = new Hashtable<String, String>();
    JSONArray songs = jobj.getJSONArray("songs");
    if (songs.length() == 0) didNotFindMatchForCode(code);
```

```
        else {
            JSONObject song = songs.getJSONObject(0);
            match.put(song.getString("title"), song.getString("artist_name"));
        }
            didFindMatchForCode(match, code);
    }
        else didFailWithException(new Exception("no match found"));
```

7. Copy the `EchoprintTestActivity.java` file from the EchoprintTest project to VoiceAndAudio's `com.morkout.voiceandaudio` package and rename it to `MusicRecognitionActivity.java`.

8. Copy the `main.xml` file from EchoprintTest's `res/layout` folder to VoiceAndAudio's `res/layout` and rename it to `musicrecognition.xml`.

9. In VoiceAndAudio, add a new menu item called Music Recognition in menu's `main.xml` and value's `strings.xml`; then update `MenuActivity.java` and `AndroidManifest.xml`.

10. Add in `AndriodManifest.xml` the following permissions because you need to access the Echonest server:

```
<uses-permission android:name="android.permission.INTERNET" />
<uses-permission android:name="android.permission.ACCESS_NETWORK_STATE" />
```

You're all set! Run the app, select Music Recognition, tap the Start button to set your Glass in the listening mode, and play a YouTube song such as `www.youtube.com/watch?v=wxSfojergh0`. After about 10 seconds, you'll see the matched result, as shown in Figure 6-5.

Figure 6-5. Recognizing a song

> **Note**   If you see an error like "java.lang.UnsatisfiedLinkError: Couldn't load echoprint-jni: findLibrary returned null," it means somehow the native library `libechoprint-jni.so` didn't get saved into your Glass app's `lib` directory at `/data/data/com.morkout.voiceandaudio/lib`. You can fix this by copying the file from EchoprintLib's `libs/armeabi` folder to VoiceAndAudio's `libs/armeabi-v7a` folder.

It's possible you may not get a match for some songs, although the Echoprint database has about 1 million popular fingerprinted songs (`http://echoprint-data.s3.amazonaws.com/list_of_songs.txt`). If you do plan to build your own commercial-level song recognition app for Glass, you may want to look into how to build your own server at `http://echoprint.me/server` and add new songs to the current data at `http://echoprint.me/data`.

Summary

In this chapter, I covered a lot of voice- and audio-related topics, from the standard Glass voice input, both high-level and low-level audio capture and playback, to various audio-processing examples, including musical note detection, DTMF touchtone detection, and, finally, song identification. Voice and audio are essential parts of our communication with each other and with devices, so you can expect to see many innovative apps in this area, developed by people like you.

Chapter 7

Networking, Bluetooth, and Social

We live in a world that is getting more and more connected, in terms of both people and products. Social networking sites abound—Facebook, Twitter, Google Plus, and LinkedIn, to name a few. Mobile social apps, such as Instagram, WhatsApp, and WeChat, have seen historic user growth. The wearable technology and Internet of Things, a term used to denote the "advanced connectivity of devices, systems, and services" (`http://en.wikipedia.org/wiki/Internet_of_Things`), are regarded as the next wave of technology after phases such as the PC, Internet, and mobile. Devices such as smartphones, tablets, and many Bluetooth-based classic and smart devices can all be connected to help us lead better lives. How Glass can join this connected world, using Bluetooth and other networking technologies, is the topic of this chapter.

Common solutions with step-by-step tutorials and working code to be covered include the following:

- How to make common HTTP requests from Glass to send and receive data
- How to do socket programming to let Glass exchange data with smartphones and tablets (iOS and Android) while Glass is connected to wi-fi
- How to use Bluetooth Classic (also known as Classic Bluetooth) to let Glass do data transfer with other Android devices while your Glass is not connected with wi-fi
- How to allow Glass to act as a Bluetooth Low Energy (BLE) client and get data from a BLE device
- How to use Classic Bluetooth and socket programming to receive data from Android and iOS devices, which have better support for Bluetooth Low Energy
- How to share your Glass picture to your WhatsApp and WeChat friends using Apple push notification and an iOS app

In this chapter, you'll see some iOS and Android projects and code other than Glass apps. In a connected world, apps running on different platforms often need to work together to accomplish something impossible for a stand-alone app. Smartphones, tablets, and Glass can be used as hubs and gateways to send the data from your connected devices and sensors to the cloud for further analysis. I won't cover the cloud part here, but you'll see many examples of how devices connect and transfer data to each other.

Making HTTP Requests

If you're not familiar with HTTP and its GET and POST methods, you should check out some online tutorials (for example, www.w3schools.com/tags/ref_httpmethods.asp) first. There are two main ways to develop HTTP clients in Android: DefaultHttpClient and HttpURLConnection. Both of them work well in Glass. DefaultHttpClient works best with earlier versions of Android (API level 8 or earlier), and HttpURLConnection is the best for API level 9 or newer. A more detailed comparison of the two methods is available at http://android-developers.blogspot.com/2011/09/androids-http-clients.html.

Actually, you have already used both methods in previous apps. For example, in the VideoSearchActivity.java file of MyVideoApps in Chapter 5, DefaultHttpClient is used to query YouTube's data API, which returns a JSON object. In the SearchActivity.java file of SmartCamera in Chapter 4, HttpURLConnection is used to upload a picture taken on Glass to Google for image search. For your convenience, I'll show you simple yet complete code samples to make HTTP GET and POST requests, including file uploading, from Glass, all using the preferred HttpURLConnection class, which you should also use for your new Glass apps.

Before getting started, follow the same steps from previous chapters to create a new Glass app, called NBSocial, based on GlasswareTemplate. Then create three new menu options in MenuActivity.java and add their string definitions in strings.xml.

```
case R.id.httpget:
    Intent intent = new Intent(this, HTTPRequestActivity.class);
    intent.putExtra( "WHAT", "GET" );
    startActivity(intent);
    return true;

case R.id.httppost:
    Intent intent2 = new Intent(this, HTTPRequestActivity.class);
    intent2.putExtra( "WHAT", "POST" );
    startActivity(intent2);
    return true;

case R.id.httpupload:
    Intent intent3 = new Intent(this, HTTPRequestActivity.class);
    intent3.putExtra( "WHAT", "UPLOAD" );
    startActivity(intent3);
    return true;

<string name="httpget">HTTP GET</string>
<string name="httppost">HTTP POST</string>
<string name="httpupload">HTTP UPLOAD</string>
```

Create a new Activity subclass file called HTTPRequestActivity.java. Don't forget to add its activity declaration in AndroidManifest.xml. If you're a little lost, you may want to go back to previous chapters or check out the complete source code for the chapter from the book's source code.

HTTP GET

Add the code in Listing 7-1 to HTTPRequestActivity.java to implement an HTTP GET request to my demo web site at http://morkout.com, which just returns some simple text.

Listing 7-1. Making an HTTP GET Request in HTTPRequestActivity.java

```java
TextView mTvInfo;
String mWhat;
HttpURLConnection mUrlConnection;
String mResult;

public void onCreate(Bundle savedInstanceState) {
    super.onCreate(savedInstanceState);

    setContentView(R.layout.main);
    mTvInfo = (TextView) findViewById(R.id.info);
    Intent intent = getIntent();
    mWhat = intent.getStringExtra("WHAT");
    mTvInfo.setText("Making HTTP "+ mWhat + " request...");
    new HTTPRequest().execute();
}

// Async task class to make HTTP Get, Post and upload

private class HTTPRequest extends AsyncTask<Void, Void, Void> {
    @Override
    protected Void doInBackground(Void... arg0) {
        try {
            if (mWhat.equalsIgnoreCase("GET")) {
                // get json via YouTube API
                URL url = new URL("http://morkout.com");
                mUrlConnection = (HttpURLConnection)
                        url.openConnection();
                InputStream in = new BufferedInputStream(
                        mUrlConnection.getInputStream());
                int ch;
                StringBuffer b = new StringBuffer();
                while ((ch = in.read()) != -1) {
                        b.append((char) ch);
                }

                mResult = new String(b);
            }
        } catch (Exception e) {}
        return null;
    }
```

```
@Override
protected void onPostExecute(Void result) {
    super.onPostExecute(result);
    mTvInfo.setText(mResult);
}
```

Don't forget to add `<uses-permission android:name="android.permission.INTERNET"/>`to your `AndroidManifest.xml` file. Now run the app and tap to select HTTP GET. You'll see the message "Making HTTP GET request. . .," followed by the GET result, as shown in Figure 7-1.

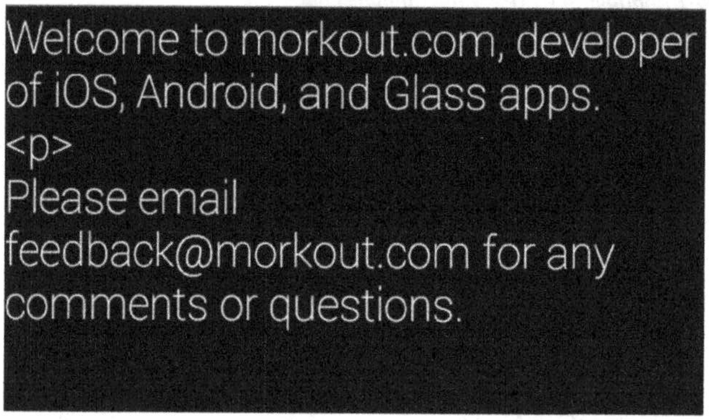

Figure 7-1. *HTTP GET request response*

So, with just a few lines of code, you can make an HTTP GET call and get its returned result.

> **Note** You cannot perform the request or, generally speaking, a networking operation on an app's main thread because the main thread is for UI and you always want to keep a responsive UI. In fact, your Glass app will throw an exception and crash if you try to run the networking code in the main thread (for more information on the topic, see `www.androiddesignpatterns.com/2012/06/app-force-close-honeycomb-ics.html`). That's why you should run your HTTP request code in an `AsyncTask`.

HTTP POST

Similarly, you can make an HTTP POST request with `DefaultHttpClient`. Simply add the code in Listing 7-2 after the `if` statement in `doInBackground` of Listing 7-1.

Listing 7-2. Making an HTTP POST Request in HTTPRequestActivity.java

```
else if (mWhat.equalsIgnoreCase("POST")) {

    URL url = new URL("http://morkout.com/glass/posttest.php");
    mUrlConnection = (HttpURLConnection) url.openConnection();
    mUrlConnection.setRequestMethod("POST");
    String urlParameters = "email=jeff.x.tang@gmail.com&name=Jeff
            Tang&pwd=1234567&vcode=2014";
```

```
OutputStreamWriter writer = new
    OutputStreamWriter(mUrlConnection.getOutputStream());
writer.write(urlParameters);
writer.flush();

InputStream in = new BufferedInputStream(
            mUrlConnection.getInputStream());
int ch;
StringBuffer b = new StringBuffer();
while ((ch = in.read()) != -1) {
    b.append((char) ch);
}

mResult = new String(b);

in.close();
writer.close();
}
```

The server code posttest.php, if you are curious, is extremely simple, used here only for demo purposes (you don't need to implement this; it's set up on my demo server morkout.com).

```php
<?php

$email = $_REQUEST["email"];
$pwd = md5($_REQUEST["pwd"]);
$name = $_REQUEST["name"];
$vcode = md5(uniqid(time()));

echo "POST returns: email=$email, pwd=$pwd, name=$name, vcode=$vcode";

?>
```

Run the app and select HTTP POST this time. You'll see after "Making HTTP Post request . . ." the message shown in Figure 7-2.

Figure 7-2. HTTP POST request response

HTTP File Uploading

The code in Listing 7-3 shows how to implement file uploading using HttpURLConnection. First copy an image file called marchmadness.png from the project's asset file to Glass's external storage directory using the same copyAsset method you used in Chapter 5; then send the file to the server and display the response message from the server.

Listing 7-3. HTTP File Uploading in HTTPRequestActivity.java

```
else if (mWhat.equalsIgnoreCase("UPLOAD")) {
    int serverResponseCode = 0;
    File sourceFile = new File(copyAsset("marchmadness.png"));
    DataOutputStream dos = null;
    String lineEnd = "\r\n";
    String twoHyphens = "--";
    String boundary = "*****";
    int bytesRead, bytesAvailable, bufferSize;
    byte[] buffer;
    int maxBufferSize = 1024 * 1024;
    int REQUEST_SUCCESS_CODE = 200; // for all possible response codes and messages, see
    http://www.w3.org/Protocols/rfc2616/rfc2616-sec10.html

    FileInputStream fileInputStream = new FileInputStream(sourceFile);
    URL url = new URL("http://www.morkout.com/glass/upload.php");

    mUrlConnection = (HttpURLConnection) url.openConnection();
    mUrlConnection.setRequestMethod("POST");
    mUrlConnection.setRequestProperty("Content-Type", "multipart/form-data;boundary=" + boundary);
    // Content-Type has to be set like this to support HTTP file uploading, which originates from
    HTML form-based file uploading

    mUrlConnection.setRequestProperty("Filedata", sourceFile.getName()); // "Filedata" needs to
    match the server code that handles file uploading. For example, in PHP, $_FILES["Filedata"]
    ["tmp_name"] is used to access the uploaded file

    dos = new DataOutputStream(mUrlConnection.getOutputStream());
    dos.writeBytes(twoHyphens + boundary + lineEnd);
    dos.writeBytes("Content-Disposition: form-data; name=Filedata;filename="+ sourceFile.getName() +
    lineEnd);
    dos.writeBytes(lineEnd);

    bytesAvailable = fileInputStream.available();
    bufferSize = Math.min(bytesAvailable, maxBufferSize);
    buffer = new byte[bufferSize];
    bytesRead = fileInputStream.read(buffer, 0, bufferSize);
    while (bytesRead > 0) {
        dos.write(buffer, 0, bufferSize);
        bytesAvailable = fileInputStream.available();
        bufferSize = Math.min(bytesAvailable, maxBufferSize);
        bytesRead = fileInputStream.read(buffer, 0, bufferSize);
    }
```

```
        dos.writeBytes(lineEnd);
        dos.writeBytes(twoHyphens + boundary + twoHyphens + lineEnd);

        // Responses from the server (code and message)
        serverResponseCode = mUrlConnection.getResponseCode();
        String serverResponseMessage = mUrlConnection.getResponseMessage();

        if(serverResponseCode == REQUEST_SUCCESS_CODE) {
            InputStream is = mUrlConnection.getInputStream();
            int ch;
            StringBuffer b = new StringBuffer();
            while ((ch = is.read()) != -1) {
            b.append((char) ch);
            }

            final String uploadedFilename = b.toString();
            mResult = "uploaded file at http://www.morkout.com/glass/uploads/" + uploadedFilename;
        }
        is.close();
        fileInputStream.close();
        dos.close();
```

The server code upload.php is also pretty straightforward. (Again, this is just for reference; you don't need to set up your web server or implement this code.)

```php
<?
if (!isset($_FILES["Filedata"]) || !is_uploaded_file($_FILES["Filedata"]["tmp_name"]) ||
$_FILES["Filedata"]["error"] != 0) {
    echo 0;
}
else {
    $uploaded_filename = "glassupoad-" . md5($_FILES["Filedata"]["tmp_name"] . uniqid("")) . ".jpg";
    move_uploaded_file($_FILES["Filedata"]["tmp_name"], "uploads/" . $uploaded_filename);
    echo $uploaded_filename;
}
?>
```

Run the app and select HTTP UPLOAD, and you'll see the uploaded file URL on your Glass, as shown in Figure 7-3. It will be something like http://www.morkout.com/glass/uploads/glassupoad-075cb1d03db3e039cbb5643ac1ea2740.png.

Figure 7-3. HTTP file uploading response

You can easily replace the code that copies a file from the project's asset folder with code that uses a picture taken on your Glass and then upload the picture to your server for further processing or sharing. You'll see how this works for sharing your Glass pictures with your WhatsApp or WeChat friends later in the chapter.

Now that you have the working code running on Glass that does the most common HTTP client tasks, the next step is to go a little lower level. Socket programming is a powerful networking solution that may work best for your own client-server requirements, such as a chat app or a Bluetooth-based app.

Socket Programming

If you use Glass indoors, most likely you'll have wi-fi connection for your Glass. In the section, I'll show you how to let your Glass communicate with other smartphones and tablets via wi-fi.

> **Note**   To test the socket examples with Glass, ideally you need to have another Android or iOS device, but you can also use an Android virtual device or iOS simulator on your computer. Make sure you connect your Glass and other device (smartphone or tablet) or computer to the same wi-fi network.

Glass Client vs. Android Server

Let's first run a socket client on Glass talking to a socket server running on another Android device (real or virtual). In the Glass project NBSocial, create a new activity file, called SocketClientActivity.java, with the code in Listing 7-4.

Listing 7-4. Socket Client Code in SocketClientActivity.java

```
public class SocketClientActivity extends Activity implements Runnable {
    private TextView mTvInfo;
    String mResult;
    Socket mClientSocket;
```

```java
@Override
public void onCreate(Bundle savedInstanceState) {
    super.onCreate(savedInstanceState);
    setContentView(R.layout.main);
    mTvInfo = (TextView) findViewById(R.id.info);
    mTvInfo.setText("Connecting to server ...");
    Thread thread = new Thread(this);
    thread.start();
}

@Override
protected void onStop() {
    super.onStop();
    try {
        if (mClientSocket != null) mClientSocket.close();
    }
    catch (IOException e) {
        e.printStackTrace();
    }
}

public void run() {
    // This is the IP address of Android server running on an actual device or virtual device on
    // computer. It's likely to be different on your device and if so, you should replace this with
    // your IP
    String serverIP = "192.168.1.9";

    // This is the server socket port that client will connect to. It should be the same as in
    // SocketServerActivity.java in Listing 7-5.
    int port = SocketServerActivity.PORT;
    try {
        mClientSocket = new Socket(serverIP, port);
        BufferedReader input = new BufferedReader(new InputStreamReader(mClientSocket.
        getInputStream()));
        mResult = input.readLine();
        runOnUiThread(new Runnable() {
            public void run() {
                // This is used to get client's connection info including IP address
                WifiManager wim= (WifiManager) getSystemService(WIFI_SERVICE);
                List<WifiConfiguration> l =  wim.getConfiguredNetworks();
                WifiConfiguration wc = l.get(0);
                mTvInfo.setText("CLIENT IP: " + Formatter.formatIpAddress
                (wim.getConnectionInfo().getIpAddress()) + ", connected to " + mClientSocket.
                getRemoteSocketAddress() + ", received: "+mResult);
            }
        });

        PrintWriter out = new PrintWriter(mClientSocket.getOutputStream(), true);
        // add the number received from server by 50 and send to server
        out.println(Integer.parseInt(mResult)+50);
        mClientSocket.close();
    }
```

```
                    catch(IOException e) {
                        final IOException ex = e;
                        runOnUiThread(new Runnable() {
                            public void run() {
                                // let users know if socket exception occurs
                                mTvInfo.setText(ex.getMessage());
                            }
                        });
                    }
                }
            }
}
```

Now create a new Android app called SocketAndroidApp and add a file called SocketServerActivity.java with the code in Listing 7-5. Then copy the SocketServerActivity.java file to NBSocial to make the client app use the port defined in the server app (I have int port = SocketServerActivity.PORT; in Listing 7-4). Similarly, copy SocketClientActivity.java from NBSocial to AndroidSocketApp. In the next section, you'll see Glass acting as a server and another Android device acting as a client.

Listing 7-5. Socket Server Code in SocketServerActivity.java

```java
public class SocketServerActivity extends Activity implements Runnable {
    public final static int PORT = 6604;
    private TextView mTvInfo;
    private ServerSocket mServerSocket;
    private Socket mClientSocket;
    String mResult;

    @Override
    public void onCreate(Bundle savedInstanceState) {
        super.onCreate(savedInstanceState);
        setContentView(R.layout.main);
        mTvInfo = (TextView) findViewById(R.id.info);
        Thread thread = new Thread(this);
        thread.start();
    }

    @Override
    protected void onStop() {
        super.onStop();

        try {
            if (mClientSocket != null) mClientSocket.close();
            if (mServerSocket != null) mServerSocket.close();
        }
        catch (IOException e) {
            e.printStackTrace();
        }
    }
```

```java
public void run() {
    try {
        serverSocket = new ServerSocket(PORT);
        while(true)
        {
            mServerSocket = new ServerSocket(PORT);
            runOnUiThread(new Runnable() {
                public void run() {
                    WifiManager wim= (WifiManager) getSystemService(WIFI_SERVICE);
                    List<WifiConfiguration> l =  wim.getConfiguredNetworks();
                    WifiConfiguration wc = l.get(0);
                    mTvInfo.setText(mTvInfo.getText() + "\n\nServer IP: " + Formatter.
                    formatIpAddress(wim.getConnectionInfo().getIpAddress())  + ". Waiting for
                    client on port " + PORT);
                }
            });
            mClientSocket = mServerSocket.accept();

            runOnUiThread(new Runnable() {
                public void run() {
                    mTvInfo.setText(mTvInfo.getText() + "\nJust connected from client" +
                    mClientSocket.getRemoteSocketAddress());
                }
            });

            OutputStream oStream = mClientSocket.getOutputStream();
            PrintWriter out = new PrintWriter(oStream, true);
            BufferedReader input = new BufferedReader(new InputStreamReader(mClientSocket.
            getInputStream()));

            out.println(2014);
            mResult = input.readLine();

            runOnUiThread(new Runnable() {
                public void run() {
                    mTvInfo.setText(mTvInfo.getText() + "\nSent: 2014. Received: "+mResult);
                }
            });

            mClientSocket.close();
            mServerSocket.close();
        }
    }
    catch(SocketTimeoutException s)
    {
        runOnUiThread(new Runnable() {
            public void run() {
                mTvInfo.setText("Socket timed out!");
            }
        });
    }
    catch(IOException e)
```

```
            {
                final IOException ex = e;
                runOnUiThread(new Runnable() {
                    public void run() {
                        mTvInfo.setText(ex.getMessage());
                    }
                });
            }
        }
    }
}
```

In Listings 7-4 and 7-5, after a socket connection is established between a client and a server, the server sends the number 2014 to the client. The client adds 50 to it and returns 2064 to the server.

The layout/main.xml file for both NBSocial and SocketAndroidApp has just a simple TextView.

```xml
<?xml version="1.0" encoding="utf-8"?>
<LinearLayout xmlns:android="http://schemas.android.com/apk/res/android"
    android:orientation="vertical"
    android:layout_width="fill_parent"
    android:layout_height="fill_parent"
    >
<TextView
    android:id="@+id/info"
    android:layout_width="fill_parent"
    android:layout_height="wrap_content"
    android:text="@string/info"
    />
</LinearLayout>
```

Now in NBSocial, add two new menu entries in menu.xml, add the string definitions for socketclient and socketserver to strings.xml, and add the two activities in AndroidManifest.xml.

```
        case R.id.socketclient:
            Intent intent4 = new Intent(this, SocketClientActivity.class);
            startActivity(intent4);
            return true;

        case R.id.socketserver:
            Intent intent5 = new Intent(this, SocketServerActivity.class);
            startActivity(intent5);
            return true;

<string name="socketclient">SOCKET CLIENT</string>
<string name="socketserver">SOCKET SERVER</string>
```

In AndroidSocketApp's AndroidManifest.xml file, make SocketServerActivity your MAIN action.

```
<activity
    android:name=".SocketServerActivity"
    android:label="@string/app_name" >
    <intent-filter>
        <action android:name="android.intent.action.MAIN" />

        <category android:name="android.intent.category.LAUNCHER" />
    </intent-filter>
</activity>
```

Note   If you don't have a Nexus or other Android phone or tablet, you can easily test the code here using a Nexus 7 emulator from Eclipse on your computer. Just make sure your computer and Glass are on the same wi-fi network.

Finally, make sure both your Glass and Android device are connected to the same wi-fi network and change the serverIP value in NBSocial's SocketClientActivity.java file from 192.168.1.9 to your Android device's IP or, if you use simulator (Android virtual device), your computer's IP address. (You can find the IP address in Settings by selecting Wi-Fi and then your connected wi-fi network name.)

Now run the server app on your non-Glass Android device first. You'll see a message like "Server IP: 192.168.1.9. Waiting for client on port 6604." Start the Glass app NBSocial and select "SOCKET CLIENT." You'll see on your Glass a message similar to "CLIENT IP: 192.168.1.9, connected to /192.168.1.8:6680, received: 2014," as shown in Figure 7-4.

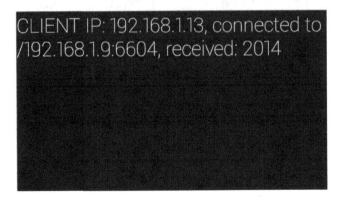

Figure 7-4. Glass client message

On your Android device you'll see new message like "Just connected from client/192.168.1.13:60787. Sent: 2014. Received: 2064," followed by "Server IP: 192.168.1.9. Waiting for client on port 6604" again. The server code is in a loop that keeps waiting for a new client connection after a connection is established, data gets exchanged, and both client and server sockets are closed. You can swipe down on Glass to exit the client activity and then select SOCKET CLIENT to connect to the Android server again. Figure 7-5 shows the server messages.

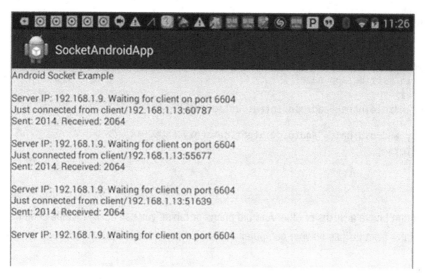

Figure 7-5. Android server messages

If your Glass and Android device are not on the same wi-fi network and Glass cannot reach the Android device's IP address, you'll see on Glass a "No route to host" exception, as shown in Figure 7-6.

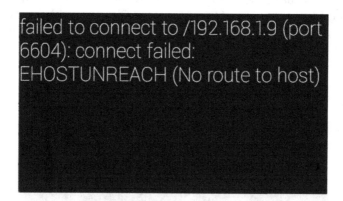

Figure 7-6. Glass unable to reach Android device's IP address

If your Glass and Android device are on the same wi-fi but the Android server app is running on a different port or is not running, you'll see the message shown in Figure 7-7.

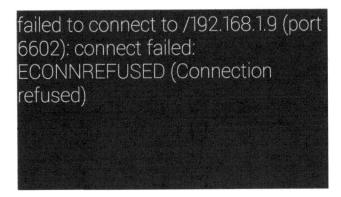

Figure 7-7. *Glass unable to connect to server's port*

Based on the simple client and server interaction between Glass and another Android device shown here, you can build much richer interaction for your own apps.

Glass Server vs. Android Client

The steps to build a Glass server and an Android client are similar. You just need to run the NBSocial app on Glass first, select SOCKET SERVER, and then replace SocketServerActivity in your Android app's AndroidManifest.xml file with SocketClientActivity (make sure you set serverIP in AndroidSocketApp's SocketClientActivity.java file to your Glass's IP address, shown earlier as "client IP" in Figures 7-4 and 7-5). Then run the app on Android. You'll see on Android a message similar to Figure 7-4. Figure 7-8 shows a message similar to what you'll see on Glass.

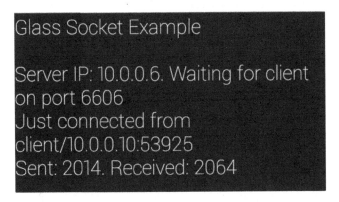

Figure 7-8. *Glass socket server log message*

Glass Client vs. iOS Server

If you're also an iOS developer, you may be interested to know how to let Glass talk to an iOS device. The good news is that using a C-level socket, you can easily connect to Glass as a client or server. There are some open source Objective-C socket libraries you can use too. Listing 7-6 is the code snippet that you can use on your iOS app to act as a socket server (the complete iOS project, called SocketiOSApp, is included in the book's source code) to talk to the Glass socket client, as shown earlier in Listing 7-4.

Listing 7-6. iOS Socket Server Code to Talk to Glass Client

```objectivec
- (IBAction)socketTapped:(id)sender {
    [self runSocketServer];
}

- (void) runSocketServer {
    int listenfd = 0;
    __block int connfd = 0;
    struct sockaddr_in serv_addr;

    __block char sendBuff[1024];
    __block NSString *info;

    listenfd = socket(AF_INET, SOCK_STREAM, 0);
    memset(&serv_addr, '0', sizeof(serv_addr));
    memset(sendBuff, '0', sizeof(sendBuff));

    serv_addr.sin_family = AF_INET;
    serv_addr.sin_addr.s_addr = htonl(INADDR_ANY);
    serv_addr.sin_port = htons(6606);

    bind(listenfd, (struct sockaddr*)&serv_addr, sizeof(serv_addr));

    listen(listenfd, 10);

    _lblInfo.text = @"Waiting for client on port 6606";

    dispatch_async(dispatch_get_global_queue(0, 0), ^{
        struct sockaddr_in client_addr;
        socklen_t addrlen=sizeof(client_addr);
        connfd = accept(listenfd, (struct sockaddr*)&client_addr, &addrlen);
        write(connfd, "2014\n", 5);
        char recvBuff[1024];
        int n = read(connfd, recvBuff, sizeof(recvBuff)-1);
        recvBuff[n] = '\0';

        struct sockaddr_in localAddress;
        socklen_t addressLength = sizeof(localAddress);
        getsockname(connfd, (struct sockaddr*)&localAddress, &addressLength);

        info = [NSString stringWithFormat:@"SERVER IP: %@, connected from %@, received: %s",
            [NSString stringWithCString:inet_ntoa(localAddress.sin_addr)
                encoding:NSUTF8StringEncoding],
            [NSString stringWithCString:inet_ntoa(client_addr.sin_addr)
                encoding:NSUTF8StringEncoding],
            recvBuff];
        close(connfd);
        close(listenfd);
```

```
        dispatch_async(dispatch_get_main_queue(), ^{
            _lblInfo.text = [NSString stringWithFormat:@"%@\n%@", _lblInfo.text, info];
        });
    });
}
```

After the iOS app runs on an iOS device or simulator, you tap or click the "run as server" button shown in Figure 7-9 to start the socket server. A UILabel is used to show the information "Waiting for client connection. . .." Then you use the iOS device's IP, or computer's IP if you use the iOS simulator, to set serverIP in NBSocial's SocketClientActivity.java file. Run the Glass app and then choose SOCKET CLIENT, and you'll see the same numbers, 2014 and 2064, sent between your iOS app and Glass app. Figure 7-9 shows the server log in the iOS simulator.

Figure 7-9. iOS socket server log message

Glass Server vs. iOS Client

Listing 7-7 shows the iOS code that acts as a socket client to communicate with the Glass server code shown earlier in Listing 7-5.

Listing 7-7. iOS Socket Client Code to Talk to Glass Server

```
- (IBAction)clientTapped:(id)sender {
    [self runSocketClient];
}
```

```objc
- (void) runSocketClient {
    int sockfd = 0, n = 0;
    char recvBuff[1024];
    struct sockaddr_in serv_addr;

    memset(recvBuff, '0',sizeof(recvBuff));
    if((sockfd = socket(AF_INET, SOCK_STREAM, 0)) < 0)
    {
        printf("unable to create socket\n");
        return;
    }

    memset(&serv_addr, '0', sizeof(serv_addr));

    serv_addr.sin_family = AF_INET;
    serv_addr.sin_port = htons(6604); // replace 6604 with Glass server port defined in
    "public final static int PORT = 6604;" of SocketServerActivity.java

    // Replace "10.0.0.6" with your Glass IP
    if(inet_pton(AF_INET, "10.0.0.6", &serv_addr.sin_addr)<=0)
    {
        printf("inet_pton error occurred\n");
        return;
    }

    if( connect(sockfd, (struct sockaddr *)&serv_addr, sizeof(serv_addr)) < 0)
    {
        printf("unable to connect\n");
    }

    if ( (n = read(sockfd, recvBuff, sizeof(recvBuff)-1)) > 0)
    {
        recvBuff[n] = 0;
        char result[1024];
        sprintf(result, "%d\n", atoi(recvBuff)+50);
        write(sockfd, result, 5);

        // get server IP address
        struct sockaddr_in localAddress;
        socklen_t addressLength = sizeof(localAddress);
        getsockname(sockfd, (struct sockaddr*)&localAddress, &addressLength);

        _lblInfo.text = [NSString stringWithFormat:@"CLIENT IP: %@, connected to %@, received: %s",
                            [NSString stringWithCString:inet_ntoa(localAddress.sin_addr)
                            encoding:NSUTF8StringEncoding],
                            [NSString stringWithCString:inet_ntoa(serv_addr.sin_addr)
                            encoding:NSUTF8StringEncoding],
                            recvBuff];
        close(sockfd);
    }
}
```

Run the NBSocial app on Glass, select SOCKET SERVER, and then run the iOS app (make sure in Listing 7-7 to use your Glass's IP and port). Tap or click the "run as client" button shown in Figure 7-10 to connect to the Glass socket server. After data exchange, you'll see on Glass the message shown earlier in Figure 7-8, and you'll see on an iOS device or in the simulator the message shown in Figure 7-10.

Figure 7-10. iOS socket client log message

Let's move on to another interesting topic that can be useful when you don't have wi-fi available and you still want to transfer data between your Glass and other Android/iOS devices, or even some smart sensors.

Bluetooth

If you have used Glass for a while, chances are you have paired your Glass with your iPhone or Android phone via Bluetooth, which allows Glass to be able to access your smartphone's cellular data while wi-fi is not available or to accept phone calls made to your smartphone.

You may also have used some Bluetooth devices such as headsets, earphones, speakers, or heart rate monitors. How do you let Glass use Android Bluetooth APIs to talk to other Bluetooth devices? It turns out there are two types of Bluetooth technologies with different Bluetooth API support in Android and Glass: Classic Bluetooth (also known as Bluetooth Classic) and Bluetooth Low Energy (also known as Bluetooth Smart). Classic Bluetooth is typically used for a high volume of data, such as audio and video streaming or Internet access. Bluetooth Low Energy is primarily for small sensor devices such as health or temperature monitors that need low power and small intermittent data transfers. Bluetooth Low Energy is one of the essential technologies for the hot Internet of Things trend. Android developer's site has pretty good API documentation and sample code on both Classic Bluetooth and Bluetooth Low Energy: `http://developer.android.com/guide/topics/connectivity/bluetooth.html`. In this section, I'll focus on how to make Glass exchange data via both Bluetooth technologies with other Bluetooth-enabled devices, including smartphones, tablets, and a popular Polar heart rate monitor.

Classic Bluetooth

If you haven't already, you should review the Android developer site's API documentation on Bluetooth first (again, `http://developer.android.com/guide/topics/connectivity/bluetooth.html`), or you could be lost. In this section, I'll show you how Glass can act as a Classic Bluetooth client and talk to another Android app as a Classic Bluetooth server, and the other way around (Glass as a server and another Android app as a client).

Follow these steps to add the Classic Bluetooth feature to the Glass app NBSocial, which allows you to transfer a large file between Glass and another Android device:

1. Create two new menu entries in NBSocial by updating `res/menu/main.xml` and `res/values/strings.xml` and update `MenuActivity.java`.

```
<item
    android:id="@+id/cbtclient"
    android:title="@string/cbtclient" />

<item
    android:id="@+id/cbtserver"
    android:title="@string/cbtserver" />
*****
<string name="cbtclient">CBT CLIENT</string>
<string name="cbtserver">CBT SERVER</string>

*****
        case R.id.cbtclient:
            Intent intent6 = new Intent(this, ClassicBluetoothClient.class);
            startActivity(intent6);
            return true;

        case R.id.cbtserver:
            Intent intent7 = new Intent(this, ClassicBluetoothServer.class);
            startActivity(intent7);
            return true;
```

2. Add the following content to `AndroidManifest.xml`:

```
<uses-permission android:name="android.permission.BLUETOOTH" />
<uses-permission android:name="android.permission.BLUETOOTH_ADMIN" />
```

```
<activity
    android:name="com.morkout.nbsocial.ClassicBluetoothClient"
    android:enabled="true"
    android:label="@string/app_name" >
</activity>
<activity
    android:name="com.morkout.nbsocial.ClassicBluetoothServer"
    android:enabled="true"
    android:label="@string/app_name" >
```

The BLUETOOTH permission is needed to perform any Bluetooth communication, including requesting a connection, accepting a connection, and transferring data. The BLUETOOTH_ADMIN permission is needed to initiate Bluetooth device discovery or change Bluetooth settings.

3. Create a new Activity file called ClassicBluetoothServer.java in NBSocial with the code in Listing 7-8.

Listing 7-8. Classic Bluetooth Server Code

```java
public class ClassicBluetoothServer extends Activity {

    public final static String TAG = "ClassicBluetoothServer";
    BluetoothAdapter mBluetoothAdapter;
    BluetoothServerSocket mBluetoothServerSocket;
    public static final int REQUEST_TO_START_BT = 100;
    public static final int REQUEST_FOR_SELF_DISCOVERY = 200;
    private TextView mTvInfo;

    UUID MY_UUID = UUID.fromString("D04E3068-E15B-4482-8306-4CABFA1726E7");

    @Override
    public void onCreate(Bundle savedInstanceState) {
        super.onCreate(savedInstanceState);
        setContentView(R.layout.main);
        mTvInfo = (TextView) findViewById(R.id.info);

        // initialize BluetoothAdapter, for API 18 or above
        final BluetoothManager bluetoothManager =
            (BluetoothManager) getSystemService(Context.BLUETOOTH_SERVICE);
        mBluetoothAdapter = bluetoothManager.getAdapter();

        if (mBluetoothAdapter == null) {
            return;
        } else {
            if (!mBluetoothAdapter.isEnabled()) {
                Intent enableBtIntent = new Intent(BluetoothAdapter.ACTION_REQUEST_ENABLE);
                startActivityForResult(enableBtIntent, REQUEST_TO_START_BT);
            } else {
                new AcceptThread().start();
            }
        }
    }
}
```

```java
// the thread that waits for Bluetooth client connection
private class AcceptThread extends Thread {
    private BluetoothServerSocket mServerSocket;

    public AcceptThread() {
        try {
            // client should use the same MY_UUID to make connection request
            mServerSocket = mBluetoothAdapter.listenUsingRfcommWithServiceRecord("Cla
            ssicBluetoothServer", MY_UUID);
        }
        catch (IOException e) {
            Log.e(TAG, e.getMessage());
        }
    }

    public void run() {
        BluetoothSocket socket = null;
        while (true) {
            try {
                runOnUiThread(new Runnable() {
                    public void run() {
                        mTvInfo.setText(mTvInfo.getText() + "\n\nWaiting for
                        Bluetooth Client ...");
                    }
                });
                // blocking call
                socket = mServerSocket.accept();

            } catch (IOException e) {
                Log.v(TAG, e.getMessage());
                break;
            }

            if (socket != null) {
                new ConnectedThread(socket).start();

                try {
                    mServerSocket.close();
                } catch (IOException e) {
                    Log.v(TAG, e.getMessage());
                }
                break;
            }
        }
    }
}
```

```java
// the thread that sends file to client
private class ConnectedThread extends Thread {
    private final BluetoothSocket mSocket;
    private final OutputStream mOutStream;
    private int bytesRead;
    final private String FILE_TO_BE_TRANSFERRED = "marchmadness.png";
    final private String PATH = Environment.getExternalStorageDirectory().toString() +
    "/nbsocial/";

    public ConnectedThread(BluetoothSocket socket) {
        mSocket = socket;
        OutputStream tmpOut = null;

        try {
            tmpOut = socket.getOutputStream();
        } catch (IOException e) {
            Log.e(TAG, e.getMessage());
        }
        mOutStream = tmpOut;
    }

    // save as the function in MyVideoApps in Chapter 5
    String copyAsset(String filename) {
        ...
    }

    public void run() {
        byte[] buffer = new byte[1024];
        if (mOutStream != null) {
            // copy a file from app asset folder
            File myFile = new File( copyAsset("marchmadness.png") );
            FileInputStream fis = null;

            try {
                fis = new FileInputStream(myFile);
            } catch (FileNotFoundException e) {
                Log.e(TAG, e.getMessage());
            }
            BufferedInputStream bis = new BufferedInputStream(fis);
            runOnUiThread(new Runnable() {
                public void run() {
                    mTvInfo.setText(mTvInfo.getText() + "\nbefore sending file "+
                    PATH + FILE_TO_BE_TRANSFERRED
                        + " of " + new File( PATH + FILE_TO_BE_TRANSFERRED ).
                        length() + " bytes");
                }
            });
```

```
                    // use standard streaming code to send socket data
                    try {
                        bytesRead = 0;
                        for (int read = bis.read(buffer); read >=0; read = bis.read(buffer))
                        {
                            mOutStream.write(buffer, 0, read);
                            bytesRead += read;
                        }

                        mSocket.close();
                        runOnUiThread(new Runnable() {
                            public void run() {
                                mTvInfo.setText(bytesRead + " bytes of file " +  PATH +
                                FILE_TO_BE_TRANSFERRED + " has been sent.");
                            }
                        });

                    } catch (IOException e) {
                        Log.e(TAG, e.getMessage());
                    }
                }
                // wait for new client connection
                new AcceptThread().start();
            }
        }
    }
```

4. Create another `Activity ClassicBluetoothClient.java` in NBSocial with
    the code in Listing 7-9. Note that to test the Bluetooth client and server
    communication using Glass and another Android device, you'll need to
    create a new Android app (called `AndroidBluetooth` in the book's source
    code) and copy the two files in Listings 7-8 and 7-9 to the app. You'll find
    more on this after this step.

Listing 7-9. Classic Bluetooth Client Code

```
public class ClassicBluetoothClient extends Activity {

    public final static String TAG = "ClassicBluetoothClient";
    public static final int REQUEST_TO_ENABLE_BT = 100;
    private BluetoothAdapter mBluetoothAdapter;
    private TextView mTvInfo;
    private UUID MY_UUID = UUID.fromString("D04E3068-E15B-4482-8306-4CABFA1726E7");
    // notice this UUID is the same as the server's
    private final static String FILE_PATH_RECEIVED = Environment.
    getExternalStorageDirectory().getPath() +"/filefromCBTserver";

    // NOTE!!! you need to replace this with your own device name
    private final static String CBT_SERVER_DEVICE_NAME = "Jeff Tang's Glass";
```

```java
@Override
public void onCreate(Bundle savedInstanceState) {
    super.onCreate(savedInstanceState);
    setContentView(R.layout.main);
    mTvInfo = (TextView) findViewById(R.id.info);
    mTvInfo.setText("Classic Bluetooth Client");

    final BluetoothManager bluetoothManager =
        (BluetoothManager) getSystemService(Context.BLUETOOTH_SERVICE);
    mBluetoothAdapter = bluetoothManager.getAdapter();
    if (mBluetoothAdapter == null) {
        return;
    }
    else {
        if (!mBluetoothAdapter.isEnabled()) {
            Intent enableBtIntent = new Intent(BluetoothAdapter.ACTION_REQUEST_ENABLE);
            startActivityForResult(enableBtIntent, REQUEST_TO_ENABLE_BT);
        }
        else{
            // two ways to find and connect to server
            // discover new Bluetooth devices
            discoverBluetoothDevices();

            // find devices that have been paired
            getBondedDevices();
        }
    }

}


@Override
protected void onActivityResult(int requestCode, int resultCode, Intent data) {
    if (requestCode == REQUEST_TO_ENABLE_BT) {
        discoverBluetoothDevices();
        getBondedDevices();
        return;
    }
}

void discoverBluetoothDevices () {
    // register a BroadcastReceiver for the ACTION_FOUND Intent
    // to receive info about each Bluetooth device discovered.
    IntentFilter filter = new IntentFilter(BluetoothDevice.ACTION_FOUND);
    registerReceiver(mReceiver, filter);
    mBluetoothAdapter.startDiscovery();
}
```

```java
    // for each device discovered, the broadcast info is received
    private final BroadcastReceiver mReceiver = new BroadcastReceiver() {
        public void onReceive(Context context, Intent intent) {
            String action = intent.getAction();
            // When discovery finds a device
            if (BluetoothDevice.ACTION_FOUND.equals(action)) {
                // Get the BluetoothDevice object from the Intent
                BluetoothDevice device = intent.getParcelableExtra
                (BluetoothDevice.EXTRA_DEVICE);

                String name = device.getName();
                // found Glass or an Android device running server
                if (name != null && name.equalsIgnoreCase(CBT_SERVER_DEVICE_NAME)) {
                    new ConnectThread(device).start();
                }
            }
        }
    };

    protected void onDestroy() {
        unregisterReceiver(mReceiver);
        super.onDestroy();
    }

    // bonded devices are those that have already paired with the current device sometime
    in the past
    void getBondedDevices () {
        Set<BluetoothDevice> pairedDevices = mBluetoothAdapter.getBondedDevices();
        if (pairedDevices.size() > 0) {
            for (BluetoothDevice device : pairedDevices) {
                if (device.getName().equalsIgnoreCase(CBT_SERVER_DEVICE_NAME)) {
                    new ConnectThread(device).start();
                    break;
                }
            }
        }
        else {
            Toast.makeText(ClassicBluetoothClient.this, "No bonded devices",
            Toast.LENGTH_LONG).show();
        }
    }

    private class ConnectThread extends Thread {
        int bytesRead;
        int total;
        private final BluetoothSocket mmSocket;
        public ConnectThread(BluetoothDevice device) {
            BluetoothSocket tmp = null;
```

```java
        try {
            tmp = device.createRfcommSocketToServiceRecord(MY_UUID);
        } catch (IOException e) {
            Log.v(TAG, e.getMessage());
        }
        mmSocket = tmp;
    }
    public void run() {
        try {
            // blocking call to connect to server
            mmSocket.connect();
        } catch (IOException e) {
            Log.v(TAG, e.getMessage());
            try {
                mmSocket.close();
            } catch (IOException closeException) { }
            return;
        }
        manageConnectedSocket(mmSocket);
    }

    // receive file from server
    private void manageConnectedSocket(BluetoothSocket socket) {
        int bufferSize = 1024;
        byte[] buffer = new byte[bufferSize];
        FileOutputStream fos = null;
        BufferedOutputStream bos = null;

        try {
            InputStream instream = socket.getInputStream();
            fos = new FileOutputStream( FILE_PATH_RECEIVED );
            bos = new BufferedOutputStream(fos);
            bytesRead = -1;
            total = 0;
            while ((bytesRead = instream.read(buffer)) > 0) {
                total += bytesRead;
                bos.write(buffer, 0, bytesRead);
            }
            bos.close();
            socket.close();
        } catch (IOException e) {
            try {
                socket.close();
                bos.close();}
            catch (IOException e2) {
                Log.e(TAG, "socket close exception:", e2);
            }
        }
    }
}
}
```

5. Create a new Android app called AndroidBluetooth, and copy the ClassicBluetoothClient.java and ClassicBluetoothServer.java files from NBSocial to AndroidBluetooth. Update the AndroidBluetooth app's AndroidManifest.xml file to include the two Bluetooth permissions and make ClassicBluetoothClient the app's MAIN LAUNCHER activity (ideally, the app should present a UI to let you choose whether to run it as a client or server).

6. In your Android device's settings, choose Bluetooth and pair the device with your Glass. This is optional but recommended; if you don't pair your devices in advance, Glass can still discover your Android device and prompt you if you want to pair, but this later process is not very reliable and may not work all the time. Also remember to change CBT_SERVER_DEVICE_NAME in ClassicBluetoothClient.java to your actual Glass name, shown in your Android device Bluetooth settings' Paired Devices list. Figure 7-11 shows the Bluetooth settings on my Nexus 7 tablet.

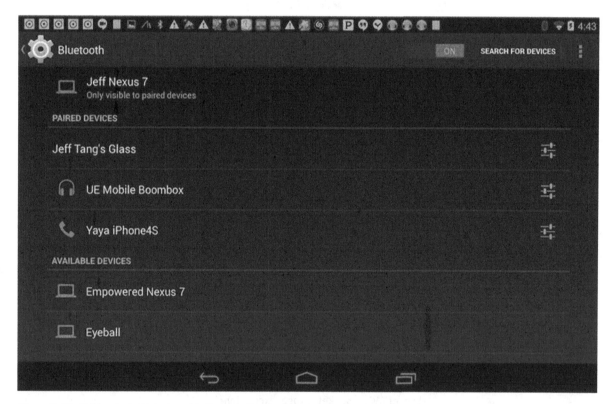

Figure 7-11. Pairing Android device with Glass via Bluetooth

7. Run the Glass app NBSocial and select CBT SERVER to run the Bluetooth server. Then start the AndroidBluetooth app on your Android device, and you'll see the `marchmadness.png` file gets transferred via Classic Bluetooth from your Glass to your Android device, saved as `/sdcard/filefromCBTserver` in your Android device. Figure 7-12 shows what you see on your Glass.

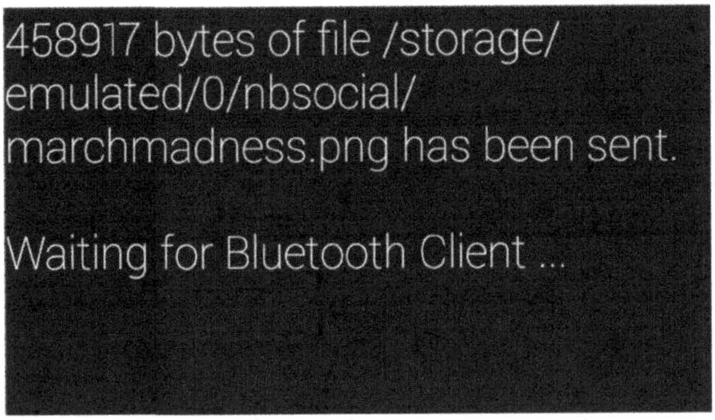

Figure 7-12. Sending file from Bluetooth server to client

8. Similarly, you can run the server on your Android device and client on your Glass. First, change AndroidBluetooth's `AndroidManifest.xml` file to set `ClassicBluetoothServer` as its LAUNCHER activity. Then start the app on your Android device, run NBSocial on your Glass app, and select CBT CLIENT. You'll see the `marchmadness.png` file gets transferred via Classic Bluetooth from your Android device to Glass, saved as `/sdcard/filefromCBTserver` in your Glass.

Here are a few points to note about the code in Listings 7-8 and 7-9:

1. The same universally unique identifier (UUID) is used in both the client's `createRfcommSocketToServiceRecord` call and the server's `listenUsingRfcommWithServiceRecord` call. By matching the UUID, the server accepts the client's connection request. You can use a command-line tool called uuidgen to generate a unique UUID for your own app (for more information, see the "About UUID" note at `http://developer.android.com/guide/topics/connectivity/bluetooth.html`).

2. After a paired device is found, `new ConnectThread(device).start();` is called, which uses `createRfcommSocketToServiceRecord` to create a socket and the socket's `connect` method to establish a socket connection with the server.

3. After a connection request from the client is accepted by the server, the standard socket programming that you saw earlier can be used to transfer data between the client and the server. Here you transfer a relatively large file instead of some short text characters.

You can think of many use cases, such as audio or video streaming, that require a large amount of data transfer between Glass and smartphones or tablets based on Classic Bluetooth. Other use cases would require small but crucial data transfer between Glass and smart sensors, which is the next topic.

Bluetooth Low Energy

BLE is also called Bluetooth Smart, and it's poised for explosive growth. More than 1 billion BLE devices in healthcare, sports, fitness, security, toys, home entertainment, and many other areas were shipped in 2013. BLE is an essential communication technology in all kinds of smart devices because of its low cost, widely adopted standard, and, of course, low energy. It is of essential importance to wearable computing, which is believed to be the next big thing after PC, Internet, and mobile computing. Apple has supported BLE in all its products since iPhone 4s and iOS 5. Google started the BLE support in Android 4.3, API Level 18.

Before proceeding, you have to check out the great Android BLE API guide at `http://developer.android.com/guide/topics/connectivity/bluetooth-le.html` to get yourself familiar with key BLE terms and concepts and sample Android code. Three most important BLE terms are *generic attribute profile* (GATT, such as the Heart Rate Profile), *service* (such as the Heart Rate Monitor service), and *Characteristic* (such as the Heart Rate Measurement characteristic). Each GATT can have one or more services, and each service can have one or more characteristics from which BLE client reads data. The BLE API guide also shows you how to set up BLE, find BLE devices, connect to a GATT server, read BLE attributes, and receive GATT notifications when a characteristic changes, but it doesn't offer a direct and simple example to get data you're interested from a BLE device. This is what I'll do in this section; I'll show you how to let Glass act as a BLE client and read heart rate data from a popular BLE sensor, the Polar H7 Heart Rate Sensor, available for purchase at `http://amzn.to/1h6RjLY`.

Reading Heart Rate from Glass

The complete code is in the NBSocial app of the book's source code. The `BLEClientActivity.java` and `BluetoothLeService.java` files cover the process of finding the Polar H7 BLE device, connecting to its heart rate service, and reading from the service's heart rate measurement characteristic.

1. In BLEClientActivity's onCreate, the following code checks for BLE support and initializes the Bluetooth adapter, before starting the device scan process:

```
// determine whether BLE is supported on the device
if (!getPackageManager().hasSystemFeature
        (PackageManager.FEATURE_BLUETOOTH_LE)) {
   Toast.makeText(this, "BLE not supported.", Toast.LENGTH_SHORT).show();
   finish();
}

// Initializes a Bluetooth adapter
final BluetoothManager bluetoothManager = (BluetoothManager)
        getSystemService(Context.BLUETOOTH_SERVICE);
mBluetoothAdapter = bluetoothManager.getAdapter();
```

```
if (mBluetoothAdapter == null) {
    Toast.makeText(this, "Cannot initialize Bluetooth adapter", Toast.LENGTH_SHORT).
    show();
    finish();
    return;
}

mTvLog.setText("Initialized Bluetooth adapter");

mHandler = new Handler();
scanPolarH7(true);
```

2. A specific UUID for the Polar H7 device is used to start the BLE device
    scan because in this app you're interested only in getting the heart rate
    (specific UUIDs for HEART_RATE_SERVICE_UUID and HEART_RATE_MEASUREMENT_
    CHARACTERISTIC_UUID are defined in SampleGattAttributes.java).

```
private void scanPolarH7(final boolean enable) {
    if (enable) {
        // Stops scanning after a pre-defined scan period.
        mHandler.postDelayed(new Runnable() {
            @Override
            public void run() {
                mScanning = false;
                mBluetoothAdapter.stopLeScan(mLeScanCallback);
                invalidateOptionsMenu();
            }
        }, SCAN_PERIOD);

        mScanning = true;
        UUID[] uuids = new UUID[1];
        uuids[0] = UUID.fromString(SampleGattAttributes.HEART_RATE_SERVICE_UUID);
        // use a UUID array to search for specific services
        // callback is used to get device info when one is found
        mBluetoothAdapter.startLeScan(uuids, mLeScanCallback);
    } else {
        mScanning = false;
        mBluetoothAdapter.stopLeScan(mLeScanCallback);
    }
}
```

3. If you found a device with the requested UUID, you show the device name on
    Glass. Then connect to the device's GATT, passing a GATT callback.

```
private BluetoothAdapter.LeScanCallback mLeScanCallback =
        new BluetoothAdapter.LeScanCallback() {

    @Override
    public void onLeScan(final BluetoothDevice device, int rssi, byte[] scanRecord) {
        runOnUiThread(new Runnable() {
            @Override
```

```
                    public void run() {
                        mTvLog.setText("Found Device: " + device.getName());

                        if (mScanning) {
                            mBluetoothAdapter.stopLeScan(mLeScanCallback);
                            mScanning = false;
                        }
                        mDeviceName = device.getName();
                        mDeviceAddress = device.getAddress();
                        mBluetoothGatt = device.connectGatt(BLEClientActivity.this, true,
                            mGattCallback);
                    }
                });
            }
        };
```

4. In the GATT callback, after successful connection to the device, you
    broadcast the connected intent.

```
    private final BluetoothGattCallback mGattCallback = new BluetoothGattCallback() {
        @Override
        public void onConnectionStateChange(BluetoothGatt gatt, int status, int newState) {
            String intentAction;

            if (newState == BluetoothProfile.STATE_CONNECTED) {
                intentAction = BluetoothLeService.ACTION_GATT_CONNECTED;
                broadcastUpdate(intentAction);
            } else if (newState == BluetoothProfile.STATE_DISCONNECTED) {
                intentAction = BluetoothLeService.ACTION_GATT_DISCONNECTED;
                broadcastUpdate(intentAction);
            }
        }

        private void broadcastUpdate(final String action) {
            final Intent intent = new Intent(action);
            sendBroadcast(intent);
        }
        ...
    }
```

5. In the broadcast receiver, you search for the specific HEART_RATE_SERVICE_
    UUID and HEART_RATE_MEASUREMENT_CHARACTERISTIC_UUID IDs and then read
    the heart rate data from the characteristic.

```
    private final BroadcastReceiver mGattUpdateReceiver = new BroadcastReceiver() {
        @Override
        public void onReceive(Context context, Intent intent) {
            final String action = intent.getAction();
```

```java
if (BluetoothLeService.ACTION_GATT_CONNECTED.equals(action)) {
    mConnected = true;
    mTvLog.setText("Connected");
    invalidateOptionsMenu();
} else if (BluetoothLeService.ACTION_GATT_DISCONNECTED.equals(action)) {
    mConnected = false;
    mTvLog.setText("Disconnected");
    invalidateOptionsMenu();
    clearUI();
} else if (BluetoothLeService.ACTION_GATT_SERVICES_DISCOVERED.equals(action)) {
    // find our interested service and characteristic (HEART_RATE_SERVICE_UUID
    and HEART_RATE_MEASUREMENT_CHARACTERISTIC_UUID)
    for (BluetoothGattService gattService : mBluetoothGatt.getServices()) {
        String uuid = gattService.getUuid().toString();
        if (!uuid.equalsIgnoreCase(SampleGattAttributes.HEART_RATE_SERVICE_UUID))
            continue;

        List<BluetoothGattCharacteristic> gattCharacteristics =
                gattService.getCharacteristics();
        ArrayList<BluetoothGattCharacteristic> charas =
                new ArrayList<BluetoothGattCharacteristic>();

        // Loops through available Characteristics.
        for (BluetoothGattCharacteristic gattCharacteristic :
        gattCharacteristics) {
            charas.add(gattCharacteristic);
            HashMap<String, String> currentCharaData = new HashMap<String, String>();
            uuid = gattCharacteristic.getUuid().toString();
            Log.i(TAG, "characterstic:"+uuid);

            if (!uuid.equalsIgnoreCase(SampleGattAttributes.HEART_RATE_
            MEASUREMENT_CHARACTERISTIC_UUID)) continue;

            if (mBluetoothAdapter == null || mBluetoothGatt == null) {
                return;
            }

            int flag = gattCharacteristic.getProperties();
            int format = -1;
            if ((flag & 0x01) != 0) {
                format = BluetoothGattCharacteristic.FORMAT_UINT16;
            } else {
                format = BluetoothGattCharacteristic.FORMAT_UINT8;
            }
            final int heartRate = gattCharacteristic.getIntValue(format, 1);
```

```
                        mTvLog.setText(heartRate);
                        break;
                }
                break;
            }
        }
    }
};
```

If you run the NBSocial app on Glass now, you'll see a new menu item called BLE CLIENT. Don't forget to wear your Polar H7 device first. Now select BLE CLIENT, and you'll see on your Glass device messages that say "found Polar device" and "connected," and the actual heart rate Glass reads from the device.

> **Note**   Debugging with a BLE device on Glass and Android devices can be a pain sometimes. The support for BLE in Glass is not reliable, and the BLE devices such as Polar H7 can get into the state of not operating correctly, in which case you'll have to remove the battery and wait for some time before putting it back and hope it'll work again.

As of March 2014 when the first draft of this section was written, Glass supported only Android 4.0.3, API Level 15, so I presented two workarounds to let Glass get updates from the Polar H7 BLE device: using an Android device with Android version 4.4.2 and using an iOS device with iOS 7. Now with the release of Android 4.4.2 and API Level 19 on Glass (BLE requires Android 4.3 and API Level 18), it seems that the workarounds are not needed anymore. But I decided to keep the content for two considerations:

- The support for BLE in Glass is still not reliable, while the support for BLE in other Android devices such as Samsung S4 and in iOS devices is excellent.

- This is a good example of showing how to use the connectivity technology you saw earlier in the chapter (socket and Classic Bluetooth) to achieve the goal of an overall better solution. Let other devices with better support for BLE get the data and then use socket or Classic Bluetooth to send Glass the data.

Using Android Device as Delegate

Overall, the Nexus 7 tablet is a great Android tablet for development and daily use. But it can be a real pain when developing and testing BLE apps, if you're not aware that its support for BLE is unstable, even with the latest Android 4.4.2 and API Level 19. The Samsung Galaxy S4 has much better support for BLE. That's why the official Android app in Google Play, called Polar Beat - Fitness Coach, from the manufacturer of the Polar H7 sensor runs only on the Samsung Galaxy S4. I hope the next upgrade of Glass will fix the issues so it can connect, disconnect, and reconnect with BLE devices and discover the services and characteristics reliably and consistently.

Follow these steps to use Glass, acting as a Classic Bluetooth client, to read your heart rate using the Polar H7 sensor:

1. Import the Android project called BLEServiceWithSocketAndCBServer in the `AndroidBLESample-ModifiedWithSocketServerAndClassicBluetoothServe r` folder of the book's source code. The project is based on the sample BLE project located at `<adt-directory>/sdk/samples/android-19/connectivity/ bluetooth/BluetoothLeGatt/BluetoothLeGatt` and modified to make it act as a Classic Bluetooth server.

2. Modify NBSocial's `ClassicBluetoothClientActivity.java` file to keep receiving the heart rate data. The completed source code is in the `HeartrateClassicBluetoothClient.java` file of the NBSocial app.

3. Set up and wear your Polar H7 sensor, run the BLEServiceWithSocketAndCBServer app on Samsung Galaxy S4, and see your heart rate updates.

4. Run the NBSocial Glass app and select the BL HEART RATE menu item. After your Glass connects to the Samsung Galaxy S4, if everything works, you'll see your heart beat updates in your Glass, as shown in Figure 7-13.

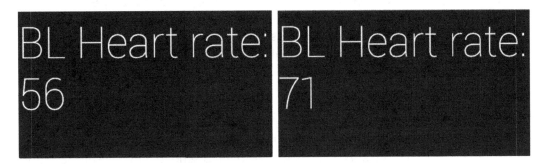

Figure 7-13. Getting heart rate updates from iOS to Glass via a socket

I can disclose a little personal information here: Most of the time while I am writing the book, my heart rate is between 55 and 65. When I sneeze in the allergy season, the rate goes up to 70 something. When I do push-ups after the team I picked in my NCAA bracket loses, it can go all the way up to 160. During the last seconds of the final game of the Spurs vs. Thunders series or while I was fighting some frustrating issue of being unable to pair with the Polar device, I wish I could have seen my heart rates!

Using iOS Device as a Delegate

The steps for building an iOS app that talks to the Polar H7 sensor and then lets your Glass app talk to the iOS app via a socket to get the heart rate information are as follows:

1. Follow the excellent iOS BLE tutorial at www.raywenderlich.com/52080/ introduction-core-bluetooth-building-heart-rate-monitor to build your iOS app.

2. Use your C socket code to make the app a socket server and keep reading and sending heart rate, available in the getHeartBPMData method of HRMViewController.m, to a connected socket client. The complete iOS project called HeartMonitor is in the iOSHeartMonitor-ModifiedWithSocketServer folder of the book's source code.

3. Modify NBSocial's SocketClientActivity.java file to keep receiving the heart rate data. The completed source code is in the HeartrateSocketClientActivity.java file of the NBSocial app.

4. Wear your Polar H7 Heart Rate Sensor. Run the iOS app in an iPhone 4s, 5, 5s, or iPod touch (third-generation or newer) and see your heart rate updates. Make sure the serverName and port values in HeartrateSocketClientActivity.java match the IP address of your iOS device and the serv_addr.sin_port in the HRMViewController.m file of the HeartMonitor project. Then run the Glass app and select SOCKET HEART RATE. You should see your heart rate values on your Glass, also similar to what Figure 7-13 shows.

BLE Peripheral

If you follow the previous steps and check out the iOS BLE tutorial, you know what a BLE peripheral is. It's just any BLE device (like Polar H7) that has some data to send to a BLE client, also known as BLE central. A BLE central, such as the Glass, Android, and iOS apps you saw earlier in this section, connects to and requests data from a BLE peripheral. As of Android 4.4.2, you can only write BLE central, not peripheral. iOS has better and more reliable API support for BLE, and you can easily create a BLE peripheral by following another good tutorial at http://code.tutsplus.com/tutorials/ios-7-sdk-core-bluetooth-practical-lesson--mobile-20741 and the GitHub project at https://github.com/orepereira/CoreBluetooth.

What this means is if you want to take advantage of some new iOS sensors, you can build a BLE peripheral app and publish services and characteristics for Glass to discover and get data from. If Glass cannot talk reliably and directly to an iOS peripheral (or any BLE device as a BLE peripheral), you know what to do: Just let Glass talk to an iOS or another Android device such as the Samsung Galaxy S4 via a socket or Classic Bluetooth, which works as a delegate to send Glass the data of interest.

Other Tips

If you're new to Classic Bluetooth or BLE, you may find it confusing sometimes how to pair Glass with a Bluetooth device. The truth is that with Classic Bluetooth, you have to pair another Bluetooth device, for example Google Glass, smartphone, or tablet, from your non-Glass Bluetooth device's (most likely a smartphone or tablet) Bluetooth settings. With BLE, you don't see the BLE devices in your smartphone or tablet's Bluetooth settings; you discover and add the devices from your app.

Also, by default, Glass can only be discovered, meaning it can be seen and initiated for pairing only by your phone or tablet. To make Glass be able to go search and connect to other Classic Bluetooth devices, such as a Bluetooth keyboard or Logitech Boombox speaker, you can follow the steps in this Google I/O video: https://www.youtube.com/watch?v=OPethpwuYEk&feature=youtu.be&t=7m35s. Although the video is called *Voiding Your Warranty: Hacking Glass*, the part that makes your Glass discover other Bluetooth devices only requires you to install two apps and then use your familiar Android Settings app to pair your Glass with a device such as the Boombox speaker, which obviously cannot pair with your Glass proactively.

Going Social

On February 19, 2014, Facebook acquired WhatsApp, the world's most popular messaging app with 450 million users, for a stunning $19 billion. WeChat, WhatsApp's China-based competitor, has about 300 million users. It seems to make sense to share a picture taken on your Glass to your WhatsApp or WeChat friends. The bad news is that as of now, both companies have only iOS/Android API/SDK support, which requires a native WhatsApp or WeChat app to be installed and used for sharing. The good news is that before a native WhatsApp or WeChat Glass app is available, you can use what you have learned in this chapter to connect Glass with an iOS/Android device, which acts as a delegate to share the content on Glass to your friends on WhatsApp or WeChat.

In this section, I'll show a new way to connect Glass and iOS for social sharing. The reason iOS was chosen instead of Android is that as of June 1, 2014, WhatsApp offers the official integration documentation only for iOS (https://www.whatsapp.com/faq/iphone/23559013). The technique I'll use is the Apple Push Notification Service, a service offered by Apple that can send notifications to an app without requiring the app to keep pulling for updates. The following is the workflow: First Glass uploads a picture to the server. Then it makes an HTTP GET request to your server, triggering a push notification sent to your iOS device, which then triggers the WhatsApp or WeChat app installed on the iOS device for user confirmation of the content to be shared and giving the choice of whom to share with.

Follow these steps to update your Glass app and create a corresponding iOS project. If you're not an iOS developer, you may want to skip the iOS part, but at least you'll get an idea of what can be done to make Glass more connectable.

1. Go back to the SmartCamera project in Chapter 4. In `ImageViewActivity.java`, which is used by `ZoomActivity.java` to upload or e-mail a picture taken after zooming, add the following code in `onOptionsItemSelected`:

```
case R.id.wechat:
    shareTo = "wechat";
    new SharingTask().execute();
    return true;
```

```
        case R.id.whatsapp:
            shareTo = "whatsapp";
            new SharingTask().execute();
```

2. Add a new AsyncTask to make an HTTP GET call (the uploadFile method is
    defined in Listing 7-3).

```
private class SharingTask extends AsyncTask<Void, Void, Void> {
    @Override
    protected void onPreExecute() {
        super.onPreExecute();
    }

    @Override
    protected Void doInBackground(Void... arg0) {
        try {
            String uploadedFilename = uploadFile(mPictureFilePath);
            new URL("http://www.morkout.com/iapps/social/notif.php?shareto="
                    + shareTo + "&uname=jeff&imagename="
                    + URLEncoder.encode(uploadedFilename, "UTF-8")).openConnection();
        } catch (IOException e) {
            Toast.makeText(ImageViewActivity.this, e.getMessage(), Toast.LENGTH_LONG).show();

        }
        return null;
    }

    @Override
    protected void onPostExecute(Void result) {
        super.onPostExecute(result);
    }
}
```

3. The server notif.php file is based on the tutorial at https://blog.
    serverdensity.com/how-to-build-an-apple-push-notification-provider-
    server-tutorial/, which is called to send an Apple push notification to a
    registered iOS device, with the payload defined like this:

```
$payload['aps'] = array('alert' =>$uname . ' sharing a Google Glass picture ', 'shareto'
=> $shareto, 'imagename' => $imagename, 'badge' => 1, 'sound' => 'default');
```

4. Create a new iOS project and follow the previous WhatsApp documentation
    URL and the WeChat SDK installation guide at http://dev.wechat.com/
    wechatapi/installguide to configure the project.

5. Create an Apple push provisioning profile to be used by your iOS project.

6. Add the iOS code in Listing 7-10 in the iOS project's AppDelegate.m.

Listing 7-10. iOS Code That Gets Push Notification and Launches WhatsApp/WeChat App to Share Glass Image

```
- (void)application:(UIApplication *)application didReceiveRemoteNotification:
(NSDictionary *)userInfo
{
    NSString *message = nil;
    NSString *imagename = nil;
    NSString *shareto = nil;
    id payload = [userInfo objectForKey:@"aps"];
    if ([payload isKindOfClass:[NSString class]]) {
        message = payload;
    } else if ([payload isKindOfClass:[NSDictionary class]]) {
        message = [payload objectForKey:@"alert"];
        imagename = [payload objectForKey:@"imagename"];
        shareto = [payload objectForKey:@"shareto"];
    }

    if ([shareto isEqualToString:@"wechat"]) {
        // with ext, error sending the message (wechat server issue! ok next morning);
        without ext, wechat doesn't even get launched
        WXMediaMessage *msg = [WXMediaMessage message];
        msg.title = message;
        msg.description = @"Tap to see image shared from google glass";

        // tap this on iPhone, WeChat will open this link
        WXWebpageObject *ext = [WXWebpageObject object];
        ext.webpageUrl = [NSString stringWithFormat:
        @"http://www.morkout.com/iapps/social/uploads/%@", imagename];
        msg.mediaObject = ext;

        SendMessageToWXReq* req = [[SendMessageToWXReq alloc] init];
        req.bText = NO;
        req.message = msg;
        req.scene = WXSceneSession; // WXSceneTimeline;
        req.text = message;
        [WXApi sendReq:req];
    }
    else if ([shareto isEqualToString:@"whatsapp"]) {
        NSURL *url = [NSURL URLWithString:[NSString stringWithFormat:
        @"http://www.morkout.com/iapps/social/uploads/%@", imagename]];
        NSData *data = [NSData dataWithContentsOfURL:url];

        NSArray *dirPaths = NSSearchPathForDirectoriesInDomains(NSDocumentDirectory,
        NSUserDomainMask, YES);
        NSString *docsDir = [dirPaths objectAtIndex:0];
        NSString *glassimage = [[NSString alloc] initWithString:
        [docsDir stringByAppendingPathComponent:@"glass.wai"]];
        [data writeToFile:glassimage atomically:YES];

        NSURL *imageFileURL = [NSURL fileURLWithPath:glassimage];
```

```
                 _documentController = [UIDocumentInteractionController interactionControllerWithU
                 RL:imageFileURL];
                 _documentController.delegate = self;
                 _documentController.UTI = @"net.whatsapp.image";
                 [_documentController presentOpenInMenuFromRect:CGRectZero inView:_firstVC.view
                 animated:YES];
            }
        }
```

Now install and run your iOS app on an iOS device. Then start the SmartCamera app on Glass, select Zoom, and take a picture. In the next picture view screen, tap to choose either WhatsApp or WeChat to share. Your picture will be uploaded to my demo server, and an Apple push notification will be sent to your iOS device, which will parse the notification payload to get the uploaded image URL and open the iOS WhatsApp or WeChat app, based on your selection, with the picture attached. After you choose the friends to share, your Glass picture will be shared to them right away.

The whole process may look a little complicated, but after you get everything set up correctly, it takes only seconds to share a picture taken on your Glass with your friends on WhatsApp or WeChat.

Summary

In this chapter, I first covered how to implement the basic HTTP GET, POST, and file uploading operations using the recommended HttpURLConnection class. Then I discussed how to accomplish low-level socket programming and let Glass talk with another Android or iOS device for data exchange, both as a client and as a server. After that, I illustrated in detail how to use Classic Bluetooth for communication between Glass and another Android device, without the need of wi-fi. I then introduced the exciting topic of BLE support and how to let Glass act as a BLE client and also how to use the Samsung Galaxy S4 smartphone or an iOS device as a bridge between Glass and BLE devices. Finally, I showed you how to use Apple's push technology to let you share your new picture taken on Glass with your WhatsApp or WeChat friends in seconds.

Chapter 8

Location, Map, and Sensors

If you have seen the Glass introduction videos by Google, you may have noticed that many use cases of Glass are for outdoor activities. So naturally, location and map services on Glass would be commonly desired. Furthermore, as a wearable device powered by Android, Glass is expected to support a variety of sensors for apps to get interesting data and better interact with the world around us. How to use the GDK to develop location, map, and sensor-aware apps is the topic of this chapter.

The solutions, sample code, and discussions covered in this chapter include the following:

- How to get your current location based on GPS provider and network provider (and when to use which provider)

- How to show the address and map of your current location and how to zoom in and out of the map

- How to develop interesting Location Based Service (LBS) Glass apps such as finding nearby business information or what pictures other Instagram users have shared about a specific tourist attraction

- What sensors Glass supports, what each means, and what the use cases are

- How to use the orientation sensors to detect head position (pitch, roll, and yaw) and movement

- How to use the magnetic field sensor to develop a metal detector

- How to use the rotation vector to develop a compass

- How to use the gyroscope, accelerometer, and magnetic field sensors to determine the planet positions in the sky

Location

Google offers a brief developer guide on location and sensors, based on the standard Android APIs, at https://developers.google.com/glass/develop/gdk/location-sensors/. To see how the Android location-based APIs actually work on Glass and what special considerations need to be taken while getting location information for Glass, let's start by creating a new project for this chapter.

Getting Location

Follow the same steps as in previous chapters and create a new Android application project called LocationSensors based on your old friend GlasswareTemplate. Then create a new menu item location in the res/menu/main.xml file, create a new string named location, and update MenuActivity.java.

```
<item
    android:id="@+id/location"
    android:title="@string/location" />
```

```
<string name="location">LOCATION</string>
```

```
case R.id.location:
    Intent intent = new Intent(this, LocationActivity.class);
    startActivity(intent);
    return true;
```

Now create a new LocationActivity.java file, as shown in Listing 8-1.

Listing 8-1. Getting Location Provider and Latitude and Longitude

```java
public class LocationActivity extends Activity implements LocationListener{
    LocationManager mLocationManager;
    Location mLocation;
    TextView mTvLocation;

    @Override
    public void onCreate(Bundle savedInstanceState) {
        super.onCreate(savedInstanceState);
        setContentView(R.layout.location);
        mTvLocation = (TextView) findViewById(R.id.tvLocation);
        mLocationManager = (LocationManager)getSystemService(Context.LOCATION_SERVICE);
    }

    protected void onStart() {
        super.onStart();
        Criteria criteria = new Criteria();
        criteria.setAccuracy(Criteria.NO_REQUIREMENT); // 1
        // criteria.setAccuracy(Criteria.ACCURACY_FINE);
        // criteria.setAccuracy(Criteria.ACCURACY_COARSE);
        System.out.println("best provider:" + mLocationManager.getBestProvider(criteria, true)); // 2
        String allString = "";
```

```
        List<String> providers = mLocationManager.getProviders(criteria, false);
        for (String p : providers) {
            allString += p+":";
            if (mLocationManager.isProviderEnabled(p)) { // 3
                allString += "Y;";
                mLocationManager.requestLocationUpdates(p, 10000, 0, this); // 4
                Location location = mLocationManager.getLastKnownLocation(p); // 5
                if (location == null)
                    System.out.println("getLastKnownLocation for provider " + p + " returns null");
                else {
                    System.out.println("getLastKnownLocation for provider " + p + " returns NOT null");
                    mTvLocation.setText(location.getLatitude() + ", " + location.getLongitude());
                }
            }
            else allString += "N;";
        }

        // on Glass, allString is: remote_gps:Y;remote_network:Y;network:Y;passive:Y
        mTvLocation.setText(allString);
    }

    @Override
    public void onStatusChanged(String provider, int status, Bundle extras) {
    }

    @Override
    public void onProviderEnabled(String provider) {
    }

    @Override
    public void onProviderDisabled(String provider) {
    }

    @Override
    public void onLocationChanged(Location location) {
        mLocation = location;
        mTvLocation.setText(mLocation.getLatitude() + ", " + mLocation.getLongitude());
    }
}
```

After a LocationManager is created, Criteria.NO_REQUIREMENT is set on commented line 1. You can also use other criteria such as ACCURACY_FINE and ACCURACY_COARSE. NO_REQUIREMENT and ACCURACY_COARSE require only the built-in network provider on Glass, meaning both wi-fi and Bluetooth on Glass can be disconnected, but Glass can still get the location data. ACCURACY_FINE, however, requires a remote GPS provider, which is possible only if you pair Glass with a smartphone or tablet where the MyGlass app is installed. If this is a little confusing, the sample output you'll see when you run the app (which I'll describe in detail shortly) will help you understand it better.

A location provider supplies periodic updates on the device location. getBestProvider in // 2 returns the best provider to meet the criteria specified in // 1. This doesn't mean the provider is available on your Glass to return the last known location in // 5, even though it's enabled in // 3. requestLocationUpdates in // 4 asks the provider to send a location update every ten seconds; if the third parameter is greater than zero, then the provider will send an update only when the location has changed by at least that many meters *and* at least the number of milliseconds specified by the second parameter have passed. You may want to check out the documentation of requestLocationUpdates at http://developer.android.com/reference/android/location/LocationManager.html to get more information, especially on how to choose an appropriate value for the second parameter to conserve battery life.

Now add a new layout file called location.xml as follows:

```xml
<?xml version="1.0" encoding="utf-8"?>
<FrameLayout xmlns:android="http://schemas.android.com/apk/res/android"
    android:layout_width="match_parent"
    android:layout_height="match_parent"
    android:background="@color/black" >

    <TextView
        android:id="@+id/tvLocation"
        android:layout_width="match_parent"
        android:layout_height="match_parent"
        android:layout_gravity="center"
        android:layout_marginTop="-10px"
        android:gravity="center"
        android:textSize="100px" />
</FrameLayout>
```

Run the LocationSensors app on Glass and select LOCATION from the menu. You'll see the latitude and longitude of your current locations, updated about every ten seconds. In Eclipse's LogCat, you'll see different outputs for different cases.

1. If Criteria.NO_REQUIREMENT or ACCURACY_COARSE is set, then whether you have wi-fi and Bluetooth enabled on your Glass or not and whether Bluetooth is paired with another Android or iOS device or not, you'll see the following result:

   ```
   best provider:remote_network
   getLastKnownLocation for provider remote_gps returns null
   getLastKnownLocation for provider remote_network returns null
   getLastKnownLocation for provider network returns NOT null
   remote_gps:Y;remote_network:Y;network:Y;
   ```

2. If your paired Android or iOS device has the MyGlass app up and running
    and its screencast successfully shows your Glass content, you'll see the
    following:

```
best provider:remote_network
getLastKnownLocation for provider remote_gps returns NOT null
getLastKnownLocation for provider remote_network returns null
getLastKnownLocation for provider network returns NOT null
remote_gps:Y;remote_network:Y;network:Y;
```

3. If you use ACCURACY_FINE in the criteria, you'll see only the remote_gps
    provider, not the network or remote_network provider anymore.

```
best provider:remote_gps
getLastKnownLocation for provider remote_gps returns NOT null
remote_gps:Y;
```

For many types of location-based apps, such as retrieving an address, showing a map of the current
location, finding nearby information of interest, or viewing pictures shared for the location, the network
provider and Criteria.NO_REQUIREMENT are good enough. Those are exactly what I'll discuss next.

Showing Address

Follow these steps to show the address of your current location:

1. In class LocationActivity, add private GestureDetector mGestureDetector;
    then at the end of onCreate, add the following:

```
mGestureDetector = new GestureDetector(this);
mGestureDetector.setBaseListener(new GestureDetector.BaseListener() {
    @Override
    public boolean onGesture(Gesture gesture) {
        if (gesture == Gesture.TAP) {
            openOptionsMenu();
            return true;
        }
        return false;
    }
});
```

2. Then add the following code to the class:

```
// this method is required for tap touchpad to work!
public boolean onGenericMotionEvent(MotionEvent event) {
    if (mGestureDetector != null) {
        return mGestureDetector.onMotionEvent(event);
    }
    return false;
}
```

```java
@Override
public boolean onCreateOptionsMenu(Menu menu) {

    MenuInflater inflater = getMenuInflater();
    inflater.inflate(R.menu.location, menu);
    return true;
}

@Override
public boolean onOptionsItemSelected(MenuItem item) {
    switch (item.getItemId()) {
    case R.id.address:
        Geocoder geocoder;
        List<Address> addresses;
        geocoder = new Geocoder(this, Locale.getDefault());
        try {
            addresses = geocoder.getFromLocation(mLocation.getLatitude(),
            mLocation.getLongitude(), 1);
            String address = addresses.get(0).getAddressLine(0);
            String city = addresses.get(0).getAddressLine(1);
            String country = addresses.get(0).getAddressLine(2);
            mTvLocation.setText(address + "," + city + "," + country);
        }
        catch (IOException e) {
            e.printStackTrace();
        }

        return true;

    default:
        return super.onOptionsItemSelected(item);
    }
}
```

3. Create a new location.xml file in res/menu and update strings.xml.

```xml
<?xml version="1.0" encoding="utf-8"?>
<menu xmlns:android="http://schemas.android.com/apk/res/android" >

    <item
        android:id="@+id/address"
        android:title="@string/address"/>
</menu>

<string name="address">ADDRESS</string>
```

Run the app now. After selecting LOCATION and seeing the latitude and longitude, tap the touchpad to see a menu with the single item ADDRESS. Tap it again, and you'll see the address information for the current location.

What the code did was to add the support for gesture recognition, as shown in Chapter 3, so tapping the touchpad will launch a menu for LocationActivity. Then you use the Geocoder class and pass in the latitude and longitude values to get the address.

Showing and Resizing Map

A more interesting use case would be to see a map of your location and be able to zoom in and out on the map. Google offers a simple-to-use Maps API to show a static map based on, yes, latitude and longitude, exactly what you need: https://developers.google.com/maps/documentation/imageapis/. You can use its zoom parameter to make the static map a little dynamic. The steps to do this in the app are as follows:

1. Declare three constants and two new variables in the LocationActivity class and initialize the variables in the onCreate method.

    ```
    ImageView mIvMap;
    int mZoom;
    private static final int MAX_ZOOM = 20;
    private static final int MIN_ZOOM = 2;
    private static final int START_ZOOM = 10;

    mIvMap = (ImageView) findViewById(R.id.ivMap);
    mZoom = START_ZOOM;
    ```

2. Add the following code to res/layout/location.xml, after the TextView element.

    ```
    <ImageView
        android:id="@+id/ivMap"
        android:layout_width="match_parent"
        android:layout_height="match_parent" />
    ```

3. Back in LocationActivity's onGesture method, add two new if statements.

    ```
    else if (gesture == Gesture.SWIPE_RIGHT) {
        if (mZoom < MAX_ZOOM)
            new ImageLoadingTask().execute("http://maps.googleapis.com/maps/api/
            staticmap?zoom=" + ++mZoom + "&size=640x360&markers=color:red%7C"+mLocation.
            getLatitude() + "," + mLocation.getLongitude() + "&sensor=false");
        else
            Toast.makeText(LocationActivity.this, "Max zoom reached...",
            Toast.LENGTH_LONG).show();

        return true;
    } else if (gesture == Gesture.SWIPE_LEFT) {
    ```

```
    if (mZoom > MIN_ZOOM)
        new ImageLoadingTask().execute("http://maps.googleapis.com/maps/api/
        staticmap?zoom=" + --mZoom + "&size=640x360&markers=color:red%7C"+mLocation.
        getLatitude() + "," + mLocation.getLongitude() + "&sensor=false");
    else
        Toast.makeText(LocationActivity.this, "Min zoom reached...",
        Toast.LENGTH_LONG).show();

    return true;
    }
```

4. In the onOptionsItemSelected method, add the code to process the MAP
    menu item.

```
case R.id.map:
    // create an async task to get the image since network access isn't allowed on the
main thread:
    new ImageLoadingTask().execute("http://maps.googleapis.com/maps/api/staticmap?zoom="
    + mZoom + "&size=640x360&markers=color:red%7C"+mLocation.getLatitude() + "," +
    mLocation.getLongitude() + "&sensor=false");
    return true;
```

5. The AsyncTask ImageLoadingTask is defined in Listing 8-2.

Listing 8-2. Downloading an Image Asynchronously

```
private class ImageLoadingTask extends AsyncTask<String, Void, Bitmap> {

@Override
protected Bitmap doInBackground(String... stringURL) {
    Bitmap bmp = null;
    try {
        URL url = new URL(stringURL[0]);
        HttpURLConnection conn = (HttpURLConnection) url.openConnection();
        conn.setDoInput(true);
        conn.connect();
        InputStream is = conn.getInputStream();
        BitmapFactory.Options options = new BitmapFactory.Options();
        bmp = BitmapFactory.decodeStream(is, null, options);
    } catch (Exception e) {
        e.printStackTrace();
    }

    return bmp;
}

@Override
protected void onPostExecute(Bitmap result) {
    mTvLocation.setVisibility(View.GONE);
    mIvMap.setVisibility(View.VISIBLE);
```

```
            mIvMap.setImageBitmap(result);
            super.onPostExecute(result);
        }

    }
```

6. Add a new menu item map in res/menu/location.xml and a new string to strings.xml.

```
<item
    android:id="@+id/map"
    android:title="@string/map"/>
<string name="map">MAP</string>
```

7. Your AndroidManifest.xml file should have these user permissions now:

```
<uses-permission android:name="com.google.android.glass.permission.DEVELOPMENT" />
<uses-permission android:name="android.permission.ACCESS_FINE_LOCATION" />
<uses-permission android:name="android.permission.INTERNET" />
```

Now run the app and select LOCATION. Then tap and choose MAP. You'll see a map as in Figure 8-1.

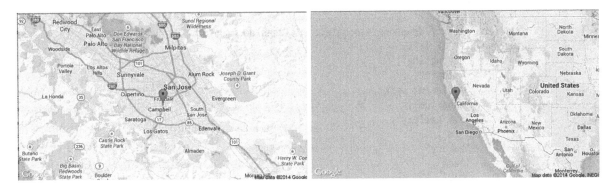

Figure 8-1. *Showing a map of my current location and zooming in*

Swipe left and right, and you'll see the resized map!

Finding Places Nearby

Google offers a more sophisticated API called the Places API for you to build more advanced location-based apps: https://developers.google.com/places/documentation/index. You can search for any of the 100 or so supported types, listed at https://developers.google.com/places/documentation/supported_types, based on your location. You should definitely check out the type list to get inspired.

The following steps describe how to use the Google Places API in a Glass app.

1. Follow the authentication step for the Google Places API at
   https://developers.google.com/places/documentation/index to create a
   new API key.

2. Replace <YOUR_API_KEY>, <LATITUDE,LONGITUDE>, in the following URL to
   make your place search: https://maps.googleapis.com/maps/api/place/
   nearbysearch/json?location=<LATITUDE,LONGITUDE>&radius=500&types=rest
   aurant&sensor=false&key=<YOUR_API_KEY>;.

3. Create a new menu item called NEARBY PLACES in menu's main.xml and
   update strings.xml and MenuActivity.java.

4. Copy LocationActivity.java and rename it to NearbyPlacesActivity.java,
   making its content look like Listing 8-3.

Listing 8-3. Showing Place Types and Launching Activity to Show Matched Places Nearby

```java
public class NearbyPlacesActivity extends Activity {
    LocationManager mLocationManager;
    Location mLocation;
    TextView mTvLocation;
    private GestureDetector mGestureDetector;

    // from https://developers.google.com/places/documentation/supported_types
    String[] PLACE_TYPES = {
            "accounting",
            "airport",
            "amusement_park",
            "aquarium",
            "art_gallery",
            "atm",
            "bakery",
            "bank",
            "bar",
            ...
            };

    @Override
    public void onCreate(Bundle savedInstanceState) {
        super.onCreate(savedInstanceState);

        setContentView(R.layout.location);
        mTvLocation =  (TextView) findViewById(R.id.tvLocation);
        mLocationManager = (LocationManager)getSystemService(Context.LOCATION_SERVICE);
```

```java
        mGestureDetector = new GestureDetector(this);
        mGestureDetector.setBaseListener(new GestureDetector.BaseListener() {
            @Override
            public boolean onGesture(Gesture gesture) {
                if (gesture == Gesture.TAP) {
                    openOptionsMenu();
                    return true;
                }
                return false;
            }
        });
    }

    public boolean onGenericMotionEvent(MotionEvent event) {
        if (mGestureDetector != null) {
            return mGestureDetector.onMotionEvent(event);
        }
        return false;
    }

    @Override
    public boolean onCreateOptionsMenu(Menu menu) {

        MenuInflater inflater = getMenuInflater();
        inflater.inflate(R.menu.juststop, menu);

        for (int i=1; i<=PLACE_TYPES.length; i++)
            menu.add(PLACE_TYPES[i-1].toUpperCase());

        return true;
    }
    @Override
    public boolean onOptionsItemSelected(MenuItem item) {
        String ptype = item.getTitle().toString().toLowerCase();
        if (ptype.equals("stop")) {
            finish();
            return true;
        }

        Intent intent = new Intent(this, ScrollingCardsActivity.class);
        intent.putExtra("ptype", ptype);
        intent.putExtra("latitude", Double.valueOf(mLocation.getLatitude()));
        intent.putExtra("longitude", Double.valueOf(mLocation.getLongitude()));
        startActivity(intent);

        return super.onOptionsItemSelected(item);

    }
```

```
            protected void onStart() {
                super.onStart();
                Criteria criteria = new Criteria();
                criteria.setAccuracy(Criteria.NO_REQUIREMENT);

                List<String> providers = mLocationManager.getProviders(criteria, false);
                for (String p : providers) {
                    if (mLocationManager.isProviderEnabled(p)) {
                        mLocation = mLocationManager.getLastKnownLocation(p);
                        if (mLocation != null) {
                            mTvLocation.setText(mLocation.getLatitude() + ", " +
                                                mLocation.getLongitude());
                            break;
                        }
                    }
                }
            }
        }
```

5. Copy juststop.xml from the GlassUIElements project in Chapter 3 and copy ScrollingCardsActivity.java as well, making its content the same as Listing 8-4.

Listing 8-4. Calling the Google Places API and Showing Search Results

```
public class ScrollingCardsActivity extends Activity {
    private List<View> mCards;
    private CardScrollView mCardScrollView;
    private ExampleCardScrollAdapter mAdapter;

    @Override
    protected void onCreate(Bundle savedInstanceState) {
        super.onCreate(savedInstanceState);

        Bundle extras = getIntent().getExtras();
        String ptype = (String)extras.get("ptype");
        Double latitude = (Double)extras.get("latitude");
        Double longitude = (Double)extras.get("longitude");

        mCardScrollView = new CardScrollView(this);
        new QueryPlacesTask().execute("https://maps.googleapis.com/maps/api/place/
                nearbysearch/json?location="+
                latitude.doubleValue()+","+
                longitude.doubleValue()+"&radius=1500&types="+ptype
                +"&sensor=false&key=<YOUR_API_KEY>");
    }

    private class QueryPlacesTask extends AsyncTask<String, Void, JSONArray> {
        @Override
        protected void onPreExecute() {
            super.onPreExecute();
        }
```

```java
@Override
protected JSONArray doInBackground(String... stringURL) {
    JSONArray entries = null;
    try {
        DefaultHttpClient httpClient = new DefaultHttpClient();
        HttpGet httpGet = new HttpGet(stringURL[0]);
        HttpResponse httpResponse = httpClient.execute(httpGet);
        HttpEntity httpEntity = httpResponse.getEntity();

        String jsonStr = EntityUtils.toString(httpEntity);
        if (jsonStr != null) {
            JSONObject jsonObj = new JSONObject(jsonStr);
            entries = jsonObj.getJSONArray("results");
        }
    } catch (IOException e) {
    } catch (JSONException e) {
    }

    return entries;
}

@Override
protected void onPostExecute(JSONArray entries) {
    if (entries.length() == 0) {
        Toast.makeText(ScrollingCardsActivity.this, "No Results Found",
        Toast.LENGTH_LONG).show();
        return;
    }

    mCards = new ArrayList<View>();
    try {
        for (int i = 0; i < entries.length(); i++) {
            JSONObject entry = entries.getJSONObject(i);

            String name = entry.getString("name");
            String address = entry.getString("vicinity");
            double lat = entry.getJSONObject("geometry").
                    getJSONObject("location").getDouble("lat");
            double lng = entry.getJSONObject("geometry").
                    getJSONObject("location").getDouble("lng");
            String id = entry.getString("id");

            Card card;
            card = new Card(ScrollingCardsActivity.this);
            card.setText(name);
            card.setFootnote(address);
```

```
                            new ImageLoadingTask().execute(id, card, "http://maps.googleapis.com/
                            maps/api/staticmap?zoom=15&size=640x360&markers=color:red%7C"+lat +
                            "," + lng + "&sensor=false");
                    }
                }
                catch (JSONException e) {
                }

                mAdapter = new ExampleCardScrollAdapter();
                mCardScrollView.setAdapter(mAdapter);
                mCardScrollView.activate();
                setContentView(mCardScrollView);

                super.onPostExecute(entries);
            }
        }

        class CardImg {
            Card mCard;
            String mFilename;

            public CardImg(Card card, String filename) {
                mCard = card;
                mFilename = filename;
            }
        }

        private class ImageLoadingTask extends AsyncTask<Object, Void, CardImg> {

            @Override
            protected CardImg doInBackground(Object... params) {
                Bitmap bmp = null;
                String id = (String)params[0];
                Card card = (Card)params[1];
                File cacheDir = null;
                try {
                    URL url = new URL((String)params[2]);
                    HttpURLConnection conn = (HttpURLConnection) url.openConnection();
                    conn.setDoInput(true);
                    conn.connect();
                    InputStream is = conn.getInputStream();
                    BitmapFactory.Options options = new BitmapFactory.Options();
                    bmp = BitmapFactory.decodeStream(is, null, options);

                    cacheDir = getCacheDir();
                    FileOutputStream out = new FileOutputStream(cacheDir + "/" + id);
                    bmp.compress(Bitmap.CompressFormat.PNG, 90, out);
                    out.close();

                } catch (IOException e) {
                }
```

```
                       return new CardImg(card, cacheDir + "/" + id);
            }

            @Override
            protected void onPostExecute(CardImg cardImg) {
                            cardImg.mCard.addImage(BitmapFactory.decodeFile
                            (cardImg.mFilename));
                            mCards.add(cardImg.mCard.getView());
                            mAdapter.notifyDataSetChanged();
                super.onPostExecute(cardImg);
            }
        }

        private class ExampleCardScrollAdapter extends CardScrollAdapter {
            @Override
                public int getPosition(Object item) {
                return mCards.indexOf(item);
            }

            @Override
            public int getCount() {
                return mCards.size();
            }

            @Override
            public Object getItem(int position) {
                return mCards.get(position);
            }

            @Override
            public View getView(int position, View convertView, ViewGroup parent) {
                return mCards.get(position);//.toView();
            }
        }
    }
```

6. Add the two activity files shown earlier to AndroidManifest.xml.

Listing 8-3 shows the place types Google API supports as menu options and, after the user selects one, passes the type name and the latitude and longitude of the current location to ScrollingCardsActivity in Listing 8-4. ScrollingCardsActivity makes an appropriate Google Place API call, parses the returned JSON result (you may want to refer to the documentation at https://developers.google.com/places/documentation/search#PlaceSearchResponses to understand how to parse the JSON result), and launches the Google Maps API you saw earlier in this chapter to show the name, the address, and a map of each result as a card in a CardScrollView, as you saw in the ScrollingCardsActivity.java in Chapter 3.

Note You use ImageLoadingTask to save each map bitmap returned from the Maps API to your app's cache directory, because you can call addImage only on a Card object with a local image resource.

Now run the app and say "OK Glass" and then "Location sensors." Select NEARBY PLACES, and you'll see the current location's coordinates. Tap and swipe left and right to see all the place types, and tap again to choose the type and see all the matched results, as shown in Figure 8-2.

Figure 8-2. Showing places of interest nearby

Searching Shared Pictures

There are many possible location-based services and apps. Let's talk about one more case before moving to the wonderful topic of sensors. Imagine you're visiting a famous place, such as the Golden Gate Bridge in San Francisco. Chances are you use Instagram to share photos with friends. So, how about letting Glass find and show photos others have shared on Instagram about the Golden Gate Bridge? Follow these steps to build such a Glass app:

1. Get yourself familiar with the Instagram APIs at `http://instagram.com/developer/endpoints/locations/`, which allow you to search for locations based on latitude and longitude and then use any location ID generated in the search result to query for a list of images and videos for that location.

2. In the Instagram's API Console at `http://instagram.com/developer/api-console/`, select OAuth 2 under Authentication to create an `access_token`.

3. Use the `access_token` and the latitude and longitude, which you obtained earlier in the chapter, in the search API. For example, this query searches for locations around the Golden Gate Bridge and returns a JSON result: `https://api.instagram.com/v1/locations/search?lat=37.819878&lng=-122.478503&access_token=<ACCESS_TOKEN>`.

4. Parse the search result for location IDs and names and use any ID in the media search API: `https://api.instagram.com/v1/locations/<ID>/media/recent?access_token=<ACCESS_TOKEN>`.

5. Parse the media search result to get image or video links for the location and present the content on your Glass timeline.

Because the `access_token` may expire any time in the future, it's better to create it in your app. But that would require the app user to log in with their Instagram username and password. This is another example of integrating your smartphone with Glass: You can develop an iOS app, for example, to ask the user to log in to Instagram, and the app will generate an `access_token` after a successful login. The `access_token` can then be sent to your Glass app using one of the several ways discussed in the previous chapter: HTTP (if you let your iOS app save the token to your server and your Glass app gets it from the server), socket, or Bluetooth.

Sensors

As a wearable device, Glass offers many sensors that let you develop apps you normally would not think of. Sensors are extremely important to wearable computing, the Internet of Things, because they allow you to better understand your environment, as well as the device in the environment. In this section, I'll cover the sensors supported by Glass in detail, offer a working sample to help you understand each of them, and build several examples to show you the power of the Glass sensors.

Supported Sensors

Glass supports the following eight sensors with the Android sensor framework:

- `TYPE_ACCELEROMETER`: Measures the acceleration applied to Glass, including the force of gravity

- `TYPE_GRAVITY`: Measures the direction and magnitude of gravity

- `TYPE_GYROSCOPE`: Measures the rate of rotation around Glass's three axes

- `TYPE_LIGHT`: Measures the ambient light level

- `TYPE_LINEAR_ACCELERATION`: Measures the acceleration applied to Glass, excluding the force of gravity

- `TYPE_MAGNETIC_FIELD`: Measures changes in the earth's magnetic field

- `TYPE_ORIENTATION` (deprecated): Measures the position of a device in the values of pitch, roll, and yaw

- `TYPE_ROTATION_VECTOR`: Measures the orientation of Glass as a combination of an angle and one of the three axes

You can also take a look at Table 1, "Sensor types supported by the Android platform," of the Android Sensors API Guide at `http://developer.android.com/guide/topics/sensors/sensors_overview.html` for an overview of each sensor listed and its common uses.

These sensors can be divided into hardware sensors and software sensors. Hardware sensors such as `ACCELEROMETER` and `GYROSCOPE` are physical components built into Glass. They derive their data by directly measuring specific environmental properties. Software sensors such as `ORIENTATION` derive their data from one or more of the hardware-based sensors.

Another more useful way to categorize the sensors, also from `http://developer.android.com/guide/topics/sensors/sensors_overview.html`, is based on how they are meant to be used.

- *Motion sensors*: These are used to monitor the motion of your Glass, and they include `ACCELEROMETER`, `GRAVITY`, `GYROSCOPE`, `LINEAR_ACCELERATION`, and `ROTATION_VECTOR`.

- *Position sensors*: These are used to determine the position of your Glass, and they include `MAGNETIC_FIELD` and `ORIENTATION`.

- *Environmental sensors*: These are used to monitor environmental properties such as light, pressure, temperature, and humidity. Glass supports only one environmental sensor: `LIGHT`.

> **Note**   If you wonder how you can use Glass to show more environmental data, you can use the Bluetooth technology, discussed in Chapter 7, and a Bluetooth Low Energe (BLE) device that supports temperature, pressure, and humidity, among other sensors. Texas Instruments' Sensor Tag, `www.ti.com/tool/cc2541dk-sensor`, is such a great device.

For a detailed explanation of what each Glass-supported sensor is used for (except the `ORIENTATION` sensor, which I'll discuss soon), go to Android's developer site at `http://developer.android.com/guide/topics/sensors/sensors_motion.html` and `http://developer.android.com/guide/topics/sensors/sensors_position.html`. It's time to see code in action!

Collecting Sensor Data

Let's create a new file called `SensorActivity.java`, as shown in Listing 8-5 and Listing 8-6, to the project, to see how each of the sensors supported by Glass collects its measured data.

Listing 8-5. Collecting and Displaying Sensor Data

```
public class SensorActivity extends Activity implements SensorEventListener {
    private static final String TAG = "SensorActivity";

    private SensorManager mSensorManager;

    private Sensor mSensorAccelerometer;
    private Sensor mSensorGravity;
```

```java
    private Sensor mSensorGyroscope;
    private Sensor mSensorLight;
    private Sensor mSensorLinearAcceleration;
    private Sensor mSensorMagneticField;
    private Sensor mSensorRotationVector;

    private static final int TYPE_ORIENTATION = 999;
    private int mSensorSelected;
    private Boolean mLogOn;
    private Date mSensorDataUpdatedTime;

    private TextView mTextView;
    private GestureDetector mGestureDetector;

    float[] mAccelerometer;
    float[] mGravity;
    float[] mGyroscope;
    float[] mLight;
    float[] mLinearAcceleration;
    float[] mMagneticField;
    float[] mOrientation;
    float[] mRotationVector;

    @Override
    public void onCreate(Bundle savedInstanceState) {
        super.onCreate(savedInstanceState);

        setContentView(R.layout.sensor);
        mTextView = (TextView) findViewById(R.id.tvSensor);
        mTextView.setText("Playing with Sensors");

        mLogOn = true;
        mSensorSelected = -1;
        getWindow().setFlags(WindowManager.LayoutParams.FLAG_KEEP_SCREEN_ON, WindowManager.
        LayoutParams.FLAG_KEEP_SCREEN_ON);

        mSensorManager = (SensorManager) getSystemService(Context.SENSOR_SERVICE); // #1
        mSensorAccelerometer = mSensorManager.getDefaultSensor(Sensor.TYPE_ACCELEROMETER);
        mSensorGravity = mSensorManager.getDefaultSensor(Sensor.TYPE_GRAVITY);
        mSensorGyroscope = mSensorManager.getDefaultSensor(Sensor.TYPE_GYROSCOPE);
        mSensorLight = mSensorManager.getDefaultSensor(Sensor.TYPE_LIGHT);
        mSensorLinearAcceleration = mSensorManager.getDefaultSensor
        (Sensor.TYPE_LINEAR_ACCELERATION);
        mSensorMagneticField = mSensorManager.getDefaultSensor(Sensor.TYPE_MAGNETIC_FIELD);
        mSensorRotationVector = mSensorManager.getDefaultSensor(Sensor.TYPE_ROTATION_VECTOR); // #2

        mGestureDetector = new GestureDetector(this);
```

```java
        mGestureDetector.setBaseListener(new GestureDetector.BaseListener() {
            @Override
            public boolean onGesture(Gesture gesture) {
                if (gesture == Gesture.TAP) {
                    openOptionsMenu();
                    return true;
                }
                return false;
            }
        });
    }

    public boolean onGenericMotionEvent(MotionEvent event) {
        if (mGestureDetector != null) {
            return mGestureDetector.onMotionEvent(event);
        }
        return false;
    }

    @Override
    public boolean onCreateOptionsMenu(Menu menu) {
        MenuInflater inflater = getMenuInflater();
        inflater.inflate(R.menu.sensors, menu);
        return true;
    }

    String display(float[] values) {
        return "\n" + values[0] + "\n" + values[1] + "\n" + values[2];
    }

    @Override
    public boolean onOptionsItemSelected(MenuItem item) {
        switch (item.getItemId()) {
        case R.id.logon:
            if (item.getTitle().equals("TURN LOG OFF")) {
                item.setTitle("TURN LOG ON");
                mLogOn = false;
            }
            else {
                item.setTitle("TURN LOG OFF");
                mLogOn = true;
            }
            return true;

        case R.id.accelerometer:
            mSensorSelected = Sensor.TYPE_ACCELEROMETER;
            if (mAccelerometer != null) mTextView.setText( getString(R.string.accelerometer) +
            ": " + display(mAccelerometer));
            return true;
```

```java
    case R.id.gravity:
        mSensorSelected = Sensor.TYPE_GRAVITY;
        if (mGravity != null) mTextView.setText( getString(R.string.gravity) + ": " +
        display(mGravity));
        return true;

    case R.id.gyroscope:
        mSensorSelected = Sensor.TYPE_GYROSCOPE;
        if (mGyroscope != null) mTextView.setText( getString(R.string.gyroscope) + ": " +
        display(mGyroscope));
        return true;

    case R.id.light:
        mSensorSelected = Sensor.TYPE_LIGHT;
        // The light sensor returns a single value.
        if (mLight != null) mTextView.setText( getString(R.string.light) + ": " + mLight[0]);
        return true;

    case R.id.linearacceleration:
        mSensorSelected = Sensor.TYPE_LINEAR_ACCELERATION;
        if (mLinearAcceleration != null) mTextView.setText( getString(R.string.
        linearacceleration) + ": " + display(mLinearAcceleration));
        return true;

    case R.id.magneticfield:
        mSensorSelected = Sensor.TYPE_MAGNETIC_FIELD;
        if (mMagneticField != null) mTextView.setText( getString(R.string.magneticfield) + ": "
        + display(mMagneticField));
        return true;

    case R.id.orientation:
        mSensorSelected = TYPE_ORIENTATION;
        if (mOrientation != null) mTextView.setText( getString(R.string.orientation) + ": \n" +
        "Yaw: " + mOrientation[0] + "°\n" + "Pitch: " + mOrientation[1] + "°\n" + "Roll:
        " + mOrientation[2] + "°");
        return true;

    case R.id.rotationvector:
        mSensorSelected = Sensor.TYPE_ROTATION_VECTOR;
        if (mRotationVector != null) mTextView.setText( getString(R.string.rotationvector) +
        ": " + display(mRotationVector));
        return true;

    default:
        return super.onOptionsItemSelected(item);
    }
}

protected void onStart() {
    super.onStart();
}
```

In the previous code, you declare a variable for each sensor, which gets initialized using a SensorManager instance's getDefaultSensor method (#1 to #2) in the activity's onCreate method. You also create menu items to let you test with the sensors. Because you'll get periodic sensor data updates, you send the WindowManager.LayoutParams.FLAG_KEEP_SCREEN_ON flag to getWindow(). setFlags so Glass won't turn off automatically when the user selects SENSORS.

Listing 8-6. Collecting and Displaying Sensor Data (Continued)

```
@Override
public final void onAccuracyChanged(Sensor sensor, int accuracy) {
    // Do something here if sensor accuracy changes.
}

@Override
public final void onSensorChanged(SensorEvent event) { // #3
    if (event.sensor.getType() == Sensor.TYPE_ACCELEROMETER) {
        mAccelerometer = event.values.clone();
        if (mLogOn && mSensorSelected == Sensor.TYPE_ACCELEROMETER) {
            if (new Date().getTime() - mSensorDataUpdatedTime.getTime() < 1000) return;
            mTextView.setText( getString(R.string.accelerator) + ": " + display(mAccelerometer));
            mSensorDataUpdatedTime = new Date();
        }
    }
    if (event.sensor.getType() == Sensor.TYPE_GRAVITY) {
        mGravity = event.values.clone();
        if (mLogOn && mSensorSelected == Sensor.TYPE_GRAVITY) {
            if (new Date().getTime() - mSensorDataUpdatedTime.getTime() < 1000) return;
            mTextView.setText( getString(R.string.gravity) + ": " + display(mGravity));
            mSensorDataUpdatedTime = new Date();
        }
    }
    if (event.sensor.getType() == Sensor.TYPE_GYROSCOPE) {
        mGyroscope = event.values.clone();
        if (mLogOn && mSensorSelected == Sensor.TYPE_GYROSCOPE) {
            if (new Date().getTime() - mSensorDataUpdatedTime.getTime() < 1000) return;
            mTextView.setText( getString(R.string.gyroscope) + ": " + display(mGyroscope));
            mSensorDataUpdatedTime = new Date();
        }
    }
    if (event.sensor.getType() == Sensor.TYPE_LIGHT) {
        mLight = event.values.clone();
        if (mLogOn && mSensorSelected == Sensor.TYPE_LIGHT) {
            if (new Date().getTime() - mSensorDataUpdatedTime.getTime() < 1000) return;
            mTextView.setText( getString(R.string.light) + ": " + mLight[0]);
            mSensorDataUpdatedTime = new Date();
        }
    }
}
```

```java
if (event.sensor.getType() == Sensor.TYPE_LINEAR_ACCELERATION) {
    mLinearAcceleration = event.values.clone();
    if (mLogOn && mSensorSelected == Sensor.TYPE_LINEAR_ACCELERATION) {
        if (new Date().getTime() - mSensorDataUpdatedTime.getTime() < 1000) return;
        mTextView.setText( getString(R.string.linearacceleration) + ": " +
        display(mLinearAcceleration));
        mSensorDataUpdatedTime = new Date();
    }
}
if (event.sensor.getType() == Sensor.TYPE_MAGNETIC_FIELD) {
    mMagneticField = event.values.clone();
    if (mLogOn && mSensorSelected == Sensor.TYPE_MAGNETIC_FIELD) {
        if (new Date().getTime() - mSensorDataUpdatedTime.getTime() < 1000) return;
        mTextView.setText( getString(R.string.magneticfield) + ": " + display(mMagneticField));
        mSensorDataUpdatedTime = new Date();
    }
}
// special handling for orientation // #4
if (mAccelerometer != null && mMagneticField != null) {
    float rotation[] = new float[16];
    float orientation[] = new float[3];
    boolean success = SensorManager.getRotationMatrix(rotation, orientation, mAccelerometer,
    mMagneticField);

    if (success) {
        mOrientation = new float[3];
        SensorManager.getOrientation(rotation, mOrientation);
        // orientation contains: azimuth, pitch and roll
        mOrientation[0] = 180 + (float) Math.toDegrees(mOrientation[0]);
        mOrientation[1] = 90 + (float) Math.toDegrees(mOrientation[1]);
        mOrientation[2] = (float) Math.toDegrees(mOrientation[2]);
        if (mLogOn && mSensorSelected == TYPE_ORIENTATION) {
            if (new Date().getTime() - mSensorDataUpdatedTime.getTime() < 1000) return;
            mTextView.setText( getString(R.string.orientation)
                    + ": \n" + "Yaw: " + mOrientation[0] + "°\n" + "Pitch: " + mOrientation[1] + "°\n"
                    + "Roll: " + mOrientation[2] + "°");
            mSensorDataUpdatedTime = new Date();
        }
    }
}
if (event.sensor.getType() == Sensor.TYPE_ROTATION_VECTOR) {
    mRotationVector = event.values.clone();
    if (mLogOn && mSensorSelected == Sensor.TYPE_ROTATION_VECTOR) {
        if (new Date().getTime() - mSensorDataUpdatedTime.getTime() < 1000) return;
        mTextView.setText( getString(R.string.rotationvector) + ": " +
        display(mRotationVector));
        mSensorDataUpdatedTime = new Date();
    }
}
}
```

```
@Override
protected void onResume() {
    super.onResume();
    mSensorManager.registerListener(this, mSensorAccelerometer, SensorManager.SENSOR_DELAY_NORMAL); // #5
    mSensorManager.registerListener(this, mSensorGravity, SensorManager.SENSOR_DELAY_NORMAL);
    mSensorManager.registerListener(this, mSensorGyroscope, SensorManager.SENSOR_DELAY_NORMAL);
    mSensorManager.registerListener(this, mSensorLight, SensorManager.SENSOR_DELAY_NORMAL);
    mSensorManager.registerListener(this, mSensorLinearAcceleration,
    SensorManager.SENSOR_DELAY_NORMAL);
    mSensorManager.registerListener(this, mSensorMagneticField, SensorManager.SENSOR_DELAY_NORMAL);
    mSensorManager.registerListener(this, mSensorRotationVector, SensorManager.SENSOR_DELAY_NORMAL);

    mSensorDataUpdatedTime = new Date();
}

@Override
protected void onPause() {
    super.onPause();
    mSensorManager.unregisterListener(this); // #6
}
}
```

In onResume, the sensor gets registered as a listener for the sensor manager, causing the methods in AccuracyChanged and onSensorChanged (#3) to be called for the sensor when the new accuracy of the sensor and the new sensor data are available, respectively.

In the onSensorChanged method, I used an instance variable called mSensorDataUpdatedTime to update the sensor data every one second; otherwise, the data will in most cases change too fast. Ideally, the sensor's sampling rate should be set when registering the listener. Android has supported passing any absolute value (in microseconds) since API Level 11 to replace SENSOR_DELAY_NORMAL, which specifies 0.2 seconds of sampling rate (other predefined values are SENSOR_DELAY_GAME for 20,000 microseconds, SENSOR_DELAY_UI for 60,000 microseconds, and SENSOR_DELAY_FASTEST for no delay at all). Unfortunately, as of XE 17.2, Glass still seems to have some bug. The passed value (for example 1,000,000 for 1 second) doesn't change the default sampling rate.

Most of the sensors return three values (one for each axis) in event.values, except the light sensor. Also, you shouldn't use TYPE_ORIENTATION directly like with other sensors because it's deprecated. Instead, treat orientation as a software sensor and get its data from the accelerator and magnetic field sensors. Code starting at #4 shows how to compute your Glass's orientation based on the rotation matrix of the accelerator and magnetic field sensor data. When SensorManager. getOrientation returns, mOrientation is filled with three interesting values in radians.

- ▪ mOrientation[0]: azimuth (yaw), rotation around the z-axis
- ▪ mOrientation[1]: pitch, rotation around the x-axis
- ▪ mOrientation[2]: roll, rotation around the y-axis

You should check out the following documentation about the Glass sensor coordinate system: https://developers.google.com/glass/develop/gdk/location-sensors#sensors. If you're unfamiliar with yaw, pitch, and roll, you'll have to check out the three wonderful animated GIFs for them at http://en.wikipedia.org/wiki/Aircraft_principal_axes. Then when you run and play with the sample app, those changed values will all make sense.

Also, using the software-based ROTATION_VECTOR sensor, you can get the yaw, pitch, and roll values. But ROTATION_VECTOR also takes the gyroscope, in addition to the accelerator and magnetic field sensors, into consideration, so the readings from the ROTATION_VECTOR sensor are more accurate (although in normal cases, the previous orientation readings are good enough).

I also used a TURN LOG ON/OFF menu item for easier debugging. By default it's on, meaning sensor data will continue to be displayed on the Glass screen. If it's turned off, then the updated data will show on Glass only if you select one of the sensors again.

Finally, in the onPause method, you must call the sensor manager's unregisterListener method. Otherwise, your sensors will continue to acquire data and drain your battery quickly. In fact, if you've been testing the sensor data for a few minutes, more likely you'll see a message showing on your Glass saying "Glass must cool down to run smoothly." In a real app you should unregister a sensor's listener as soon as you're done using it.

Now do all the little things you've done in previous chapters to get your app ready for running by following these steps:

1. Create a layout sensor.xml.

```xml
<?xml version="1.0" encoding="utf-8"?>
<FrameLayout xmlns:android="http://schemas.android.com/apk/res/android"
    android:layout_width="match_parent"
    android:layout_height="match_parent"
    android:background="@color/black" >

    <TextView
        android:id="@+id/tvSensor"
        android:layout_width="match_parent"
        android:layout_height="match_parent"
        android:layout_gravity="center"
        android:layout_marginTop="-10px"
        android:gravity="center"
        android:textSize="60px" />
</FrameLayout>
```

2. Create a menu sensor.xml.

```xml
<?xml version="1.0" encoding="utf-8"?>
<menu xmlns:android="http://schemas.android.com/apk/res/android" >

    <item
        android:id="@+id/logon"
        android:title="@string/logon"/>
```

```xml
    <item
        android:id="@+id/accelerator"
        android:title="@string/accelerator"/>
    <item
        android:id="@+id/gravity"
        android:title="@string/gravity"/>
    <item
        android:id="@+id/gyroscope"
        android:title="@string/gyroscope"/>
    <item
        android:id="@+id/light"
        android:title="@string/light"/>
    <item
        android:id="@+id/linearacceleration"
        android:title="@string/linearacceleration"/>
    <item
        android:id="@+id/magneticfield"
        android:title="@string/magneticfield"/>
    <item
        android:id="@+id/orientation"
        android:title="@string/orientation"/>
    <item
        android:id="@+id/rotationvector"
        android:title="@string/rotationvector"/>

</menu>
```

3. Update strings.xml.

```xml
<string name="sensor">SENSORS</string>
<string name="logon">TURN OFF LOG</string>
<string name="accelerator">ACCELERATOR</string>
<string name="gravity">GRAVITY</string>
<string name="gyroscope">GYROSCOPE</string>
<string name="light">LIGHT</string>
<string name="linearacceleration">LINEAR ACCELERATION</string>
<string name="magneticfield">MAGNETIC FIELD</string>
<string name="orientation">ORIENTATION</string>
<string name="rotationvector">ROTATION VECTOR</string>
```

4. Add a new item sensor in menu's main.xml, update MenuActivity.java to add a new switch case for the sensor item to start SensorActivity, and finally add the activity in AndroidManifest.xml.

Now run the app on your Glass and say "OK Glass" and then "Location sensors." Then select SENSORS, and you'll see the text "Playing with Sensors." Tap to see the menu item TURN OFF LOG and the list of all the eight Glass-supported sensors. Swipe forward to choose ORIENTATION; you'll see the data updated every one second. If you look straight ahead and then raise your head a little, you'll see the pitch value change, as shown in Figure 8-3.

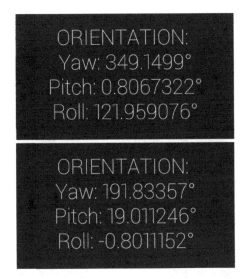

Figure 8-3. Showing Orientation's pitch value change

You can use Glass's built-in "Head wake-up" Settings to test together with the app on the pitch change. First set a new wake-up from Settings, then keep your head position unchanged, and finally select the ORIENTATION item. You should see the similar degree value in Pitch. Notice that you can set your wake-up angle to a value between 10 and 40 only, but in this app, you can raise your head as high or low as possible!

For the test of yaw and roll value changes, it's better to put your Glass on a desk and either use your Android/iOS MyGlass app's screencast or the desktop screencast app like ASM, which I covered in Chapter 2, to see the sensor data updates. Figure 8-4 shows my Glass before and after I turn it to the right about 90 degrees; notice the Yaw value change.

Figure 8-4. Showing Orientation's Yaw value change

Figure 8-5 shows the Roll value change before and after I lift the left side of Glass.

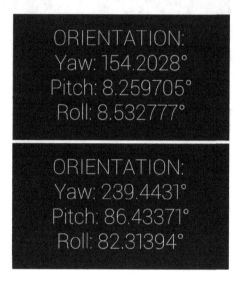

Figure 8-5. *Showing Orientation's Roll value change*

Interesting uses of pitch, yaw, and roll value changes can be built into game apps, education apps, healthcare apps, or entertainment apps to detect the head movement of a user and act accordingly.

You should play with all the other sensors and see how those values change. If you have read Android's sensor developer guides listed earlier, you may understand what each value for each sensor means; still, seeing working samples with code helps a lot. If you don't know for sure what those sensors and data are for, don't worry. More examples and explanation about the code are coming. But you should check out the SensorEvent values reference at http://developer.android.com/reference/android/hardware/SensorEvent.html#values to understand what each value means.

Shake It or Not

Chances are you have seen some Android or iOS app that can detect the shake of your smartphone. The popular WeChat app, for example, has a well-known feature called Shake that allows two people at the same place to shake their phones at the same time to easily find and add each other as friends. It turns out that detecting shake is quite simple using the ACCELEROMETER sensor. Follow these steps to see how it works:

1. In SensorActivity.java, add two new instance variables to keep track of the time the last shake was detected and the number of shakes.

    ```
    private long lastUpdate;
    private int count;
    ```

2. In onCreate, initialize the two variables.

    ```
    lastUpdate = System.currentTimeMillis();
    count = 1;
    ```

3. In onSensorChanged, add the following code after if (mLogOn &&
    mSensorSelected == Sensor.TYPE_ACCELEROMETER) { ... }:

```
else if (!mLogOn && mSensorSelected == Sensor.TYPE_ACCELEROMETER)
    getAccelerometer(event);
```

4. Add a new function as follows:

```
private void getAccelerometer(SensorEvent event) {
    float[] values = event.values;
    float x = values[0];
    float y = values[1];
    float z = values[2];

    float accelation = (x * x + y * y + z * z)
            / (SensorManager.GRAVITY_EARTH *
                SensorManager.GRAVITY_EARTH);
    long actualTime = System.currentTimeMillis();
    if (accelation >=1.2)
// 2 is a big movement of head on Glass! 1 is too sensitive. 1.2 is a good one.
    {
        if (actualTime - lastUpdate < 200) return;
        lastUpdate = actualTime;
        mTextView.setText("Glass Shaked #" + (count++));
    }
}
```

That's it. Run the app and select SENSORS, TURN LOG OFF, and ACCELEROMETER. Now play
with shaking your head fast and slow, and you'll see "Glass Shaked #1," "Glass Shaked #2," and so
on, on your Glass. If you shake fast, you'll see the count number increases by 2 instead of 1. If you
shake Glass too slow, you may not get a new shake count because of the line if (actualTime -
lastUpdate < 200) return;.

Detecting Metal

You can use the MAGNETIC_FIELD sensor, which can be influenced by nearby metal, to turn your Glass
into a metal detector (although the accuracy is not that high). Just follow these steps to try it:

1. Add the following code after if (mLogOn && mSensorSelected == Sensor.
    TYPE_MAGNETIC_FIELD) {...} in onSensorChanged of SensorActivity.java:

```
else if (!mLogOn && mSensorSelected == Sensor.TYPE_MAGNETIC_FIELD)
    getMagneticField(event);
```

2. Add the following method, also in SensorActivity.java:

```
private void getMagneticField(SensorEvent event) {
    if (LocationActivity.getCurrentLocation() == null) {
        mTextView.setText("Go Get Location First");
        return;
    }
```

```
        float[] values = event.values;
        float x = values[0];
        float y = values[1];
        float z = values[2];

        // get the intensity of the magnetic field (the magnitude of the magnetic field
        vector squared)
        float mag = (x * x + y * y + z * z);

        GeomagneticField geoField = new GeomagneticField(
                (float) LocationActivity.getCurrentLocation().getLatitude(),
                (float) LocationActivity.getCurrentLocation().getLongitude(),
                (float) LocationActivity.getCurrentLocation().getAltitude(),
                LocationActivity.getCurrentLocation().getTime());

        // get the expected value of the magnetic field at current location
        float expectedMag = (float) Math.sqrt(geoField.getX() + geoField.getY() +
                            geoField.getZ());

        if (mag > 1.4*expectedMag || mag < 0.6*expectedMag)
            mTextView.setText("Possible Metal Nearby");
        else
            mTextView.setText("No Metal Nearby");
    }
```

3. Add the following method (and modify the declaration of mLocation in the
   class as static) to LocationManager.java:

```
public static Location getCurrentLocation() {
    return mLocation;
}
```

After you run the app, you need to select LOCATION first to get the current location and then go
to SENSORS, select TURN LOG OFF, and finally select MAGNETIC FIELD. You should see the
message "No Metal Nearby." Now move your iOS or Android device close to your Glass, and you
should see "Possible Metal Nearby." You should experiment with the values 1.4 and 0.6 in the code
to see what values work better. But you shouldn't expect to see that metal detection works on Glass
all the time. Still, the example code here shows you how to use the MAGNETIC FIELD sensor and the
GeomagneticField class. A more complicated way of using GeomagneticField for a more accurate
sensor application is to build a compass app for Glass.

Developing a Compass

Google offers a GDK Compass sample, which I mentioned in Chapter 2 and you probably have
already checked out. If you haven't, stop now and follow the steps in the "Testing ADT with GDK
Samples" of Chapter 2 to import the Compass project, because you'll need to reuse one utility file in

the project. Its source code is well designed, so what if you want to add the compass feature to the example app? What sensor should you use and what minimal code do you need to port to make it happen? Just follow these steps:

1. In `SensorActivity.java`, add the following lines before `onCreate`:

```java
private final float[] mRotationMatrix = new float[16];
private GeomagneticField mGeomagneticField;
final static float ALPHA = 0.25f;
```

2. In `onCreate`, add the following:

```java
if (LocationActivity.getCurrentLocation() != null) {
mGeomagneticField = new GeomagneticField(
    (float) LocationActivity.getCurrentLocation().getLatitude(),
    (float) LocationActivity.getCurrentLocation().getLongitude(),
    (float) LocationActivity.getCurrentLocation().getAltitude(),
    LocationActivity.getCurrentLocation().getTime());
}
```

3. In your old friend `onSensorChanged`, in the "`if (event.sensor.getType() == Sensor.TYPE_ROTATION_VECTOR)`" statement, replace the following:

```java
mTextView.setText( getString(R.string.rotationvector) + ": " + display(mRotationVector));
```

with the following:

```java
showCompassReading(event);
```

4. Add the following code at the end of `SensorActivity`:

```java
private void showCompassReading(SensorEvent event) {
    if (LocationActivity.getCurrentLocation() == null) {
        mTextView.setText("Go Get Location First");
        return;
    }

    // for reference of getRotationMatrixFromVector and remapCoordinateSystem, see
    // http://developer.android.com/reference/android/hardware/SensorManager.html
    SensorManager.getRotationMatrixFromVector(mRotationMatrix, event.values);
    SensorManager.remapCoordinateSystem(mRotationMatrix, SensorManager.AXIS_X,
    SensorManager.AXIS_Z, mRotationMatrix);
    SensorManager.getOrientation(mRotationMatrix, mOrientation);

    // Convert the heading (which is relative to magnetic north) to one that is
    // relative to true north, using the user's current location to compute this.
    float magneticHeading = (float) Math.toDegrees(mOrientation[0]);
    float heading = MathUtils.mod(computeTrueNorth(magneticHeading), 360.0f) - 6;
    mTextView.setText(""+heading);
}
```

```
// Use the magnetic field to compute true (geographic) north from the specified heading
relative to magnetic north.
private float computeTrueNorth(float heading) {
    if (mGeomagneticField != null)
        return heading + mGeomagneticField.getDeclination();
    else return heading;
}
```

5. Copy the `MathUtils.java` file from the GDK Compass sample project to your project.

Now launch the app and select the LOCATION menu item to get current location data first because it's needed when creating a new `GeomagneticField` instance. Then select SENSORS and ROTATION VECTOR (the last item in the sensor list) and move your head. You'll see on your Glass different numbers, close to 0 when you face north, increased to about 90 when you face east, 180 when you face south, and 270 when you face west. I'll leave it as an exercise for you to convert those numbers to a text string such as "329 degree North, Northwest" or "1 degree North." Hint: Check out the `readHeadingAloud` method in `CompasService.java` of the Compass sample.

Finding the Planets

Because of space and time limitations, I won't discuss in detail how those pretty amazing planet-finding Android or iOS apps work and how you can use Glass to achieve the same thing. Follow these steps to build such an app. You should at least spend some time exploring the planet-finding app to be amazed by the earth we live in, the solar system, and the galaxy.

1. Understand right ascension and declination, which are the celestial equivalent of, and comparable to, our familiar geographic longitude and latitude. The URLs http://en.wikipedia.org/wiki/Right_ascension and http://en.wikipedia.org/wiki/Declination will help.

2. Check out the open source Android project at https://github.com/timgaddis/Planets-Position or the iOS project at https://github.com/paulgriffiths/planet-position to find out how to calculate each planet's right ascension and declination.

3. Use your current location (latitude and longitude) and time, combined with right ascension and declination, to get each planet's altitude and azimuth from your current observation location.

4. Use the `ORIENTATION` (`ACCELEROMETER` and `MAGNETIC_FIELD`) and `GYROSCOPE` sensor readings to get your orientation data (pitch, roll, and yaw) when you move your Glass toward the sky. The `GYROSCOPE` sensor is used in combination with `ORIENTATION` to let you respond quickly to your movements with more accurate readings.

5. Convert each planet's right ascension and declination to the pitch and roll values at your current location and date and time and then find out whether you're moving Glass closer to any of the planets.

Summary

In this chapter, I discussed in detail how to get your current location and show its address and map, how to zoom in and out the map, and how to find nearby business information based on your location information. Then I covered the eight sensors Glass supports and how to detect head movement and direction, how to detect Glass shake, how to develop a metal detector, and how to add the compass support easily to your app. Finally, I outlined the steps to build a planet-finder Glass app.

Chapter **9**

Graphics, Animation, and Games

On April 15, 2014, Google released a major update of Glass, XE 16, and five cool Glass mini-games were introduced. If you haven't tried them (`https://developers.google.com/glass/samples/mini-games`), you should definitely check them out. (Another nice Glass game released with GDK Sneak Peak in November 2013 is called Spellista, available to download at `https://glass.google.com/u/0/glassware`.) Here's what Google has to say about the five games on the Mini Games page: "With tons of tiny sensors and a screen that you can always see, we think Google Glass is an exciting new place to play… We hope our experiments inspire you to take a closer look at the Glass platform and build awesome Glassware." It's exactly what you'll do in this chapter: take a closer look at the Glass platform in the game context, do some reverse engineering, and explore common game techniques and engines.

There are already many books on Android graphics, animation, and game programming; what I'll focus on here is to show you plenty of examples and popular game engines on Glass so you can get a feeling for game development on Glass. Here is what I'll cover in this chapter:

- Graphics APIs and examples to be used in games

- Animation APIs and examples to be used in games

- How to port and use one of the most popular open source C++-based cross-platform game engines, Cocos2d-x, on Glass

- How to use another popular cross-platform game engine, libgdx, on Glass

- How to test an all Java-based Android game engine, AndEngine, on Glass

- How to port an existing Android game to Glass, with the added support of using head movement to play the game

By the end of the chapter, you'll know some of the common building blocks for game apps, be familiar with setting up and running popular open source game engines on Glass, and understand how to use head movement, or a combination of it with touch events, to control game UI. Essentially, you'll be ready to develop your own exciting Glass games.

Graphics

If you're an Android developer, you probably have checked out the ApiDemos sample project, which is full of examples of graphics and animation, among other things. If you haven't, you can first install Samples for SDK from the Android SDK Manager. Then in Eclipse, go to File ➤ New ➤ Project ➤ Android ➤ Android Sample Project, and select legacy ➤ ApiDemos. After that, run it on an emulator or a non-Glass Android device if you own one. In this section, I'll choose some typical graphics examples from the ApiDemos project and port them to Glass. Most of the code will simply work on Glass, but you'll need to add some Glass-specific touch event handling code to make some examples work on XE 17 or newer.

> **Note**   In XE 12, UI element touch and navigation for an Android app may just work fine when the app runs on Glass. But since XE 16, touch and swipe left and right gestures on an Android app running on Glass is most likely broken. You can't select or navigate like you can on a non-Glass Android device, so you have to add specific code to make touch and swipe events work on Glass.

While going through the following examples, you should also check out the Android API Guides on Graphics at http://developer.android.com/guide/topics/graphics/2d-graphics.html and http://developer.android.com/guide/topics/graphics/opengl.html to get a deeper understanding of the Graphics API.

Canvas Drawing

Let's create a new project called GraphicsAnimationApp based on the GlasswareTemplate (you can also import the completed project from the book's source code). Now copy the `Arcs.java` file from ApiDemos's `com.example.android.apis.graphics` folder to the app, and change the following line:

```
public class Arcs extends GraphicsActivity
```

to the following:

```
public class Arcs extends Activity
```

Listing 9-1 shows the main code snippet.

Listing 9-1. Using the Canvas API to Draw Arcs and Rectangles

```
private void drawArcs(Canvas canvas, RectF oval, boolean useCenter,
                      Paint paint) {
    canvas.drawRect(oval, mFramePaint);
    canvas.drawArc(oval, mStart, mSweep, useCenter, paint);
}

@Override protected void onDraw(Canvas canvas) {
    canvas.drawColor(Color.WHITE);
```

```
drawArcs(canvas, mBigOval, mUseCenters[mBigIndex],
        mPaints[mBigIndex]);

for (int i = 0; i < 4; i++) {
    drawArcs(canvas, mOvals[i], mUseCenters[i], mPaints[i]);
}

mSweep += SWEEP_INC;
if (mSweep > 360) {
    mSweep -= 360;
    mStart += START_INC;
    if (mStart >=360) {
        mStart -= 360;
    }
    mBigIndex = (mBigIndex + 1) % mOvals.length;
}
invalidate();
}
```

The `invalidate()` method in `onDraw` generates the animation effect by calling `drawArcs` with different `mStart` and `mSweep` parameters for Android Canvas class's `drawArc` API call; the same animation effect is used in the Glass mini-game Matcher. The reference of the Canvas class is at `http://developer.android.com/reference/android/graphics/Canvas.html`.

Now update the GraphicsAnimationApp project's `menu/main.xml`, `strings.xml`, `MenuActivity.java`, and `AndroidManifest.xml` files, as you've done many times in previous chapters. You may want to make the `strings.xml` file look like this:

```
<resources>
    <string name="app_name">GraphicsAnimatiom</string>
    <string name="say_glasswaretemplate">Graphics Animation</string>
    <string name="graphics_arcs">Graphics Arcs</string>
    <string name="graphics_shape">Graphics Shapes</string>
    <string name="graphics_paint">Graphics Paint</string>
    <string name="graphics_bitmap">Graphics Bitmap</string>
    <string name="opengles_cube">OpenGLES Cube</string>
    <string name="opengles_kube">OpenGLES Kube</string>
    <string name="opengles_rotate">OpenGLES Rotate</string>
    <string name="rotationvector">Rotation Vector</string>
    <string name="animation">Animation</string>
    <string name="stop">STOP</string>
</resources>
```

Install the app on Glass and run it by selecting Graphics Animation. Tap to reveal the menu and select Graphics Arcs; you'll see rectangles and an animated arc drawing, as shown in Figure 9-1. Swipe down on the touchpad to exit the activity.

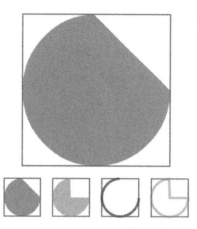

Figure 9-1. Canvas-based drawing

Drawable Shapes

Another way to draw 2D graphics is by using a ShapeDrawable object, an extension of Drawable. This gives you the benefit of using a ShapeDrawable object anywhere a Drawable object is expected, such as a View's background. The second example draws various primitive shapes based on the ShapeDrawable class (http://developer.android.com/reference/android/graphics/drawable/ShapeDrawable.html). Copy the ShapeDrawable1.java file from ApiDemos to GraphicsAnimationApp, change the base class from GraphicsActivity to Activity as you did in the previous example, update the menu's XML file, update the MenuActivity.java file, and update the AndroidManifest.xml file. Listing 9-2 shows the main code snippet, and Figure 9-2 shows what you see after running on Glass and selecting Graphics Shapes.

Listing 9-2. Using the ShapeDrawable API to Draw Shapes

```
private static class MyShapeDrawable extends ShapeDrawable {
    private Paint mStrokePaint = new Paint(Paint.ANTI_ALIAS_FLAG);
    ...
    @Override
    protected void onDraw(Shape s, Canvas c, Paint p) {
        s.draw(c, p);
        s.draw(c, mStrokePaint);
    }
}

mDrawables = new ShapeDrawable[7];
mDrawables[0] = new ShapeDrawable(new RectShape());
mDrawables[1] = new ShapeDrawable(new OvalShape());
mDrawables[2] = new ShapeDrawable(new RoundRectShape(outerR, null, null));
mDrawables[3] = new ShapeDrawable(new RoundRectShape(outerR, inset, null));
mDrawables[4] = new ShapeDrawable(new RoundRectShape(outerR, inset, innerR));
mDrawables[5] = new ShapeDrawable(new PathShape(path, 100, 100));
mDrawables[6] = new MyShapeDrawable(new ArcShape(45, -270));
```

```
mDrawables[0].getPaint().setColor(0xFFFF0000);
...
mDrawables[5].getPaint().setShader(makeTiling());
mDrawables[6].getPaint().setColor(0x88FF8844);

PathEffect pe = new DiscretePathEffect(10, 4);
PathEffect pe2 = new CornerPathEffect(4);
mDrawables[3].getPaint().setPathEffect(
        new ComposePathEffect(pe2, pe));

MyShapeDrawable msd = (MyShapeDrawable)mDrawables[6];
msd.getStrokePaint().setStrokeWidth(4);
....

for (Drawable dr : mDrawables) {
    dr.setBounds(x, y, x + width, y + height);
    dr.draw(canvas);
    y += height + 5;
}
```

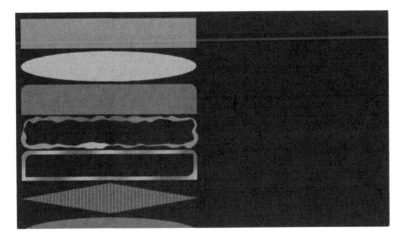

Figure 9-2. ShapeDrawable-based drawing

Finger Painting

Let's see an example that requires user interaction so you can learn what it takes to do it on Glass. This time, copy the FingerPaint.java file from the ApiDemos project, change the base class to Activity again, and then make the following changes:

1. Add the following two lines in the FingerPaint class:

    ```
    private GestureDetector mGestureDetector;
    private MyView myView;
    ```

2. In onCreate, replace setContentView(new MyView(this)); with the following:

```
myView = new MyView(this);
setContentView(myView);
```

3. At the end of onCreate, add the following:

```
mGestureDetector = createGestureDetector(this);
Toast.makeText(FingerPaint.this, "Two fingers tap to exit", Toast.LENGTH_LONG).show();
```

4. Add the following code after onCreate:

```
private GestureDetector createGestureDetector(Context context) {
    GestureDetector gestureDetector = new GestureDetector(context);
    gestureDetector.setBaseListener( new GestureDetector.BaseListener() {
        @Override
        public boolean onGesture(Gesture gesture) {
            // disable the default swipe down exiting the activity
            if (gesture == Gesture.SWIPE_DOWN) return true;
            else return false;
        }
    });

    return gestureDetector;
}

public boolean onGenericMotionEvent(MotionEvent e) {
    // two-finger tap exits the activiity
    if ((e.getAction() & MotionEvent.ACTION_MASK) == MotionEvent.ACTION_POINTER_DOWN) {
        finish();
        return true;
    }

    // pass touch event to the view's event handler!
    myView.onTouchEvent(e);

    if (mGestureDetector != null)
        return mGestureDetector.onMotionEvent(e);
    else return false;
}
```

Listing 9-3 shows the main code snippet that does the finger drawing, using the Canvas API again.

Listing 9-3. Using the Canvas API and Touch Event Handling to Do Finger Painting

```
protected void onDraw(Canvas canvas) {
    canvas.drawColor(0xFFAAAAAA);
    canvas.drawBitmap(mBitmap, 0, 0, mBitmapPaint);
    canvas.drawPath(mPath, mPaint);
}

private float mX, mY;
private static final float TOUCH_TOLERANCE = 4;
```

```java
public void touch_start(float x, float y) {
    mPath.reset();
    mPath.moveTo(x, y);
    mX = x;
    mY = y;
}
public void touch_move(float x, float y) {
    float dx = Math.abs(x - mX);
    float dy = Math.abs(y - mY);
    if (dx >=TOUCH_TOLERANCE || dy >=TOUCH_TOLERANCE) {
        mPath.quadTo(mX, mY, (x + mX)/2, (y + mY)/2);
        mX = x;
        mY = y;
    }
}
public void touch_up() {
    mPath.lineTo(mX, mY);
    // commit the path to our offscreen
    mCanvas.drawPath(mPath, mPaint);
    // kill this so we don't double draw
    mPath.reset();
}

@Override
public boolean onTouchEvent(MotionEvent event) {
    float x = event.getX();
    float y = event.getY();

    switch (event.getAction()) {
    case MotionEvent.ACTION_DOWN:
        touch_start(x, y);
        invalidate();
        break;
    case MotionEvent.ACTION_MOVE:
        touch_move(x, y);
        invalidate();
        break;
    case MotionEvent.ACTION_UP:
        touch_up();
        invalidate();
        break;
    }
    return true;
}
```

Now run the app, select Graphics Paint, and draw something with your finger, as shown in Figure 9-3.

Figure 9-3. Freehand drawing

The original FingerPaint app also supports menus for color selection, erase, and other operations. You may want to improve the app to implement those features on Glass.

Bitmap Manipulation

Manipulating bitmaps is a common task in image-related apps, and you'll see in this section a simple example of modifying a bitmap with your finger movement on Glass. Let's copy BitmapMesh.java to the project and, in BitmapMesh.java, replace beach.jpg with pet.jpg, which is contained in the book's source code. Then add the following code in the class SampleView to enable a touch event on Glass:

```
public boolean onGenericMotionEvent(MotionEvent e) {
    if ((e.getAction() & MotionEvent.ACTION_MASK) == MotionEvent.ACTION_POINTER_DOWN) {
        ((BitmapMesh)mContext).finish();
        return true;
    }

    onTouchEvent(e);
    return true;
}
```

Now add private Context mContext; in the beginning of SampleView and add mContext = context; in the SampleView constructor. Listing 9-4 shows the main graphics-related code snippet.

Listing 9-4. Manipulating and Drawing a Bitmap

```
@Override protected void onDraw(Canvas canvas) {
    canvas.drawColor(0xFFCCCCCC);

    canvas.concat(mMatrix);
    canvas.drawBitmapMesh(mBitmap, WIDTH, HEIGHT, mVerts, 0,
                          null, 0, null);
}
```

```java
private void warp(float cx, float cy) {
    final float K = 10000;
    float[] src = mOrig;
    float[] dst = mVerts;
    for (int i = 0; i < COUNT*2; i += 2) {
        float x = src[i+0];
        float y = src[i+1];
        float dx = cx - x;
        float dy = cy - y;
        float dd = dx*dx + dy*dy;
        float d = FloatMath.sqrt(dd);
        float pull = K / (dd + 0.000001f);

        pull /= (d + 0.000001f);
        if (pull >=1) {
            dst[i+0] = cx;
            dst[i+1] = cy;
        } else {
            dst[i+0] = x + dx * pull;
            dst[i+1] = y + dy * pull;
        }
    }
}

@Override public boolean onTouchEvent(MotionEvent event) {
    float[] pt = { event.getX(), event.getY() };
    mInverse.mapPoints(pt);

    int x = (int)pt[0];
    int y = (int)pt[1];
    if (mLastWarpX != x || mLastWarpY != y) {
        mLastWarpX = x;
        mLastWarpY = y;
        warp(pt[0], pt[1]);
        invalidate();
    }
    return true;
}
```

After other regular setup (update the menu XML file, MenuActivity.java, and AndroidManifest.xml), run the app, and select Graphics Bitmap; you can then move around the touchpad to see the bitmap mesh. Figure 9-4 shows the original and meshed bitmaps. Notice the change in the dog's eye. Again, a two-finger tap will close the activity.

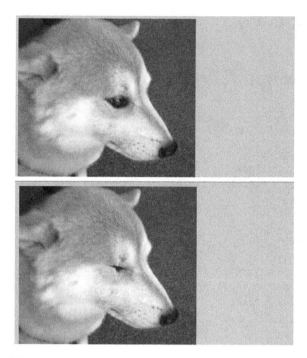

Figure 9-4. Original and meshed bitmaps

If you're interested, you should explore the drawBitmapxxx methods yourself and see how to implement a Glass app with the image-filtering features like those in Instagram.

OpenGL ES Drawing

OpenGL ES is an amazing topic but beyond the scope of this book. However, let's take a look at a few more examples of OpenGL ES rendering on Glass and how to interact with them using the Glass touchpad and the cool rotation vector sensor, which will be a key sensor to Glass game apps.

First, copy the CubeMapActivity.java file and the whole com.example.android.apis.graphics.kube folder from ApiDemos to the GraphicsAnimationApp project. Add two menu entries, OpenGLES Cube and OpenGLES Kube, to launch CubeMapActivity and Kube, respectively. Run your app and select the two menu items, and you'll see the two nice 3D animated images, as shown in Figure 9-5.

Figure 9-5. OpenGL ES drawing

Finger and Head Movement Support

Now copy two other files, TouchRotateActivity.java and Cube.java, at the end of TouchRotateActivity class, and add this method:

```
public boolean onGenericMotionEvent(MotionEvent e) {
    // this allows two-finger tap to exit the activity
    if ((e.getAction() & MotionEvent.ACTION_MASK) == MotionEvent.ACTION_POINTER_DOWN) {
        finish();
        return true;
    }

    // this enables the surfaceview to handle touch event
    mGLSurfaceView.onTouchEvent(e);
    return true;
}
```

Add a new menu entry, OpenGLES Rotate, to launch the activity. Run GraphicsAnimationApp and select OpenGLES Rotate. Touch and move on the Glass touchpad, and you'll see a cube rotating with your finger movement, as shown in Figure 9-6. (Again, to exit the activity, use a two-finger swipe down.)

Figure 9-6. Rotating a cube with finger movement on a touchpad or head movement

The next and final graphics example is even cooler. Copy the RotationVectorDemo.java file to your project. You should check out http://developer.android.com/guide/topics/graphics/opengl.html and get some OpenGL ES for Android books (for example, Pro OpenGL ES for Android by Mike Smithwick and Mayank Verma or OpenGL ES 2 for Android by Kevin Brothaler) to understand the OpenGL ES code in the example (and other examples in this section), but you've already seen the sensor-related code, shown in Listing 9-5, in the previous chapter, which will also be used later in the chapter.

Listing 9-5. Rotating Graphics with Glass Sensor

```
public class RotationVectorDemo extends Activity {
    private GLSurfaceView mGLSurfaceView;
    private SensorManager mSensorManager;
    private MyRenderer mRenderer;
```

```java
@Override
protected void onCreate(Bundle savedInstanceState) {
    super.onCreate(savedInstanceState);

    mSensorManager = (SensorManager)getSystemService(SENSOR_SERVICE);

    mRenderer = new MyRenderer();
    mGLSurfaceView = new GLSurfaceView(this);
    mGLSurfaceView.setRenderer(mRenderer);
    setContentView(mGLSurfaceView);
}

class MyRenderer implements GLSurfaceView.Renderer, SensorEventListener {
    private Cube mCube;
    private Sensor mRotationVectorSensor;
    private final float[] mRotationMatrix = new float[16];

    public MyRenderer() {
        // find the rotation-vector sensor
        mRotationVectorSensor = mSensorManager.getDefaultSensor(Sensor.TYPE_ROTATION_VECTOR);

        mCube = new Cube();
        // initialize the rotation matrix to identity
        mRotationMatrix[ 0] = 1;
        mRotationMatrix[ 4] = 1;
        mRotationMatrix[ 8] = 1;
        mRotationMatrix[12] = 1;
    }

    public void start() {
        // enable our sensor when the activity is resumed, ask for
        // 10 ms updates.
        mSensorManager.registerListener(this, mRotationVectorSensor, 10000);
    }

    public void stop() {
        // make sure to turn our sensor off when the activity is paused
        mSensorManager.unregisterListener(this);
    }

    public void onSensorChanged(SensorEvent event) {
        if (event.sensor.getType() == Sensor.TYPE_ROTATION_VECTOR) {
            SensorManager.getRotationMatrixFromVector(mRotationMatrix , event.values);
        }
    }
    ...

}
}
```

The rotation vector sensor is a composite (also known as software) sensor because it uses three base sensors (accelerometer, gyroscope, and magnetometer) to measure the orientation (yaw, pitch, and roll) of a device. For more information, you should check out Chapter 8 and additional Android resources at `https://source.android.com/devices/sensors/composite_sensors.html` and `http://developer.android.com/guide/topics/sensors/sensors_overview.html`. In a game example later in this chapter, you'll see how to use the measurement of rotation vector to display a cursor that moves with your Glass movement. This is the basis of a Glass game like Spellista.

To get a feeling of how your head movement can control the rotation of the 3D cube, simply run your app and select the Rotation Vector menu item; then move your head, and you'll see all six sides of a cube, just like Figure 9-5.

Animation

Animation is essential to game development. Google has a well-written API guide on the animation topic at `http://developer.android.com/guide/topics/graphics/prop-animation.html`, and ApiDemos has many animation examples. In the first example of the "Graphics" section, you already saw some animation in action, but the animation there was implemented using the `invalidate()` call inside onDraw.

In this section, I'll show you how property animation, the recommended and much more powerful animation framework that allows you to easily animate any object property, works. If you're not familiar with Android animation, you may want to take a quick look at the API guide link listed earlier before continuing. When you're ready, follow the steps in the next section.

Animating Properties in XML and Programmatically

Create a new AndroidAnimation activity, with the following layout file, named as animation.xml:

```xml
<?xml version="1.0" encoding="utf-8"?>
<LinearLayout xmlns:android="http://schemas.android.com/apk/res/android"
    android:layout_width="fill_parent"
    android:layout_height="fill_parent"
    android:orientation="vertical" >

    <LinearLayout
        android:layout_width="wrap_content"
        android:layout_height="wrap_content"
        android:orientation="horizontal" >

        <ImageView
            android:id="@+id/image1"
            android:layout_width="wrap_content"
            android:layout_height="wrap_content"
            android:src="@drawable/icon"
            android:visibility="visible" />

        <ImageView
            android:id="@+id/image2"
            android:layout_width="wrap_content"
            android:layout_height="wrap_content"
            android:src="@drawable/icon"
            android:visibility="visible" />
```

```
        <ImageView
            android:id="@+id/image3"
            android:layout_width="wrap_content"
            android:layout_height="wrap_content"
            android:src="@drawable/icon"
            android:visibility="visible" />
        <TextView
            android:id="@+id/mytextview"
            android:layout_width="wrap_content"
            android:layout_height="wrap_content"
            android:text="@string/hello" />
    </LinearLayout>

    <ImageView
        android:id="@+id/image4"
        android:layout_width="fill_parent"
        android:layout_height="wrap_content"
        android:src="@drawable/icon"
        android:visibility="invisible" />

    <ImageView
        android:id="@+id/image5"
        android:layout_width="fill_parent"
        android:layout_height="wrap_content"
        android:src="@drawable/icon"
        android:visibility="invisible" />

    <ImageView
        android:id="@+id/image6"
        android:layout_width="fill_parent"
        android:layout_height="wrap_content"
        android:src="@drawable/icon"
        android:visibility="visible" />

</LinearLayout>
```

Then create a new folder called animatior inside res, and add a new file called property_animator_alpha.xml with the following content:

```
<?xml version="1.0" encoding="utf-8"?>
<set xmlns:android="http://schemas.android.com/apk/res/android" >
    <objectAnimator
        android:duration="3000"
        android:propertyName="alpha"
        android:repeatCount="-1"
        android:repeatMode="reverse"
        android:valueFrom="0.0"
        android:valueTo="1.0" />
</set>
```

Now make your class implementation look like this:

```
public class AndroidAnimationActivity extends Activity {
    ImageView mImage1, mImage2, mImage3, mImage4, mImage5, mImage6;

    @Override
    public void onCreate(Bundle savedInstanceState) {
        super.onCreate(savedInstanceState);
        setContentView(R.layout.animation);
        mImage1 = (ImageView)findViewById(R.id.image1);
        mImage2 = (ImageView)findViewById(R.id.image2);
        mImage3 = (ImageView)findViewById(R.id.image3);
        mImage4 = (ImageView)findViewById(R.id.image4);
        mImage5 = (ImageView)findViewById(R.id.image5);
        mImage6 = (ImageView)findViewById(R.id.image6);

        AnimatorSet set = (AnimatorSet) AnimatorInflater.loadAnimator(this,R.animator.
        property_animator_alpha);
        set.setTarget(mImage1);
        set.start();

        ValueAnimator testAnim = ObjectAnimator.ofFloat(image2, "alpha", 1.0f, 0.0f);
        testAnim.setDuration(3000); // in milliseconds
        testAnim.setRepeatCount(ValueAnimator.INFINITE);
        testAnim.setRepeatMode(ValueAnimator.REVERSE);
        testAnim.start();
    }
}
```

Finally, add a new menu item called Animation for the activity and run the app. Select Animation, and you'll see two animated images on the top-left corner (along with two other static images and one static text; you'll animate them shortly). What happened here is that you implemented the animation on an ImageView's alpha property in two ways: the XML way and the programmatic way. The key class here is ObjectAnimator (http://developer.android.com/reference/android/animation/ObjectAnimator.html), used to animate object properties, including x, y, alpha, rotation, translation, and so on. For a list of View properties, see http://android-developers.blogspot.co.il/2011/02/animation-in-honeycomb.html. ObjectAnimator's superclass ValueAnimator is used to set timing-related properties for an animation, such as duration and repeat count. ValueAnimator's superclass Animator is used to start or end an animation and add an event listener to get start, end, cancel, and repeat notifications from an animation, which you'll see soon.

In the property_animator_alpha.xml file, you have android:valueFrom set as 0.0 and valueTo as 1.0; in the code you use ofFloat(image2, "alpha", 1.0f, 0.0f); to set the alpha value animated from 1.0 to 0.0. So, what you see is two images with the fade-in and out animation for the duration of three seconds. The animations auto-reverse and repeat infinitely, which is all defined easily in both the XML file and the code.

To see another example of simple animation, add the following code at the end of onCreate, and you'll see rotation animation for the TextView:

```
myTextView = (TextView)findViewById(R.id.mytextview);
ValueAnimator colorAnim = ObjectAnimator.ofFloat(myTextView, "rotation", 180.0f, 360.0f);
colorAnim.setDuration(3000);
colorAnim.setRepeatCount(ValueAnimator.INFINITE);
colorAnim.setRepeatMode(ValueAnimator.REVERSE);
colorAnim.start();
```

Grouping Animation in XML and Programmatically

Sometimes you need to group multiple animations either sequentially or concurrently. Let's see how you can do this. First, add a new XML file called property_animator_group.xml in the res/animator folder.

```
<?xml version="1.0" encoding="utf-8"?>
<set xmlns:android="http://schemas.android.com/apk/res/android"
    android:ordering="together" >

    <objectAnimator
        android:duration="3000"
        android:propertyName="rotation"
        android:repeatCount="-1"
        android:repeatMode="reverse"
        android:valueFrom="0.0"
        android:valueTo="180.0" />
    <objectAnimator
        android:duration="3000"
        android:propertyName="alpha"
        android:repeatCount="-1"
        android:repeatMode="reverse"
        android:valueFrom="0.0"
        android:valueTo="1.0" />
</set>
```

Then add the following code at the end of onCreate:

```
set = (AnimatorSet) AnimatorInflater.loadAnimator(this, R.animator.property_animator_group);
set.setTarget(image3);
set.start();

ObjectAnimator mover = ObjectAnimator.ofFloat(image6, "y", 0f, 360f);
mover.setDuration(3000);
ObjectAnimator rotation = ObjectAnimator.ofFloat(image6, "rotation", 0.0f, 360.0f);
rotation.setDuration(3000);
ObjectAnimator fade = ObjectAnimator.ofFloat(image6, "alpha", 0.0f, 1.0f);
fade.setDuration(3000);
```

```
ArrayList<Animator> animators = new ArrayList<Animator>();
animators.add(rotation);
animators.add(fade);
animators.add(mover);
mAnimSet = new AnimatorSet();
mAnimSet.setInterpolator(new DecelerateInterpolator());
mAnimSet.playTogether(animators);
mAnimSet.start();
```

Run the app, and you'll see two new animations, consisting of two and three animations, respectively. The first group animation, implemented in XML, is on an ImageView located on the top center, rotating and fading in and out. The second group animation, which uses three ObjectAnimator instances and AnimatorSet to combine them, is an icon falling vertically across the center of screen while rotating and fading in. Three view properties (y, rotation, and alpha) are used to achieve this effect.

Using Animation Listener

To make the animation more interesting, you'll often need to know when the animation ends and add specific code when that happens. Add the following code after mAnimSet.start():

```
mAnimSet.addListener(new AnimatorListenerAdapter() {
    @Override
    public void onAnimationEnd(Animator animation) {
        ObjectAnimator rotation = ObjectAnimator.ofFloat(image6, "rotation", 0.0f, 360.0f);
        rotation.setDuration(3000);
        ObjectAnimator mover = ObjectAnimator.ofFloat(image6, "y", 0f, 360f);
        mover.setDuration(3000);
        ObjectAnimator fade = ObjectAnimator.ofFloat(image6, "alpha", 0.0f, 1.0f);
        fade.setDuration(3000);

        ArrayList<Animator> animators = new ArrayList<Animator>();
        animators.add(rotation);
        animators.add(fade);
        animators.add(mover);
        mAnimSet.playTogether(animators);
        mAnimSet.start();

    }
});
```

Run the app again, and you'll see that the falling rotating and fading animation will repeat again and again. The key here is to use Animator's addListener and AnimatorListenerAdapter, which provides empty implementations for AnimatorListener (you'll see another example of using this next), so you don't need to provide other methods of the listener interface if you want to implement only for onAnimationEnd.

Note that you can achieve the same effect using the setRepeatCount and setRepeatMode methods, but here in onAnimationEnd, you can perform any custom operation you want.

Let's now see another example of using the animation listener. This time you'll start a new animation after the first one ends and then alternate between the two animations. Add the following declarations first:

```
Animation mAnimationIn, mAnimationOut;
ImageView mCurImage;
```

Then add the following code at the end of onCreate:

```
mAnimationIn = AnimationUtils.loadAnimation(this, android.R.anim.slide_in_left);
mAnimationOut = AnimationUtils.loadAnimation(this, android.R.anim.slide_out_right);
mAnimationIn.setDuration(1000);
mAnimationOut.setDuration(1000);
mAnimationIn.setAnimationListener(animationSlideInLeftListener);
mAnimationOut.setAnimationListener(animationSlideOutRightListener);

mCurImage = mImage4;
mImage4.startAnimation(mAnimationIn);
mImage4.setVisibility(View.VISIBLE);
```

Finally, add the following code at the end of GraphicsAnimationApp:

```
AnimationListener animationSlideInLeftListener = new AnimationListener(){

    @Override
    public void onAnimationEnd(Animation animation) {
        if(mCurImage == mImage4){
            mImage4.startAnimation(mAnimationOut);
        }else if(mCurImage == mImage5){
            mImage5.startAnimation(mAnimationOut);
        }
    }

    @Override
    public void onAnimationRepeat(Animation animation) {
    }

    @Override
    public void onAnimationStart(Animation animation) {
    }
};

AnimationListener animationSlideOutRightListener = new AnimationListener(){
    @Override
    public void onAnimationEnd(Animation animation) {
        if(mCurImage == mImage4){
            mCurImage = mImage5;
            mImage5.startAnimation(mAnimationIn);
            mImage4.setVisibility(View.INVISIBLE);
            mImage5.setVisibility(View.VISIBLE);
        }else if(mCurImage == mImage5){
            mCurImage = mImage4;
            mImage4.startAnimation(mAnimationIn);
```

```
        mImage4.setVisibility(View.VISIBLE);
        mImage5.setVisibility(View.INVISIBLE);
    }
}

@Override
public void onAnimationRepeat(Animation animation) {
}

@Override
public void onAnimationStart(Animation animation) {
}
};
```

You use `AnimationUtils.loadAnimation` this time to load the common built-in slide-in-left animation and then use the `AnimationListener`'s `onAnimatonEnd` to start a new animation after the current one ends.

Run the app now, and you'll see a new animation of an icon sliding in from left to right and, after it reaches to the center, sliding out. After this animation is done, another icon starts the same type of animation. The two animations repeat themselves infinitely.

Figure 9-7 shows the completed activity with six animations happening at the same time.

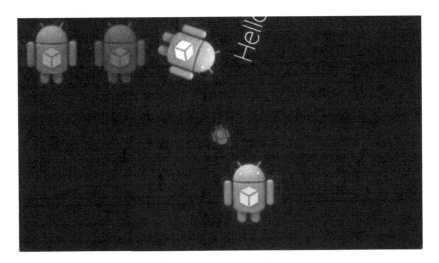

Figure 9-7. Basic and group animations with event listener in action

Game Engines on Glass

If you've developed any nontrivial Android games, chances are you're familiar with some open source game engines, which offer powerful and easy-to-use support for advanced graphics, animations, and physics so you can build professional-level games quickly. In fact, lots of commercial Android games have been built with such game engines. Although the Canvas drawing APIs and the animation techniques discussed earlier are probably good enough for some trivial small Glass games, let's take a deep look at how you can run three of the most popular open source game engines on Glass so you know what tools are available when you start porting or developing a commercial-level Glass game.

There's a long list of Android game engines at http://mobilegameengines.com/android/game_engines. I picked three of the most popular open source engines from the list.

- Cocos2d-x is a cross-platform 2D game engine (www.cocos2d-x.org), and games built with it dominate the Top Grossing charts of Google Play and Apple App Store: www.cocos2d-x.org/games. Cocos2d-x is a port of the original Cocos2d game engine, and the initial developer of Cocos2d game engine, Ricardo Quesada, recently joined Chukong, the company behind Cocos2d-x, as its chief architect, so expect it to be even more popular among game developers.

- libGDX is also a cross-platform engine (http://libgdx.badlogicgames.com) with lots of games built with it (http://libgdx.badlogicgames.com/gallery.html). Some of the Glass mini-games (https://developers.google.com/glass/samples/mini-games) also use this engine.

- AndEngine (www.andengine.org) is a Java-based game engine that's quite popular among Java developers. Glass mini-games also use this engine for rendering. I'll cover how to port a game built with AndEngine to Glass later in this chapter.

Cocos2d-x 3.0

Cocos2d-x has been around for a long time, and the 3.0 version was just released on April 23, 2014. There are some good online tutorials about developing games with Cocos2d-x 2.x and a book called *Cocos2d-x by Example*. Because 3.0 is a big improvement and highly recommended for new game development, I'll focus on 3.0 here.

Porting and Running the Demo Cocos2d-x App on Glass

These are the steps to run the sample C++ demo app that comes with Cocos2d-x 3.0:

1. Follow the how-to guide at www.cocos2d-x.org/wiki/How_to_run_cpp-tests_on_Android to get the sample app cpp-tests built.

> **Note**   You can skip the section "How to deploy it on your Android phone via command line" in the guide because you'll import the project to Eclipse and install the app to Glass from Eclipse, but you may also want to test it on your other Android devices to get the feeling of how the demo runs. Also, you'll need to cd <your-cocos2d-x-3.0>/build directory and run the command python android-build.py -p 19 cpp-tests instead of python android-build.py -p 10 cpp-tests as documented in the guide to build the app for Glass.

2. Follow the steps at www.cocos2d-x.org/wiki/How_to_Build_an_Android_Project_with_Eclipse to import the cpp-tests project and the libcocos2dx project to Eclipse. After this, you'll see something like Figure 9-8 in Eclipse.

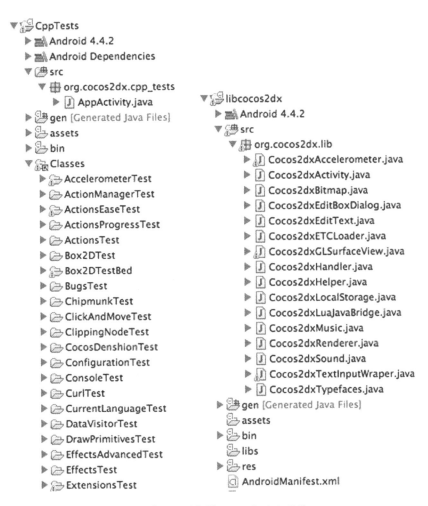

Figure 9-8. *Importing the CppTests demo and the libcocos2dx library projects to Eclipse*

3. Select CppTests and run it as an Android application with your Glass connected and turned on; you'll see something like Figure 9-9.

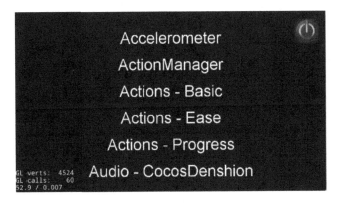

Figure 9-9. *Cocos2d-x 3.0 test app on Glass*

Unfortunately, tapping or swiping left or right won't navigate the demo menu. And what makes it worse is if your Glass screen goes off, tapping it again would take you to the OK Glass home screen instead of this CppTests app. Although the purpose of running the app on Glass is to see what features of the game engine can run on Glass so you can make a better decision on whether to use the engine when developing your next Glass games, you should have the launchy app (https://github.com/kaze0/launchy) installed and use it to easily select the CppTests to run if your Glass goes off.

4. To enable user interaction for CppTests on Glass, you need to first modify the class implementation in the AppActivity.java file shown in Figure 9-8, as shown in Listing 9-6.

Listing 9-6. Enabling and Passing a Touch Event to Cocos2d-x View on Glass

```java
public class AppActivity extends Cocos2dxActivity {
    Cocos2dxGLSurfaceView glSurfaceView;

    public Cocos2dxGLSurfaceView onCreateView() {
        glSurfaceView = new Cocos2dxGLSurfaceView(this);
        glSurfaceView.setEGLConfigChooser(5, 6, 5, 0, 16, 8);
        return glSurfaceView;
    }

    public boolean onGenericMotionEvent(MotionEvent event) {
        if ((event.getAction() & MotionEvent.ACTION_MASK) ==
        MotionEvent.ACTION_POINTER_DOWN) { // true if two-finger tap happens
            finish();
            return true;
        }

        glSurfaceView.onTouchEvent(event);
        return false;
    }
}
```

The changes are to make glSurfaceView, the view that shows each demo feature, an instance variable so in the GenericMotionEvent you can pass the touch event (except the double finger tap, which will finish the app) to the glSurfaceView.

5. To develop C++ code directly from Eclipse, you need to link the C++ source files in the Classes directory shown in Figure 9-10 to CppTests's Classes folder in Eclipse.

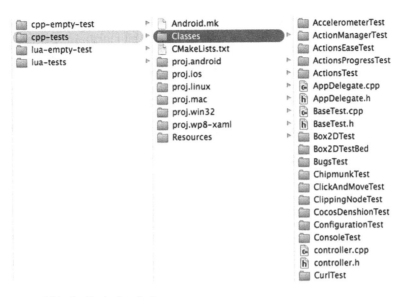

Figure 9-10. *C++ source folder for the test project*

To do this, open the project properties, select C/C++ General, and then select Paths and Symbols. You'll see the message "This project is not a CDT project" (CDT stands for C/C++ Development Tools), as shown in Figure 9-11.

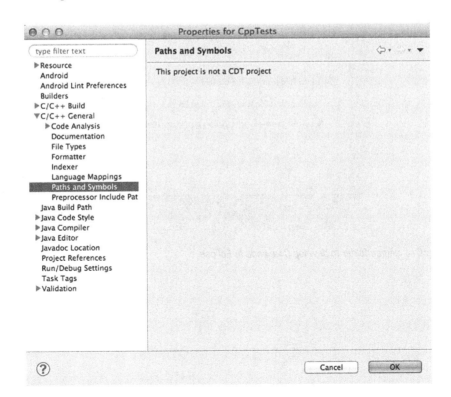

Figure 9-11. *Showing Project Properties*

To fix this, click Cancel in the Properties window. In Eclipse, select File ➤ New ➤ Project and then select C/C++ ➤ C++ Project. Enter a dummy project name and hit Finish. Now select the dummy project's Properties ➤ Resource to find its location. On Terminal, copy the .cproject file from that location to your CppTests app's proj.android directory (<path-to-cocos2d-x-3.0>/tests/cpp-tests/proj.android). You can delete the dummy project from both Eclipse and the project contents on disk now.

6. Go back to CppTests Properties ➤ C/C++ General ➤ Paths and Symbols ➤ Source Location, click Link Folder, check "Link to folder in the file system," click Browse, and select the Classes folder of CppTests (Figure 9-12).

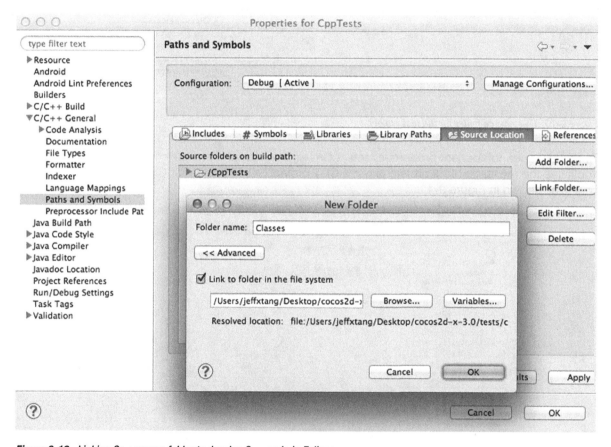

Figure 9-12. Linking C++ source folder to develop C++ code in Eclipse

Click OK, and you'll see the dialog in Figure 9-13. Click OK again, and Eclipse will show all the source folders under Classes, as in Figure 9-14.

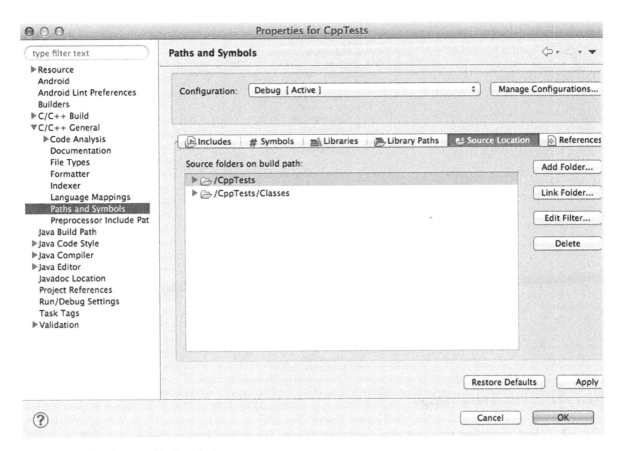

Figure 9-13. After Source Folder is Linked

Figure 9-14. C++ source folders in Eclipse

7.　Next, you need to modify the AppDelegate.cpp file in the Classes folder. But before you do this, you first need to fix the errors when you open the AppDelegate.cpp file. Eclipse, at least as of ADT version 22.6.2, incorrectly shows an error in the CppTests project and lots of errors in the AppDelegate. cpp file. If you try to build the CppTests application now (after you open the AppDelegate.cpp file), you'll get the annoying "Your project contains error(s), please fix them before running your application." error message. To fix this, open the CppTests's Properties window, go to Code Analysis under C/C++ General, select "Use project settings," and deselect Syntax and Semantic Errors, as shown in Figure 9-15. This is important because otherwise you won't be able to build the CppTests app from Eclipse after you make some C++ code change in Eclipse.

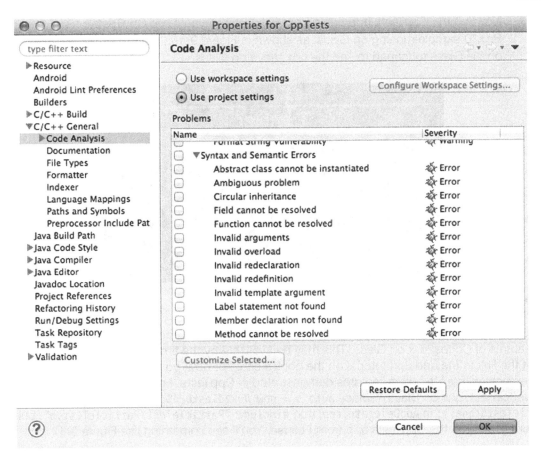

Figure 9-15. Deselecting incorrect code analysis to enable project build in Eclipse

8. The changes you need to make to AppDelegate.cpp are pretty simple.
    In the applicationDidFinishLaunching method, before return true;, add
    the following two lines of code:

```
auto s = new Box2dTestBedScene();
s->runThisTest();
```

Then add #include "Box2DTestBed/Box2dView.h" in the beginning of AppDelegate.cpp. Now open a Terminal window, cd to the cocos2d-x-3.0 build directory, and run the native C++ library build command.

```
python android-build.py -p 19 cpp-tests
```

After the "BUILD SUCCESSFUL" message, a new version of the CppTests library file, named libcpp_tests.so, will be available in the CppTests/libs/armeabi folder.

9. Now run the CppTests app again from Eclipse, and you'll see CppTests's Box2D sample running on Glass, as shown in Figure 9-16. Move your finger on the Glass touchpad to see the box move on Glass.

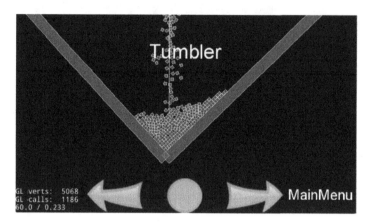

Figure 9-16. Running Cocos2d-x Box2d test code on Glass

Ideally, you would be able to use a gesture to go back to MainMenu and easily test all the other cool features of Cocos2d-x on Glass. This may be available by the time you read the book. If so, I'll post the link to the updated tutorial on the book's site. For now, you can use steps 6 and 7 to experiment with all the other features demonstrated in CppTests. For example, to check out how ParticleTest runs on Glass, replace auto s = new Box2dTestBedScene(); with auto s = new ParticleTestScene(); in AppDelegate.cpp, add #include "ParticleTest/ParticleTest.h", build the C++ library, and run the CppTests app from Eclipse. You'll see something like Figure 9-17.

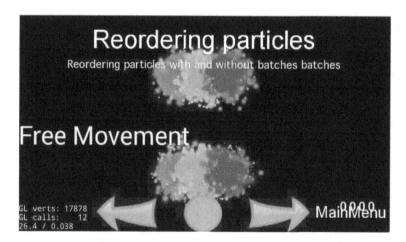

Figure 9-17. Running Cocos2d-x particle test code on Glass

After playing with CppTests, you should check out the Cocos2d-x wiki and API references at www.cocos2d-x.org for further information before you start using it to build your next Glass game. Before you move to the next game engine, let's see how you can create a new Cocos2d-x app running on Glass.

Creating a New Cocos2d-x App on Glass

Follow these steps to create a Cocos2d-x app from scratch:

1. Follow the how-to guide at www.cocos2d-x.org/wiki/How_to_Start_A_New_ Cocos2D-X_Game. To summarize, the commands I ran on my Mac are as follows:

```
cd cocos2d-x-3.0
./setup.py
source ~/.bash_profile
cocos new MyGame -p com.myCompany.myGame -l cpp -d ./MyCompany
cocos run -s ./MyCompany/MyGame -p android
```

2. In Eclipse, import the Android project located at MyCompany/MyGame/ proj.android. After importing, if you see errors in the MyGame project and AppActivity.java, you need to fix the reference to libcocos2dx. Open the project's properties, go to Android's Library section, click Add, and then select libcocos2dx there. After that, you should see something like Figure 9-18.

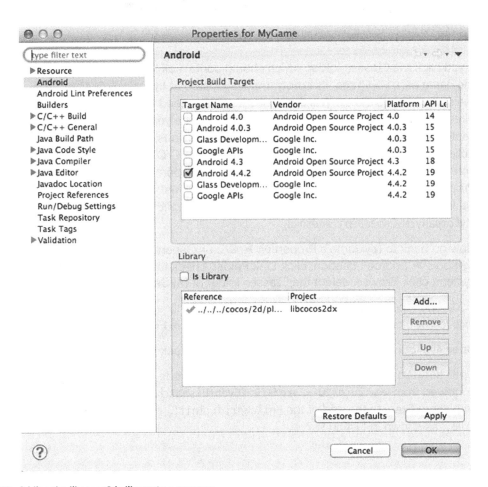

Figure 9-18. Adding the libcocos2dx library to a new app

3. Run the MyGame app on your Glass, and you'll see the Cocos2d-x version of Hello World on Glass, as shown in Figure 9-19.

Figure 9-19. Running Cocos2d-x Hello World app on Glass

4. If you click the `Classes` folder, which should contain all the C++ code for the game app, you'll see it's empty, but it's located at `MyCompany/MyGame`, at the same level as the `proj.android` directory. You need to link the `Classes` directory to MyGame's `Classes` folder in Eclipse, like you did in the previous section. To do this, simply follow step 5 in the previous section. Or, in Eclipse, select File ➤ New ➤ Project..., then select C/C++ ➤ C++ Project, enter a dummy project name, and hit Finish. Now open the dummy project's Properties ➤ Resource to find its location. On Terminal, copy the `.cproject` file from that location to your new game app's `proj.android` directory (`MyCompany/MyGame/proj.android`).

    Now go back to MyGame's Properties ➤ C/C++ General ➤ Paths and Symbols ➤ Source Location, click Link Folder, check Link to folder in the file system, click Browse, select the `Classes` folder of MyGame, and click OK.

5. If you open the `AppDelegate.cpp` file in `Classes`, you'll see lots of errors. To fix this, follow step 7 in the previous section, as shown in Figure 9-15.

6. Open `AppActivity.java` and change its content to look like Listing 9-6.

7. Open `HelloWorldScene.cpp` and add the following code, most of which is borrowed from www.cocos2d-x.org/wiki/EventDispatcher_Mechanism but with some fixes, to the end of the `HelloWorld::init()` method, before `return true;`, as shown in Listing 9-7.

Listing 9-7. Adding Sprites with a Touch Event Listener for Cocos2d-x 3.0

```
auto size = Director::getInstance()->getWinSize();

auto sprite1 = Sprite::create("CloseNormal.png");
sprite1->setPosition(origin+Point(size.width/2, size.height/2) + Point(-80, 80));
addChild(sprite1, 10);

auto sprite2 = Sprite::create("CloseNormal.png");
sprite2->setPosition(origin+Point(size.width/2, size.height/2));
addChild(sprite2, 20);

auto sprite3 = Sprite::create("HelloWorld.png");
sprite3->setPosition(Point(0, 0));
sprite2->addChild(sprite3, 1);

auto listener1 = EventListenerTouchOneByOne::create();
listener1->setSwallowTouches(true);

listener1->onTouchBegan = [](Touch* touch, Event* event){
    auto target = static_cast<Sprite*>(event->getCurrentTarget());

    //Get the position of the current point relative to the button
    Point locationInNode = target->convertToNodeSpace(touch->getLocation());
    Size s = target->getContentSize();
    Rect rect = Rect(0, 0, s.width, s.height);

    //Check the click area
    if (rect.containsPoint(locationInNode)) {
        target->setOpacity(180);
        return true;
    }
    return false;
};

//Trigger when moving touch
listener1->onTouchMoved = [](Touch* touch, Event* event){
    auto target = static_cast<Sprite*>(event->getCurrentTarget());
    //Move the position of current button sprite
    target->setPosition(target->getPosition() + touch->getDelta());
};

//Process the touch end event
listener1->onTouchEnded = [=](Touch* touch, Event* event){
    auto target = static_cast<Sprite*>(event->getCurrentTarget());
    target->setOpacity(255);
    //Reset zOrder and the display sequence will change
    if (target == sprite2)
        sprite1->setZOrder(100);
    else if(target == sprite1)
        sprite1->setZOrder(0);
};
```

```
_eventDispatcher->addEventListenerWithSceneGraphPriority(listener1, sprite1);
_eventDispatcher->addEventListenerWithSceneGraphPriority(listener1->clone(), sprite2);
_eventDispatcher->addEventListenerWithSceneGraphPriority(listener1->clone(), sprite3);
```

8. Open a Terminal window, cd to MyGame's proj.android directory, and run the python build_native.py command. You should see messages as follows:

```
[armeabi] Compile++ thumb: cocos2dcpp_shared <= HelloWorldScene.cpp
[armeabi] SharedLibrary  : libcocos2dcpp.so
[armeabi] Install        : libcocos2dcpp.so => libs/armeabi/libcocos2dcpp.so
```

9. Return to Eclipse and run the MyGame app on Glass. This time, you can move around the image on the top of the Glass touchpad, as shown in Figure 9-20. Be aware that you have to drag on the right part of the touchpad to make the move work.

Figure 9-20. Moving Cocos2d-x sprite on Glass

If you have any Cocos2d game development background, or even if you don't, you can come up to speed with Cocos2d-x quickly. It has well-documented online resources and examples. What I hope to offer here is to show you how to run the engine and samples on Glass and interact with the engine so you can see the potential of using the great engine for your next Glass game project. To get inspired, take another look at many great games developed with the engine at www.cocos2d-x.org/games.

libgdx

libgdx is a popular cross-platform (but Java-based, unlike Cocos2d-x, which is C++-based) game engine. In this section, I'll show you how to create and run a new libgdx app and how to run one cool libgdx demo on Glass and make some changes in the code so you can interact with the game on Glass.

Creating a New libgdx App on Glass

Follow these steps:

1. Follow the document at https://github.com/libgdx/libgdx/wiki/Setting-up-your-Development-Environment-%28Eclipse%2C-Intellij-IDEA%2C-NetBeans%29 to set up Eclipse. Because you've been using Eclipse for your GDK development, chances are you need to install only JDK 7 (if you use JDK 6; you can find out by running java -version on Terminal). The last step of "Setting up Eclipse" is "Eclipse Integration Gradle." Gradle (http://en.wikipedia.org/wiki/Gradle) is an automation build tool used by libgdx projects, and you also need to follow the steps at https://github.com/spring-projects/eclipse-integration-gradle, under "Installation instructions" and then "Installing Gradle Tooling from update site."

2. Download gdx-setup.jar at http://libgdx.badlogicgames.com/download.html.

3. Double-click the gdx-setup.jar or run java -jar gdx-setup.jar in the Terminal or a command-line window to run the file, and in the libgdx Project Generator window, enter values for Name, Package, Game class, Destination, and Android SDK. Select Sub Projects and Extensions and click Generate, and you'll see something like Figure 9-21.

Figure 9-21. Setting up a new libgdx project

4. In Eclipse, select File ➤ Import ➤ Gradle ➤ Gradle Project, as shown in Figure 9-22.

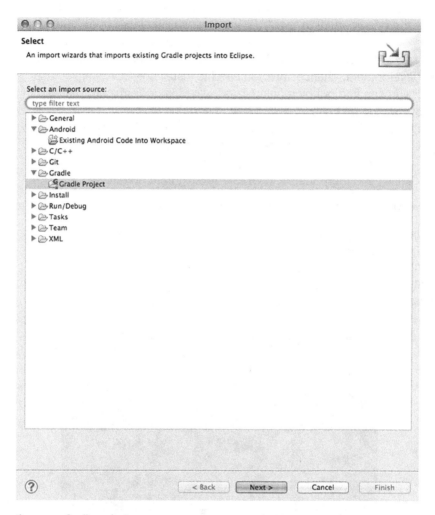

Figure 9-22. *Importing a new Gradle project*

5. Click Browse and choose the destination entered in Figure 9-21 of step 3. Then click Build Model. If you see error saying "SDK location not found," you can fix this by creating a new file called `local.properties` in the `Destination` directory and entering this single line:

    ```
    sdk.dir=<your-path-to-adt>/sdk
    ```

    Then select Build Model again. You should see something like Figure 9-23.

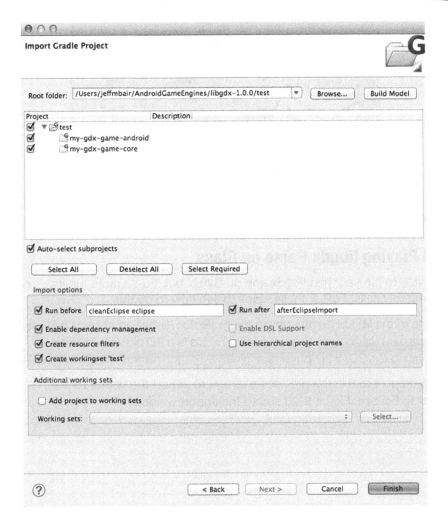

Figure 9-23. Importing a new libgdx project

6. Select the test project and click Finish; you'll see two new projects in Eclipse: my-gdx-game-android and my-gdx-game-core.

7. Connect your Glass, keep the Glass screen on, and run the app. You'll see the default home screen, as shown in Figure 9-24.

Figure 9-24. Running the libgdx test app on Glass

Running and Playing libgdx Game on Glass

It's great you're able to run your first libgdx app on Glass, but it'd be more fun if you could play an actual libgdx game on Glass. Follow these steps to see how to do this:

1. Get one of the libgdx demo apps, namely, Vector Pinball, at `https://github.com/libgdx/libgdx-demo-vector-pinball`. This is a 2D pinball simulation game using Box2D, a 2D physics engine.

2. Follow steps 4 to 6 in the previous exercise to import the Vector Pinball project to Eclipse. Figure 9-25 shows the Import window.

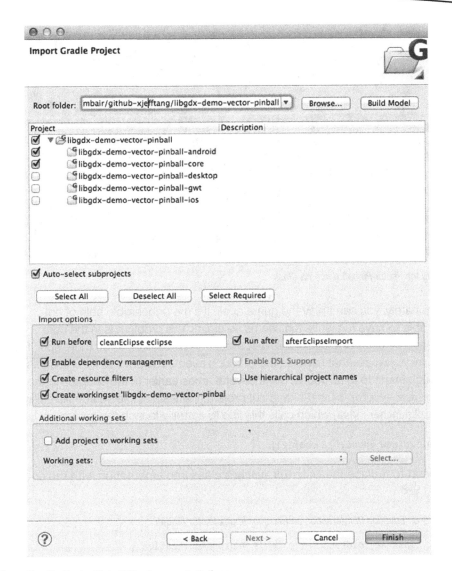

Figure 9-25. Importing the Vector Pinball libgdx game to Eclipse

3. In Eclipse, run `libgdx-demo-vector-pinball-android` on Glass. You'll see the game UI, as shown in Figure 9-26.

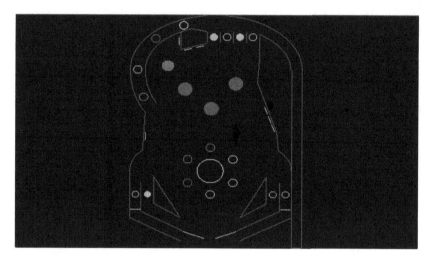

Figure 9-26. Running the Vector Pinball game on Glass

4. Unfortunately, you can't play the game at all. It's the unbearable pain of not
    being able to have fun while fun seems so close. The problem is in the core
    game source code of `libgdx-demo-vector-pinball-core` or, to be more specific,
    the `Bouncy.java` file that handles the UI touch event. You have to let Glass pass
    the touch event to it, as you've done several times earlier in the chapter. In the
    `libgdx-demo-vector-pinball-android` project, there's a single source file called
    `AndroidLauncher.java`, which calls this line to actually launch the game:

```
initialize(new Bouncy(), config);
```

You need to replace the `AndroidLauncher` class implementation with the code in
Listing 9-8.

Listing 9-8. Enabling UI interaction on Glass for libgdx Vector Pinball

```
public class AndroidLauncher extends AndroidApplication {
    Bouncy mBouncy;

    @Override
    protected void onCreate (Bundle savedInstanceState) {
        super.onCreate(savedInstanceState);
        AndroidApplicationConfiguration config = new
            AndroidApplicationConfiguration();
        mBouncy = new Bouncy();
        initialize(mBouncy, config);
    }

    public boolean onGenericMotionEvent(MotionEvent event) {
        switch (event.getActionMasked()) {
        case MotionEvent.ACTION_DOWN:
            mBouncy.touchDown(0, 0, 0, 0);
            break;
```

```
            case MotionEvent.ACTION_UP:
                mBouncy.touchUp(0, 0, 0, 0);
                break;
            case MotionEvent.ACTION_MOVE:
                mBouncy.touchDragged(0, 0, 0);
                break;
            }
            return true;
        }
    }
```

You use an instance variable of `mBouncy` here so you can call its `touchdown`, `touchup`, and `touchDragged` event handlers defined in the core project's `Bouncy.java`.

5. Now run the app again, and you'll be able to play the vector pinball game perfectly fine on Glass.

libgdx is well documented at `http://libgdx.badlogicgames.com/documentation.html` and has been used to build hundreds of cool games. Now that you know how to create a new app or port an existing one in libgdx to Glass, you're well positioned to consider it when developing your next Glass game app.

AndEngine

The last open source game engine I'll discuss is AndEngine, which is only for Android game development. AndEngine is easier to use and quicker for game development and should be good for most 2D Android game development, if you don't plan on cross-platform support. Check out a nice tutorial on using it at `www.raywenderlich.com/12065/how-to-create-a-simple-android-game`.

In this section, I'll show you how to run and interact with an AndEngine example app on Glass and how to import the AndEngine game in the previous tutorial, to which you'll add the support of a Glass sensor in the next section to replace hand gestures when controlling the game UI.

Running and Testing AndEngine Examples on Glass

Follow these steps to add and use the AndEngine library and run examples in Eclipse:

1. Get the AndEngine library at `https://github.com/nicolasgramlich/AndEngine`.

2. Import the AndEngine library downloaded to Eclipse, and that's it. You now have the AndEngine library you can use in your game app.

3. Get the AndEngine examples project at `https://github.com/nicolasgramlich/AndEngineExamples` and most of the extensions listed at the Extensions section of the AndEngine GitHub location at `https://github.com/nicolasgramlich/AndEngine` (the extensions are needed to run the AndEngineExamples). After you import the examples project and all the extensions to Eclipse, you should see something like Figure 9-27 (you may need to add the AndEngine library to each of the extension projects if you get a library error on the extension's properties).

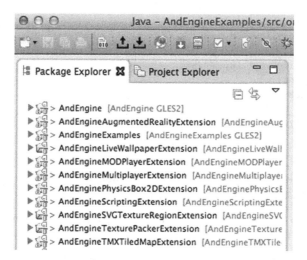

Figure 9-27. Importing the AndEngine library, examples, and extensions to Eclipse

4. Open the AndEngineExamples project's properties, change Project Build Target to Glass Development Kit Preview, and then add the AndEngine library and all the extension libraries. Figure 9-28 shows what it looks like.

Figure 9-28. Adding the AndEngine and Extension libraries to the AndEngineExamples

5. Now you can run AndEngineExamples on Glass and see the example UI as in Figure 9-29.

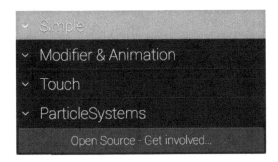

Figure 9-29. Showing AndEngineExamples UI on Glass

6. Still, you can't navigate the menu and see how all the examples work. To fix this, open ExampleLauncher.java in AndEngineExamples's org.andengine.examples.launcher package. First add four instance variables before onCreate.

```
private GestureDetector mGestureDetector;
private ExpandableListActivity mList;
private int mGroupPosition = 0;
private int mChildPosition = 0;
```

Then add two lines of code at the end of onCreate.

```
mGestureDetector = createGestureDetector(this);
mList = this;
```

Finally, add the following two methods after onCreate.

```
private GestureDetector createGestureDetector(Context context) {
  GestureDetector gestureDetector = new GestureDetector(context);
  gestureDetector.setBaseListener( new GestureDetector.BaseListener() {
      @Override
      public boolean onGesture(Gesture gesture) {
          if (gesture == Gesture.TAP) {
              if (mList.getExpandableListView().isGroupExpanded(mGroupPosition)) {
                  if (mChildPosition >=0) {
                      final Example example = mExpandableExampleLauncherListAdapter.
                      getChild(mGroupPosition, mChildPosition);
                      startActivity(new Intent(mList, example.CLASS));
                  }
              }
              else {
                  mList.getExpandableListView().expandGroup(mGroupPosition);
                  mChildPosition = 0;
                  mList.setSelectedChild(mGroupPosition, 0, true);
              }
```

```
                    return true;
            } else if (gesture == Gesture.SWIPE_RIGHT) {
                if (mList.getExpandableListView().isGroupExpanded(mGroupPosition)) {
                    if (mExpandableExampleLauncherListAdapter. getChildrenCount(mGroupPosition) >
                    mChildPosition+1)
                        mList.setSelectedChild(mGroupPosition, ++mChildPosition, true);
                }
                else if ( mExpandableExampleLauncherListAdapter.getGroupCount() > mGroupPosition+1 )
                    mList.setSelectedGroup(++mGroupPosition);
                return true;
            } else if (gesture == Gesture.SWIPE_LEFT) {
                if (mList.getExpandableListView().isGroupExpanded(mGroupPosition)) {
                    if (mChildPosition > 0)
                        mList.setSelectedChild(mGroupPosition, --mChildPosition, true);
                    else {
                        mList.getExpandableListView().collapseGroup(mGroupPosition);
                        mList.setSelectedGroup(mGroupPosition);
                    }
                }
                else if (mGroupPosition > 0) {
                    mList.setSelectedGroup(--mGroupPosition);
                    mChildPosition = 0;
                }

                return true;
            }
            return false;
        }
    });

    return gestureDetector;
}

public boolean onGenericMotionEvent(MotionEvent event) {
    if (mGestureDetector != null) {
        return mGestureDetector.onMotionEvent(event);
    }
    return false;
}
```

The previous code enables the navigation and selection of the expanded list of examples. Tapping an unexpanded group expands it and highlights the first item in the group; tapping a highlighted item runs the example associated with it. Swiping right on an unexpanded group highlights the next group, unless it's the last group. Swiping right on a highlighted group item highlights the next item in the group, unless it's the last item in the group. Swiping left on an unexpanded group highlights the previous group, unless it's the first group. Swiping left on a highlighted group item goes to the previous item, but if it's already the first item in the group, then swiping left uncollapses and highlights the group. Swiping down on an example goes back to the navigation list. This is all intuitive actually; maybe I just got inspired by the phrase "BAD Logic" in Figure 9-24 and decided to describe the good logic for navigation in detail.

7. Now run the app again and try the examples. For example, if you choose A Cool ParticleSystem and A Nexus ParticleSystem (Figure 9-30) under ParticleSystems, you'll see the effects shown in Figure 9-31.

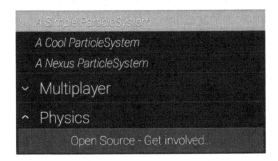

Figure 9-30. Navigating AndEngine example list on Glass

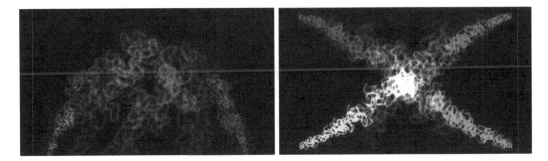

Figure 9-31. Showing AndEngine's particle effects on Glass

If you choose an example that requires touch event handling, you still need to make some code change in the xxxExample.java file. For example, if you select the second item, Using Physics, under Physics, you'll need to add code like the following in PhysicsExample.java of the org.andengine.examples package to make the touch work:

```
public boolean onGenericMotionEvent(MotionEvent event) {
    if (event.getActionMasked() == MotionEvent.ACTION_DOWN) {
        this.addFace(event.getX(), event.getY());
    }

    return false;
}
```

You've already seen examples of enabling touch in previous sections of this chapter, and you're about to explore how to use a Glass sensor and head gesture, more fitting for Glass in some cases, to control the UI, so I'll leave this to you to experiment with. Before I discuss how to enable head gesture for a game, let's first quickly check out a game built with AndEngine. I'll show you how to improve the game using a Glass sensor after that.

An AndEngine-based Tower of Hanoi Game

www.raywenderlich.com/12065/how-to-create-a-simple-android-game is a nice tutorial on how to use AndEngine to create a simple Android game. Download the project's source code from the link at the end of the tutorial, unzip and import it to Eclipse, and fix the library issue if necessary by adding the AndEngine library project in the TowerOfHanor project's properties.

If you run the app now in a non-Glass Android device or a virtual device, you can play the game. Run it on Glass, however, and you see only a static scene of the game. You can either use onGenericMotionEvent, as you've done in this chapter, to enable touch handling, or use the Glass sensor to create a hands-free experience, as I'll describe in the next section.

Developing a Sensor-Based Game

If you have played the Glass game Spellista or Matcher (one of the Glass mini-games), available to install to your Glass at https://glass.google.com/myglass, you should be familiar with how the Glass sensor works perfectly in those cases to control the game. You can move your head around to make a selector or cursor on top of a target and then stay at the target for a certain amount of time to select it or tap to select the target.

In the description of the Matcher game at https://developers.google.com/glass/samples/mini-games, Google says that "the gyroscope and accelerometer team up to precisely follow the position of the player's head." You've seen how to read the gyroscope and accelerometer sensor data in Chapter 8, and you can try to use the sensor fusion to combine the two sensors and the magnetic field sensor to calculate the accurate head position. This article covers both theory and the Android implementation pretty well: www.thousand-thoughts.com/2012/03/android-sensor-fusion-tutorial/.

But there's an easy solution, as you saw earlier in the chapter, by using the software rotation vector sensor, which already takes gyroscope, accelerometer, and magnetometer sensors into account to calculate the head position. Follow these steps to display a cursor that moves with your head movement to point to the targets (the three rings) to be selected for the Tower of Hanoi game:

1. Make the class TowerOfHanoiActivity implement the SensorEventListener interface.

2. Add the following instance variables to the class:

```
private SensorManager mSensorManager;
private Text mSelector;
private int mStartX = CAMERA_WIDTH / 2 - 5;
private int mStartY = CAMERA_HEIGHT / 2 - 5;
private Boolean mFirstTime = true; // used to save initially detected pitch and yaw
(heading) values
```

3. Add the onCreate method with the following code:

```
public void onCreate(Bundle savedInstanceState) {
    super.onCreate(savedInstanceState);
    mSensorManager = (SensorManager) getSystemService
                (Context.SENSOR_SERVICE);
}
```

4. At the end of the onCreateScene method, before return scene;, add the following:

```
final VertexBufferObjectManager vertexBufferObjectManager = this
        .getVertexBufferObjectManager();
BitmapTextureAtlas fontTexture = new BitmapTextureAtlas(
        this.getTextureManager(), 32, 32,
        TextureOptions.REPEATING_NEAREST);
final Font font = new Font(this.getFontManager(), fontTexture,
        Typeface.create(Typeface.DEFAULT, Typeface.NORMAL), 64, true,
        Color.MAGENTA);
font.load();
mSelector = new Text(mStartX, mStartY, font, buildSelector(),
        new TextOptions(HorizontalAlign.CENTER),
        vertexBufferObjectManager);
scene.attachChild(mSelector);
scene.setTouchAreaBindingOnActionDownEnabled(true);
```

And then after the onCreateScene method, add a new method.

```
private CharSequence buildSelector() {
    SpannableStringBuilder builder = new SpannableStringBuilder();
    builder.append('\u25cb');
    return builder;
}
```

The code here will add a circle-shaped red selector to the screen. Now you need to move it when you move your head.

5. Add the following code to the class:

```
@Override
public final void onAccuracyChanged(Sensor sensor, int accuracy) {
}

@Override
public final void onSensorChanged(SensorEvent event) {
    if (event.sensor.getType() == Sensor.TYPE_ROTATION_VECTOR) {
        float pitchInDegree = (float) Math.toDegrees(
                        event.values[0]);
        float headingInDegree = (float) Math.toDegrees(
                        event.values[1]);

        if (mSelector != null) {
            int x = ((int) (mStartX + 20.0 * headingInDegree))
                            % CAMERA_WIDTH;
            int y = ((int) (mStartY + 20.0 * pitchInDegree))
                            % CAMERA_HEIGHT;

            if (x > CAMERA_WIDTH - 30)
                x = CAMERA_WIDTH - 30;
```

```
                else if (x < 2)
                    x = 2;

                if (y > CAMERA_HEIGHT - 50)
                    y = CAMERA_HEIGHT - 50;
                else if (y < 2)
                    y = 2;

                mSelector.setPosition(x, y);
            }
        }
    }

    @Override
    protected void onResume() {
        super.onResume();
        mSensorManager.registerListener(this,
            mSensorManager.getDefaultSensor
                            (Sensor.TYPE_ROTATION_VECTOR),
                            SensorManager.SENSOR_DELAY_NORMAL);
    }

    @Override
    protected void onPause() {
        super.onPause();
        mSensorManager.unregisterListener(this);
    }
```

In the onSensorChanged callback, event.values[0] is the pitch angle, and event.values[1] is the heading (yaw) angle, both in radians. You convert them to degrees, and because the values changed when moving a head are pretty small, you multiple them by 20 to make the selector movement obvious.

6. Now run the app again, and this time you'll see a red cycle on the screen that moves around with your head movement.

The algorithm is as follows to add a time-based control with the selector to play the Tower of Hanoi game with just head movement:

1. If a ring that the selector stays on is at the top, then after the selector stays on the ring for a certain amount of time (for example, two seconds), the ring will be selected.

2. After a ring is selected, moving your head will move the ring, and if the new position of the selector is around a different stack, also for a certain amount of time, the ring will be placed on the stack if there's no smaller ring on the stack, or it will be returned to the stack from which it's moved and become unselected.

3. After a ring is selected, if the position of the selector remains on the same stack, also for a certain amount of time, the ring will be unselected.

I'll leave the detailed implementation to you as an exercise but will also include it in the source code for you to download.

> **Note** Artificial intelligence (AI) is always an exciting topic in the game development world. Entire books have been written about game AI. Simply search for *game ai* on Amazon and you'll see what I mean. If you want to port your existing game AI code to Glass, it should be clear to you by now, if you follow the book closely, that it's really the easy part because Glass is just another powerful Android device. If you're interested but new to AI, you should check out other game AI books or many excellent online sites such as www.gameai.com and http://ai-depot.com.

Summary

In this chapter, I covered common graphics and animation APIs and showed many demos running on Glass, which you can use in your own simple Glass apps. Then I discussed in great detail how to set up and run three popular open source game engines (Cocos2d-x, libgdx, and AndEngine) on Glass. You learned how to run and interact with many examples for the three game engines, as well as how to create new apps using the engines. Finally, you learned how to use the Glass rotation vector sensor to control your game with head movement. I hope you're well-armed with these powerful tools before you continue your own exciting game development journey.

Chapter 10

The Mirror API

So far I have focused on the GDK option of developing Glass apps, or Glassware. A second option, which is simpler and was offered earlier than the GDK option, is the Mirror API, which lets you use any web programming language, such as Java, PHP, Python, Ruby, .NET, or Go, to build web services that interact with Glass via Google's cloud-based API. With the Mirror API, you can build a Glass app that publishes content to users' Glass in a simple and elegant way. For more information on which option to use, check out Google's documentation at `https://developers.google.com/glass/develop/overview`, which also briefly covers the hybrid way to build Glass apps. Basically, a Mirror API app can launch a GDK app through a menu item on a static card inserted by the Mirror app.

In this chapter, I'll present step-by-step tutorials on how to set up your environment and test and deploy apps. I'll also cover many examples of using the Mirror API. The following are the topics included in this chapter:

- How to set up your environment and deploy and play with the Mirror API's quick-start projects on Google App Engine (for free) or your own server

- The details of the Mirror API, including the timeline, static cards, contacts, subscriptions, locations, and authorization, with Java examples

- How to build a hybrid app that uses the Mirror API to launch a GDK app

- Image processing the Mirror API way, including how to upload a picture to a server of your own (you'll reuse some Java code from Chapter 7)

- A Mirror app of an NBA 2014 roster that you can browse and use voice to query for any player on the 2014 playoff teams

Setting Up Your Environment

If you're new to the Mirror API, the best place to start is to check out Google's Mirror API quick-start guide at `https://developers.google.com/glass/develop/mirror/quickstart/index`. Before I walk you through the detailed steps of setting up your development environment and deploying to Google App Engine or your own server, you should follow the steps in the guide to see how a demo project deployed on Google App Engine (`https://glass-python-starter-demo.appspot.com`) works.

Because of the scope of the book, I won't be able to cover all the languages demoed in the Google quick-start project. I'll start with PHP, the most-used language on the Web (running about 75 percent of the Web) and show you how to deploy the project and run it on your own server and why it can't be deployed to Google App Engine yet (at least as of May 2014). Then I'll focus on Java, the main language used for GDK Glassware development (native C/C++ can also be used in GDK development, as you have seen in the book). If you're a web developer of another language such as Ruby, Python, or .NET and want to get serious about Glass development, I strongly recommend you use Java as your main language for the Mirror API app development so you can be better prepared for GDK development when you want to expand the possibilities of your Glassware.

If you still want to start with other languages, PHP and Python are your second best choice because on May 13, 2014, Google removed the links to Ruby, .NET, and Go on the quick-start page at `https://developers.google.com/glass/develop/mirror/quickstart/index`, although the GitHub project links to the three languages are still available at `https://github.com/googleglass`.

> **Note** Google App Engine is my preferred way to host the Mirror Glassware developed in this chapter. It's free and easy to use, so everyone can see the Mirror apps in action easily. It also has great support for logging. If you already have a hosted service, you can certainly deploy the Mirror apps there. I'll briefly cover how to do this for the Glass sample PHP project.

Using PHP

Google's quick-start guide for PHP at `https://developers.google.com/glass/develop/mirror/quickstart/php` is pretty good, but it misses some steps and presents some incorrect information (as of April 15, 2014, when it was last updated), which can cause you headache when trying to deploy and run the project. So, I'm offering the following notes on how to start, deploy, and test the Mirror API PHP quick-start project (you should still follow the quick-start guide first and then refer to these notes when necessary):

1. In step 6 of the guide, under Authorized Redirect URIs, an App Engine URI is shown as an example: `https://myappengineinstance.appspot.com/oauth2callback` (xxx.appspot.com refers to an app hosted on the Google App Engine). But you'll see soon why App Engine won't work for hosting the PHP quick-start project, which, by the way, you can get using the following command (if you are new to Git and GitHub, the most popular open source version control system, check out `https://help.github.com/articles/set-up-git` first):

    `git clone https://github.com/googleglass/mirror-quickstart-php`

    Because the Google App Engine PHP is still in Preview mode, if in the future Google improves it to actually support the quick-start project, you can replace myappengineinstance in the URI with an app name created at `https://appengine.google.com`.

Note   If you want to host on Google App Engine, you should create an App Engine app (with a unique application identifier) at `https://appengine.google.com` first and then go to `https://code.google.com/apis/console` to open that app project and create the OAuth 2.0 client ID–related information; the Mirror quick-start guide for PHP (and Java) doesn't specify the first step. Then you can use the application identifier created at `https://appengine.google.com` for your host URI such as `https://myappengineinstance.appspot.com`, and refer to the client ID and secret in your app's code.

2. Make sure the authorized redirect URIs match exactly the URI to `oauth2callback.php`, including `http` or `https`. That is, if your web server supports HTTPS, you need to put `https` in the URI; but if your web server doesn't support HTTPS, then just use `http`. Otherwise, you'll get an "Error: redirect_uri_mismatch" message when loading the app. For example, I copied the whole `mirror-quickstart-php` folder to the root directory of my test web server, which supports only HTTP, so I have this defined in the redirect URIs:

    `http://morkout.com/mirror-quickstart-php/oauth2callback.php`

3. The simple API key for the API project used by the PHP quick-start app will be available only after you enable the Google Mirror API for the project.

4. You need to modify the quick-start project, which is not an App Engine project, and add an App Engine configuration file called `app.yaml` with the following content:

```
application: <replace_this_with_your_App_Engine_application_identifier>
version: 1
runtime: php
api_version: 1

handlers:
- url: (.+).php
  script: \1.php

- url: /.*
  script: index.php
```

    For details on the configuration file, see the "Creating the Configuration File" section in the Google PHP App Engine document at `https://developers.google.com/appengine/docs/php/gettingstarted/helloworld`.

5. You should install the App Engine PHP SDK, available for download at
    `https://developers.google.com/appengine/docs/php/gettingstarted/`
    `installing`, and use the Google App Engine Launcher in the SDK to upload
    the quick-start project to App Engine. Then when you load https, you'll
    first see the error message "Google CurlIO client requires the CURL PHP
    extension." To fix this, open the `mirror-quickstart-php/google-api-php-`
    `client/src/config.php` file and replace these two lines:

    ```
    'ioClass'      => 'Google_CurlIO',
    'cacheClass'   => 'Google_FileCache',
    ```

    with the following:

    ```
    'ioClass'=>'Google_HttpStreamIO',
    'cacheClass'=>'Google_MemcacheCache',
    ```

    Then add the following two lines:

    ```
    'ioMemCacheCache_host'=>'does_not_matter',
    'ioMemCacheCache_port'=>'37337',
    ```

    After this, redeploy the PHP project to App Engine using the Google App
    Engine Launcher, and launch the PHP app at `https://<your_app_engine_`
    `app_name>.appspot.com` again. This time you'll get a blank page. Go to
    `https://appengine.google.com`, select your application, and then under Main
    – Logs, you'll see the dirty little secret, which is the error message "PHP Fatal
    error: Class 'SQLite3' not found." The problem is that according to Google
    (under "Enabled extensions" at `https://developers.google.com/appengine/`
    `docs/php/`), the SQLite extension for PHP is not enabled in the Google PHP
    App Engine.

Note   The PHP App Engine is still in Preview mode, but support for SQLite may be added in the future. If that
does happen, what's covered here will help you deploy the Mirror PHP quick-start project to App Engine more
easily. But for your own apps, you can use MySQL and deploy them to Google App Engine.

For now, you can ignore notes 4 and 5 and deploy the quick-start PHP
app to your own Apache/PHP server. But you need to install the PHP `curl`
extension and SQLite; both are required to run the app. On Ubuntu, simply
run the following two commands:

```
sudo apt-get install curl libcurl3 libcurl3-dev php5-curl
sudo apt-get install php5-sqlite
```

For example, I created an App Engine app called glassdbquery and followed the Google's quick-start guide for PHP and my notes (without 4 and 5), and then I deployed the quick-start project to my server. You can test it at `http://morkout.com/mirror-quickstart-php`. Authenticate with OAuth 2.0 using your Google account associated with your Glass, and you'll see the same UI as in the Google's demo project at `https://glass-python-starter-demo.appspot.com`, as shown in Figure 10-1. You can perform the timeline and contacts-related operations, which I'll discuss in detail soon.

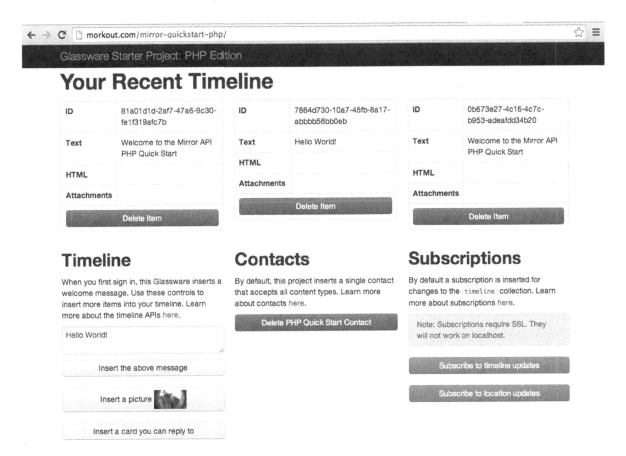

Figure 10-1. Testing the deployed Mirror PHP quick-start project

Using Java

Similar to the PHP guide, Google's quick-start guide for Java at `https://developers.google.com/glass/develop/mirror/quickstart/java` contains a lot of good information you can use to start with, but it misses some important information on how to deploy the Mirror quick-start Java project, available at `https://github.com/googleglass/mirror-quickstart-java`, to Google App Engine. I'll show you how to set up the Eclipse environment to import the quick-start Java project and what it takes to run the project both locally and on App Engine.

Setting Up Eclipse

The Mirror quick-start Java project is a project managed by Maven, a project build management tool. You'll see soon how you can use Maven to build the project, run it locally, and deploy it to Google App Engine. Eclipse is no doubt the best IDE for Java app development, but unfortunately, you can't use the ADT bundle for the Android app development, which I covered in Chapter 2 and have used in all the previous GDK development chapters, to import the Mirror quick-start Java project. So, follow these steps to set up the original Eclipse and related tools:

1. Download Eclipse Juno or newer at `www.eclipse.org/downloads`.

2. After Eclipse is downloaded and unzipped, launch Eclipse and then drag and drop the Maven to Eclipse plug-in Install icon at `http://eclipse.org/m2e/download/` to the Eclipse workspace, as shown in Figure 10-2.

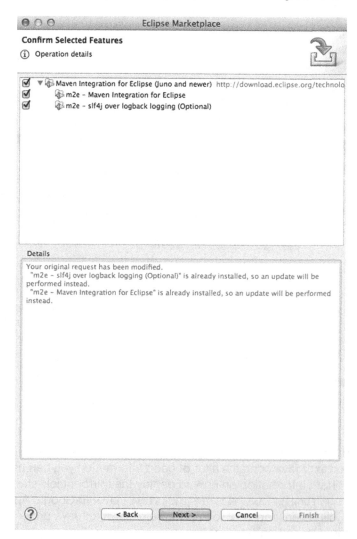

Figure 10-2. Adding the Maven to Eclipse plug-in

3. Get the Mirror quick-start Java project using the following command:

```
git clone https://github.com/googleglass/mirror-quickstart-java
```

4. Import the project to Eclipse by selecting File ➤ Import ➤ Maven ➤ Existing Maven Projects. Then choose the folder for the mirror-quickstart-java project and select the pom.xml file, which is the XML file that contains project information and configuration details. Then click Finish, as shown Figure 10-3. Figure 10-4 shows the imported project in Eclipse.

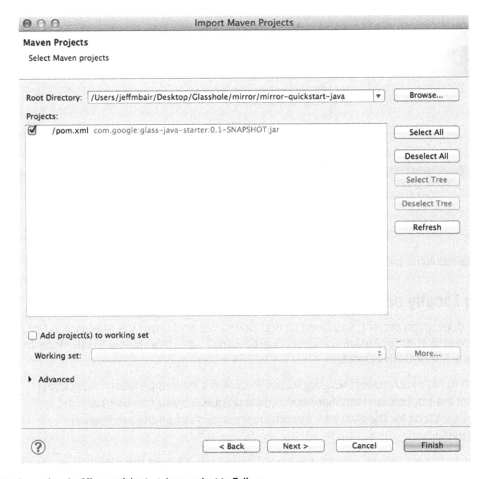

Figure 10-3. Importing the Mirror quick-start Java project to Eclipse

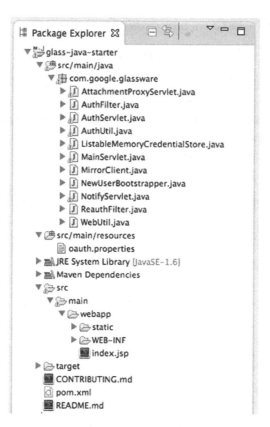

Figure 10-4. Imported Mirror quick-start Java project in Eclipse

Deploying Locally and to App Engine

To build and deploy the project, you need to first download and unzip the Maven 3.2.1 or newer command-line tool at `http://maven.apache.org/download.cgi`. Now follow these steps to modify and deploy the Mirror Java project:

1. Go to `https://appengine.google.com` to create a new application. Note again that the application identifier needs to be unique, so you can use `<appid>. appspot.com` for the web site. I used `jave-mirror-api` as the application identifier.

2. Go to `https://code.google.com/apis/console` and select the project you created in the previous step (you may need to choose Open under "Other projects" to find it).

3. Follow steps 2 to 7 at the Google's Mirror quick-start guide for Java (`https://developers.google.com/glass/develop/mirror/quickstart/ java`). In my case, after step 6, the redirect URIs after my client ID for web applications look like Figure 10-5.

Redirect URIs: `https://java-mirror-api.appspot.com/oauth2callback`
                        `http://localhost:8080/oauth2callback`

JavaScript origins: `https://java-mirror-api.appspot.com`
                        `http://localhost`

Figure 10-5. Redirect URIs setting for both App Engine and localhost

4. In Eclipse, modify oauth.properties to use client_id and client_secret, available in the "API Access" section at https://code.google.com/apis/console, for your app.

5. In Terminal, first cd to the mirror-quickstart-java folder and then launch the following command to start the app locally:

    ```
    <path-to-apache-maven>/bin/mvn jetty:run
    ```

    For example, my command is as follows:

    ```
    ~/Devtools/apache-maven-3.2.1/bin/mvn jetty:run
    ```

6. After you see "Started Jetty Server," go to a browser and launch http://localhost:8080 and log in with your Google account; you'll see the same UI as in Figure 10-1.

7. To deploy the project to App Engine, you need to create a new file called appengine-web.xml in src/main/webapp/WEB-INF, with the following content:

    ```xml
    <?xml version="1.0" encoding="utf-8"?>
    <appengine-web-app xmlns="http://appengine.google.com/ns/1.0">
        <application>java-mirror-api</application>
        <version>1</version>
        <threadsafe>true</threadsafe>
        <sessions-enabled>true</sessions-enabled>

        <system-properties>
            <property name="java.util.logging.config.file" value="WEB-INF/logging.properties" />
        </system-properties>

    </appengine-web-app>
    ```

    Of course you'll need to replace the <application> value with the app name you created in step 1.

8. Download the Google App Engine Java SDK at https://developers.google.com/appengine/downloads and install the Google plug-in for Eclipse by selecting Eclipse's Help ➤ Install New Software. Enter https://dl.google.com/eclipse/plugin/4.2, and set up the screen like Figure 10-6.

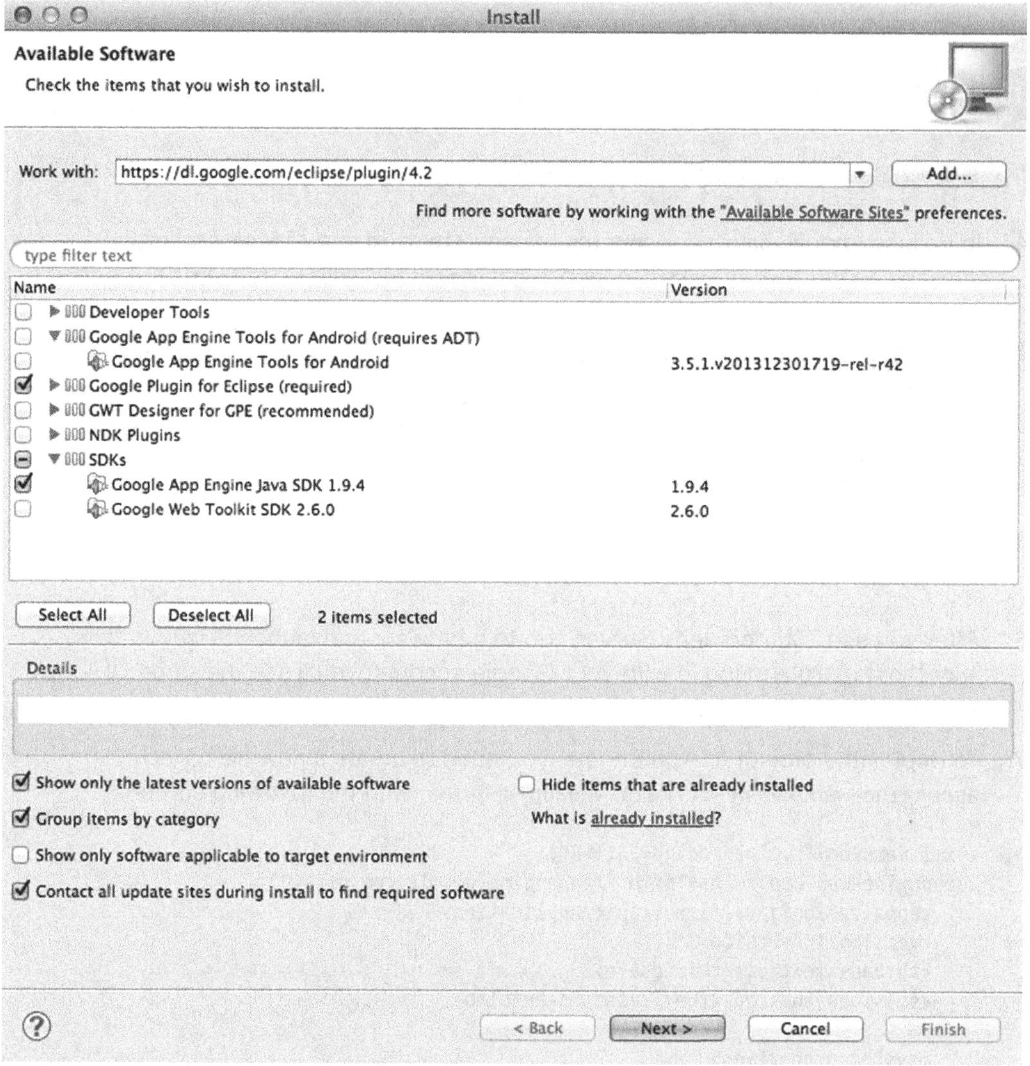

Figure 10-6. Installing Google plug-in and App Engine Java SDK

9. Return to Terminal, cd to the `mirror-quickstart-java` directory first, and then run the following command to get ready for deployment:

```
<path-to-apache-maven>/bin/mvn war:war
```

10. If you're on Mac or Linux, you may also need to add the executable permission of the following two files:

```
chmod +x <path-to-appengine-java-sdk/bin/run_java.sh
chmod +x <path-to-appengine-java-sdk>/bin/appcfg.sh
```

11. Now run the following command to deploy the Mirror quick-start Java project to App Engine:

```
<path-to-appengine-java-sdk>/bin/appcfg.sh update target/glass-java-starter-0.1-SNAPSHOT
```

You may need to enter your Google account and password to complete the deployment process. After you see the "Success" message, open a browser, launch https://<your-app-name>.appspot.com (in my case it's https://java-mirror-api.appspot.com), authenticate with OAuth 2.0, and see the Mirror quick-start Java app running on App Engine!

Before moving forward to the more interesting part of the Mirror API details, let's make sure you can make a change to the app and deploy it. Go back to Eclipse and add some text after Glassware Starter Project in index.jsp and then make some change to the line message = "A timeline item has been inserted"; for the insertItem operation in MainServlet.java. In Terminal, first run mvn war:war to build and package the app; then run the command in step 11. Now reload https://<your-app-name>.appspot.com and click the "Insert the above message" button. You'll see the changes, underlined in red, get deployed to the server, as shown in Figure 10-7.

Figure 10-7. Deployed and modified Mirror quick-start Java app on App Engine

The Mirror API

It's time to explore the nitty-gritty details of the Mirror API. You'll need to often refer to Google's Mirror API guides at https://developers.google.com/glass/develop/mirror and the Mirror API reference at https://developers.google.com/glass/v1/reference. You should also use your version of the Mirror quick-start Java app deployed as an app of your own on Google App Engine, the process discussed in the previous section, to understand and play with the Mirror API. I'll use my https://java-mirror-api.appspot.com for illustration purpose. You can also use http://localhost:8080, as shown earlier, for test purposes, but you may have noticed that in the quick-start project UI, the Mirror Subscriptions API requires SSL, and it's really easy to deploy to App Engine, so testing on App Engine is my preferred way to do things.

> **Note** If you still prefer to test on `http://localhost:8080`, you should set up the subscription proxy server as documented at `https://developers.google.com/glass/tools-downloads/subscription-proxy` so you can receive notification you subscribed to.

Overview

The main building blocks for the Mirror API apps are as follows:

- *Timeline and static cards*: You can insert, update, delete, get, and list static cards, also called *timeline items*, on the Glass timeline.

- *Contacts*: Contacts allow your app to receive timeline items shared by users, and you can also share your timeline items with other contacts.

- *Subscriptions*: You can subscribe to timeline or location notifications so your app gets notified when the user performs an action on a timeline item created by your app or when their location changes.

- *Location*: You can get the user's location, subscribe to location updates, and render maps on timeline items.

In this section, I'll provide many Java examples for each of the building blocks that you can run and test to help you get up to speed with the Mirror API. While going through the Java code, you may need to refer to the Mirror API for Java documentation, which implements the raw HTTP API in Java, at `https://developers.google.com/resources/api-libraries/documentation/mirror/v1/java/latest/`. In the Eclipse glass-java-starter project, the Mirror API for Java Library is packaged in the `google-api-services-mirror-v1-xxx.jar` file, shown in Figure 10-8.

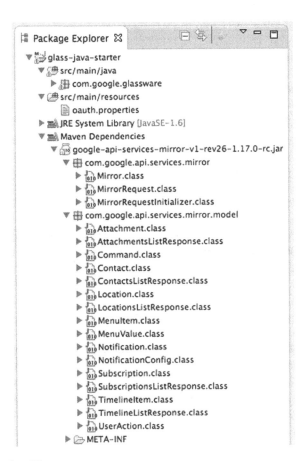

Figure 10-8. The Mirror API for Java Library

Timeline and Static Cards

If you have used Glass for a while, chances are you have seen static cards delivered to your Glass by apps like New York Times and CNN. Static cards are great for delivering periodic or important information, such as headline news, sports scores, patient data (see the healthcare video at http://wearableintelligence.com for an example), and daily quotes. Static cards can also start live cards or immersions, which I covered in great detail in the previous chapters, to create a hybrid and more interactive user experience. You'll see simple examples in this section and a complete app later in the chapter.

Inserting a Simple Text Card

Let's start with the simplest task of inserting text. Open https://developers.google.com/glass/develop/mirror/static-cards, and under "Inserting static cards," choose the Java tab. You'll see these three lines of code:

```
TimelineItem timelineItem = new TimelineItem();
timelineItem.setText("Hello world");
service.timeline().insert(timelineItem).execute();
```

To actually test this, go to Eclipse and open the `MainServlet.java` file in the `src/main/java`'s `com.google.glassware` package. Then after `TimelineItem timelineItem = new TimelineItem();` in `else if (req.getParameter("operation").equals("insertItem")) {...}`, add the code in Listing 10-1.

Listing 10-1. Inserting a New Static Card

```
timelineItem.setText("Hello again!");
MirrorClient.insertTimelineItem(credential, timelineItem);
```

The `MirrorClient` class used here is a wrap of the basic Mirror API in Java. If you look at its implementation of the `insertTimelineItem` method, you'll see a single line of code.

```
getMirror(credential).timeline().insert(item).execute();
```

Because the quick-start Java project is the basis for exploring the Mirror API and building Mirror apps, you'll use MirrorClient instead of the basic Mirror API for easier development.

Now go to Terminal and run this:

```
mvn war:war
appcfg.sh update target/glass-java-starter-0.1-SNAPSHOT
```

Then reload `https://java-mirror-api.appspot.com` (replace java-mirror-api with your own App Engine app name), and after authentication, click "Insert the above message." You'll see two new static cards inserted to your Glass timeline. One is the "Hello World!" text message, defined in `src/main/webapp/index.jsp` and added by the original code `timelineItem.setText(req.getParameter("message"));`. The other is the "Hello again!" text added by the previous code. Figure 10-9 shows this.

Figure 10-9. Inserted Timeline and static cards, mirror API:text insertiontwo timeline text items

Two plain-text cards? That's not very exciting, I know. But this shows you the process of testing the Mirror API code, and with a few more examples, you'll soon be able to explore easily the Mirror API details that I can't fully cover here.

Inserting a Card with an Image

In `index.jsp`, there's an HTML form defined as follows:

```
<form action="<%= WebUtil.buildUrl(request, "/main") %>" method="post">
  <input type="hidden" name="operation" value="insertItem">
  <input type="hidden" name="message" value="Chipotle says 'hi'!">
  <input type="hidden" name="imageUrl" value="<%= appBaseUrl +
        "static/images/chipotle-tube-640x360.jpg" %>">
  <input type="hidden" name="contentType" value="image/jpeg">

  <button class="btn btn-block" type="submit">Insert a picture
    <img class="button-icon" src="<%= appBaseUrl +
        "static/images/chipotle-tube-640x360.jpg" %>">
  </button>
</form>
```

For test purposes, I changed the message value to be "Good morning," added the new image `goodmorning.jpg` to `webapp/static/images`, and then built and deployed the project.

The input name value for `imageUrl` (on my App Engine deployment, it's `https://java-mirror-api.appspot.com/static/images/goodmorning.jpg`) is passed to the doPost method of `MainServlet.java` and processed with the following code:

```
if (req.getParameter("imageUrl") != null) {
    URL url = new URL(req.getParameter("imageUrl"));
    String contentType = req.getParameter("contentType");
    MirrorClient.insertTimelineItem(credential, timelineItem, contentType, url.openStream());
}
```

So, if you click the "Insert a picture" button in your equivalent of `https://java-mirror-api.appspot.com`, you'll see a new card with text and an image, as shown in Figure 10-10, on your Glass.

Figure 10-10. Inserted a timeline item with text and image

Attaching Video to a Card

However, you can't replace the index.jsp and MainServlet.java files shown earlier with videoUrl and contenType values of video/mp4 and expect an item with a video attachment to be inserted. The right way to attach a video is to use the built-in PLAY_VIDEO menu. Here's an example:

```
menuItemList.add(new MenuItem().setAction("PLAY_VIDEO").
setPayload("http://morkout.com/mirrortest.mp4"));

timelineItem.setMenuItems(menuItemList);
```

To test the code, you'll first need to understand how to add menu items to a static card, and you'll see in Listing 10-2 how to attach a video, among other things.

Adding Menu Items to a Card

The menu functionality makes a static card not that static and is a key in building an interactive user experience with the Mirror API. There are two types of menu items you can create to be attached to a card.

Built-in Menu Items

The Mirror API supports many built-in menu items. For a complete list with notes, see https://developers.google.com/glass/v1/reference/timeline#menuItems.action. I'll show you examples with the following common menu items (and you can play with others if needed):

- *REPLY*: Send a voice reply to the card.
- *DELETE*: Delete the card.
- *SHARE*: Share the card with contacts.
- *READ_ALOUD*: Read the card's speakableText or text field aloud.
- *TOGGLE_PINNED*: Toggle the pin state of a card. (A static card is called *pinned* if it's moved to the left of the timeline so it won't be removed. Static cards on the right are removed from the timeline after 7 days or when there are 200 newer cards.)
- *OPEN_URI*: Open the payload of the menu item, either in a browser or as a live card or immersion.
- *PLAY_VIDEO*: Play the video specified in the payload.

Let's see some menu items in action. In MainServlet.java, add the code in Listing 10-2 before if (req.getParameter("imageUrl") != null) { ... }.

Listing 10-2. Adding Built-in Menu Items

```
List<MenuItem> menuItemList = new ArrayList<MenuItem>();
menuItemList.add(new MenuItem().setAction("REPLY"));
menuItemList.add(new MenuItem().setAction("SHARE"));
menuItemList.add(new MenuItem().setAction("READ_ALOUD"));
```

```
menuItemList.add(new MenuItem().setAction("TOGGLE_PINNED"));
menuItemList.add(new MenuItem().setAction("PLAY_VIDEO").setPayload("http://morkout.com/mirrortest.mp4"));
menuItemList.add(new MenuItem().setAction("DELETE"));

timelineItem.setMenuItems(menuItemList);
```

Note that if you call TimelineItem's setHtml method instead of setText to set the content, you'll also need to call TimelineItem's setSpeakableText to make the READ_ALOUD menu item effective; otherwise, the READ_ALOUD menu item won't show.

Now build the project (mvn war:war) and redeploy it to App Engine (appcfg.sh update target/glass-java-starter-0.1-SNAPSHOT). Relaunch your app and click "Insert the above message." After you get the "Hello World!" card, tap it and swipe to see six menu items added. Figure 10-11 shows three such items. Feel free to play the first five before selecting the last one, Delete, to delete the card. Tap Play, and you'll see how a single line of code in Listing 10-2, with the menu item action set to be PLAY_VIDEO, implements attaching a video to a timeline card.

Figure 10-11. *Added menu items to a timeline item*

Another built-in menu item, OPEN_URI, is used to open a URL in a browser, or, more interestingly, as a live card or immersion. It's pretty simple to open in a browser; just add this line before the line of setMenuItems in Listing 10-2:

```
menuItemList.add(new MenuItem().setAction("OPEN_URI").setPayload ("http://www.google.com"));
```

Then you'll see a "View website" menu item with www.google.com shown at the bottom; tapping it will open the Google home page on your Glass.

Launching a GDK App from the Mirror API App

To launch a GDK immersion from a static card's OPEN_URI menu item, you also need to modify the GDK app's AndroidManifest.xml file. Follow these steps to see how this works:

1. Launch the ADT Eclipse that you've been using for developing your GDK apps in the previous chapters; then open the GraphicsAnimationApp project from Chapter 9.

2. In the project's AndroidManifest.xml file, add an intent-filter to the RotationVectorDemo activity, so it'll become the following:

```
<activity
    android:name="com.morkout.graphicsanimation.RotationVectorDemo"
    android:enabled="true"
    android:label="@string/app_name" >

    <intent-filter>
        <action android:name="android.intent.action.VIEW" />
        <category android:name="android.intent.category.DEFAULT" />
        <data android:scheme="com.morkout.graphicsanimation.scheme" />
    </intent-filter>
</activity>
```

Note that android:scheme's value, com.morkout.graphicsanimation.scheme, can be set to any unique string value (for example, immersion_scheme works too); it doesn't have to include the package name com.morkout. graphicsanimation as a prefix, although it's a good idea to do so (to make it less likely to have name conflict).

3. Back in MainServlet.java in Eclipse for the Mirror API Java starter project, add the code in Listing 10-3 before the setAction("DELETE") line in Listing 10-2.

Listing 10-3. Creating OPEN_URI Menu Item to Launch GDK Activity

```
List<MenuValue> menuValues = new ArrayList<MenuValue>();
menuValues.add(new MenuValue().setDisplayName("Graphics").setState("DEFAULT"));
menuItemList.add(new MenuItem().setValues(menuValues).setAction("OPEN_URI").
setPayload("com.morkout.graphicsanimation.scheme://open"));
```

Notice setPayload here uses com.morkout.graphicsanimation.scheme, which matches android:scheme in step 2. Also, to just launch the GDK app, :// is required, but open can be any name, such as xxxx. In other words, the payload needs to be in a format of <scheme_value_that_matches_GDK_ activity_scheme>://<action_name><optional_parameters>. I'll talk about the scheme-specific part (the content after ://) in more detail shortly.

4. Reinstall the GraphicsAnimationApp GDK app to Glass and redeploy the Java Mirror app (mvn, appcfg). Now reload your App Engine app and click "Insert the above message," and you'll see a new menu item called Graphics. Tapping it will launch the RotationVectorDemo activity, shown in Figure 9-5, with running OpenGL ES and Glass sensor event handling code, as in Listing 9-5. Move your head, and you'll see, as you saw in previous chapter, all six sides of the cube, which is something you can't possibly do with just the Mirror API. Take a break and let your imagination go a little wide with this hybrid model of launching a GDK app from a Mirror app.

As stated in step 3, the <action_name> in the scheme-specific part can be any value if your goal is just to launch a GDK app from your Mirror API app. But if you want your GDK app to retrieve the action name or accept parameters passed from the Mirror API app, then you need to set a meaningful <action_name> with parameters. Let's try this:

1. In MainServlet.java, replace the code in Listing 10-3 with the code in Listing 10-4.

   Listing 10-4. Passing Action Name and Parameters to GDK App

   ```
   List<MenuValue> menuValues = new ArrayList<MenuValue>();
   menuValues = new ArrayList<MenuValue>();
   menuValues.add(new MenuValue().setDisplayName("Hybrid2").setState("DEFAULT"));
   menuItemList.add(new MenuItem ().setValues(menuValues).setAction("OPEN_URI").
   setPayload("com.morkout.graphicsanimation.scheme://xxxx/pa/pb/pc"));

   menuValues = new ArrayList<MenuValue>();
   menuValues.add(new MenuValue().setDisplayName("Hybrid3").setState("DEFAULT"));
   menuItemList.add(new MenuItem().setValues(menuValues).setAction("OPEN_URI").
   setPayload("com.morkout.graphicsanimation.scheme://open/p1/p2/p3"));
   ```

2. In the GDK GraphicsAnimation app's RotationVectorDemo.java file, make onCreate, onResume, and onPause look like the code in Listing 10-5 (note that for easy demonstration, I commented out the code that shows the graphics and sets the sensor manager).

   Listing 10-5. Accepting Parameters Passed from the Mirror API App

   ```
   @Override
   protected void onCreate(Bundle savedInstanceState) {
       super.onCreate(savedInstanceState);

       Uri data = getIntent().getData();
       List params = data.getPathSegments();
       String param0 = (String)params.get(0);
       String param1 = (String)params.get(1);
       String param2 = (String)params.get(2);

       String msg = data.getPath() + ":" +  param0+" to "+param1;
       Card card =new Card(this);
       card.setText(msg);
       card.setFootnote(data.getSchemeSpecificPart() + "," + param2);
       View view =card.getView();

       //          // Get an instance of the SensorManager
       //          mSensorManager = (SensorManager)getSystemService(SENSOR_SERVICE);
       //
       //          // Create our Preview view and set it as the content of our
       //          // Activity
       //          mRenderer = new MyRenderer();
       //          mGLSurfaceView = new GLSurfaceView(this);
   ```

```
//          mGLSurfaceView.setRenderer(mRenderer);
//          setContentView(mGLSurfaceView);

    setContentView(view);
}

@Override
protected void onResume() {
    super.onResume();
//      mRenderer.start();
//      mGLSurfaceView.onResume();
}

@Override
protected void onPause() {
    super.onPause();
//      mRenderer.stop();
//      mGLSurfaceView.onPause();
}
```

3.   Install the GraphicsAnimation GDK app to Glass.

4.   Rebuild, redeploy, and reload the Java starter Mirror app. Then click "Insert the above message," and you'll see a new "Hello World!" card inserted to your Glass. Tap it and select the menu items Hybrid2 and Hybrid3. You'll see two cards created by your GDK app code in Listing 10-5, as shown in Figure 10-12. The cards' text shows the parameters, and the footer shows the schema-specific part sent from the Mirror app.

Figure 10-12. Displaying action name and parameters from Mirror app in GDK app

Custom Menu Items

To create custom menu items, add the code in Listing 10-6 after the code in Listing 10-4.

Listing 10-6. Creating Custom Menu Item

```
menuValues = new ArrayList<MenuValue>();
menuValues.add(new MenuValue().setIconUrl(WebUtil.buildUrl(req,
    "/static/images/drill.png")).setDisplayName("Drill In"));
menuItemList.add(new MenuItem().setValues(menuValues).setId("drill").setAction("CUSTOM"));
```

> **Note** In MenuValues, the icon needs to be a 50x50 PNG file with a transparent background and white-only foreground, or it may not show in the card. Google offers a set of menu icons, available for download at https://developers.google.com/glass/tools-downloads/menu_icons.zip, for your custom menu items so your app can be consistent with the Glass UI.

Build and deploy the app again and click "Insert the above message." You'll see a new "Drill In" menu item. Tap it, and NotifyServlet will get a notification. If you look at the app logs on App Engine, you'll see the following message:

```
com.google.glassware.NotifyServlet doPost: got raw notification {
"collection": "timeline", "itemId": "4494834b-dba9-4309-af7d-f555192984d9",
"operation": "UPDATE", "userToken": "107295550450648165922", "userActions": [
{   "type": "CUSTOM",    "payload": "drill"  } ]}
```

By the way, the log for SHARE shows that there's only a single type attribute in the userActions array.

```
com.google.glassware.NotifyServlet doPost: got raw notification {
"collection": "timeline", "itemId": "0d325a9e-77ad-4ce8-a535-bb9cd667d7f4",
"operation": "INSERT", "userToken": "107295550450648165922", "userActions":
[  {   "type": "SHARE"  } ]}
```

The NotifyServlet.java file that comes with the Java starter project does not have code that handles the notification, so you'll see "I don't know what to do with this notification, so I'm ignoring it." in the app log. How about adding more details when user selected Drill In? To do that, just add the code in Listing 10-7 to the doPost method of NotifyServlet.java, inside else if (notification.getCollection().equals("timeline")).

Listing 10-7. Handling Custom Menu Item Selection Notification

```
else if (notification.getUserActions().contains(new UserAction().setType("CUSTOM").
setPayload("drill"))) {
    TimelineItem timelineItem = new TimelineItem();
    timelineItem.setTitle("Drill In Requested");
    timelineItem.setHtml("<article><section><p>First page</p></section></article><article><section>
    <p>Second page</p></section></article><article><section><p>Third page</p></section></article>");
    MirrorClient.insertTimelineItem(credential, item);
}
```

The next time you select Drill In, a new card of HTML content will be inserted, showing "First page" at first. Tap the new card, and you'll see a "Read more" menu item, which lets you see other articles ("Second page" and "Third page"). You'll see in the next subsection a detailed introduction to what can be used for the HTML content.

Inserting an HTML Card

Most of the static cards you have probably seen on your Glass are in HTML instead of plain text. Supported and blocked HTML elements are listed in detail at https://developers.google.com/glass/v1/reference/timeline#html. Here's a quick summary of all the supported elements: h1, h2, h3, h4, h5, h6, img, li, ol, ul, article, aside, details, figure, figcaption, footer, header, nav, section, summary, time, blockquote, br, div, hr, p, span, b, big, center, em, i, u, s, small, strike, strong, style, sub, sup, table, tbody, td, tfoot, th, thead, and tr. For details, see https://developers.google.com/glass/v1/reference/timeline#html.

To get familiar with the HTML support by Glass, you should definitely check out the Mirror API Playground at https://developers.google.com/glass/tools-downloads/playground, which offers many common templates with HTML source code: TEXT, AUTO RESIZE, HYBRID, HYBRID MOSAIC, MULTIPAGE, SIMPLE EVENT, LIST, IMAGE LIST, MOSAIC LIST, STOCK, SPORTS, FLIGHT, MOVIE, TRANSIT, SIMPLE MESSAGE, and AUTHOR. You can play with any template you choose for your card and test changes to the HTML content for the template right there at the Mirror API Playground. After you feel good about the UI of your card content, you can then apply the HTML content to your code and test the deployed version.

Google also offers a neat CSS file with the style definitions for many elements and classes if you want to dig deep and see how the templates are implemented: https://mirror-api-playground.appspot.com/assets/css/base_style.css.

Let's see an example of using the FLIGHT template for an NBA Roster app that I'll discuss soon. Go to https://developers.google.com/glass/tools-downloads/playground, scroll down and choose to see the Templates list, and then scroll horizontally and select the FLIGHT template. Click the HTML tab, and replace the HTML source code there with the following code:

```
<article><section><div class='layout-figure'><div class='align-center yellow'><p class='text-auto-
size'>Chris Paul</p><p class='green'>Age: 29</p></div><div class='text-normal'><p>No. 3, PG</p><p>6-0,
175lb</p><p>Wake Forest</p><p class='red'>$18,668,431</p></div></div></section></article>
```

Figure 10-13 shows what you'll see on the screen.

Figure 10-13. Playing with the HTML template

Now that you know how to find and refine a cool template for your card, I'll move on and let you have all the fun in the Mirror API Playground. Just remember that using the templates is highly encouraged because it ensures that your app layout meets the Glass design style guidelines; see `https://developers.google.com/glass/design/style` for details.

Getting a Card

To see how to get a timeline item and call its methods, first add the following code at the end of `MirrorClient.java`:

```
public static TimelineItem getTimelineItem
                              (Credential credential, String itemId)
      throws IOException {
              return getMirror(credential).timeline().get(itemId).execute();
}
```

Then in `MainServlet.java`, after `timelineItem.setMenuItems(menuItemList);` in Listing 10-2, use the code in Listing 10-8.

Listing 10-8. Getting a Timeline Item

```
if (req.getParameter("imageUrl") != null) {
...
} else {
    TimelineItem item = MirrorClient.insertTimelineItem(credential, timelineItem);
    TimelineItem insertedItem = MirrorClient.getTimelineItem(credential, item.getId());
    message = "A timeline item " + insertedItem.getText() + ", " + insertedItem.getTitle() +
" has been inserted.";
}
```

For demo purpose, you just use the newly inserted item's `itemid` to retrieve it. Now if you click the "Insert the above message" button, you'll see this message at the top of the browser window: "A timeline item Hello World! has been inserted."

`https://developers.google.com/glass/v1/reference/timeline/get` shows more examples of other methods you can call on a timeline item: `getIsDeleted`, `getCreator`, `getDisplayTime`, `getInReplyTo`, `getRecipients`, `getNotification`, and `getAttachments`. A complete list of available methods is at `https://developers.google.com/resources/api-libraries/documentation/mirror/v1/java/latest/com/google/api/services/mirror/model/TimelineItem.html`.

Getting a List of Cards

To get a list of timeline items for the authenticated user, meaning all the items successfully inserted to the user's timeline by the app, add the code in Listing 10-9 after Listing 10-8.

Listing 10-9. Getting a List of Timeline Items

```
List<TimelineItem> result = new ArrayList<TimelineItem>();
TimelineListResponse timelineItems = MirrorClient.listItems(credential, 100);
LOG.info("timelineItems size="+timelineItems.getItems().size());
```

```
if (timelineItems.getItems() != null && timelineItems.getItems().size() > 0) {
    result.addAll(timelineItems.getItems());
    for (int i=0; i<timelineItems.getItems().size(); i++) {
        LOG.info("timelineItem: "+timelineItems.getItems().get(i).toString());
    }
}
```

After you insert the "Hello World!" message, open `https://appengine.google.com` in your browser and select your app for the Java starter project. In Logs below Main, you'll see a bunch of items like the following:

com.google.glassware.MainServlet doPost: timelineItem: {"created":"2014-05-15T16:32:34.268Z","etag":"1400171554268","id":"4635d0b7-ffef-4b0f-8a90-ff7c

com.google.glassware.MainServlet doPost: timelineItem: {"created":"2014-05-15T16:32:25.968Z","etag":"1400171545968","id":"cc6b3193-a185-4f50-81ea-859a

com.google.glassware.MainServlet doPost: timelineItem: {"created":"2014-05-15T16:28:17.432Z","etag":"1400171297432","id":"8cdf49a0-4c77-4adf-a804-8659

com.google.glassware.MainServlet doPost: timelineItem: {"created":"2014-05-15T16:28:07.022Z","etag":"1400171287022","id":"b9dca7f2-4672-491b-a4a3-e328

com.google.glassware.MainServlet doPost: timelineItem: {"created":"2014-05-15T15:19:31.029Z","etag":"1400167171029","html":"<article><section><p>First

com.google.glassware.MainServlet doPost: timelineItem: {"created":"2014-05-15T07:28:57.601Z","etag":"1400167169480","id":"06729c02-0ab7-41d9-80e3-9f9c

com.google.glassware.MainServlet doPost: timelineItem: {"created":"2014-05-15T07:29:09.728Z","etag":"1400138949728","html":"<article><section><p>First

Each item's detail information is like this:

```
com.google.glassware.MainServlet doPost: timelineItem: {"created":"2014-05-15T16:32:34.268Z","etag":
"1400171554268","id":"4635d0b7-ffef-4b0f-8a90-ff7cdbc52edf","kind":"mirror#timelineItem",
"menuItems":[{"action":"REPLY"},{"action":"SHARE"},{"action":"READ_ALOUD"},{"action":"TOGGLE_PINNED"},
{"action":"PLAY_VIDEO","payload":"http://morkout.com/mirrortest.mp4"},{"action":"OPEN_URI",
"payload":"immersion_scheme://open","values":[{"displayName":"Graphics","state":"DEFAULT"}]},
{"action":"CUSTOM","id":"drill","values":[{"displayName":"Drill In","iconUrl":"https://java-mirror-
api.appspot.com/static/images/drill.png"}]},{"action":"OPEN_URI","payload":"http://www.google.com"},
{"action":"DELETE"}],"notification":{"level":"DEFAULT"},"selfLink":"https://www.googleapis.com/
mirror/v1/timeline/4635d0b7-ffef-4b0f-8a90-ff7cdbc52edf","text":"Hello World!","updated":"2014-05-
15T16:32:34.268Z"}
```

Updating and Patching a Card

The following code in `NotifyServlet.java` inside `if (notification.getUserActions().contains(new UserAction().setType("LAUNCH")))` lets you update an already inserted timeline card. Here is the card inserted with the transcribed text as content, after one of the two voice commands "Take a note" or "Post an update" is said:

```
TimelineItem timelineItem = mirrorClient.timeline().get(notification.getItemId()).execute();
String noteText = timelineItem.getText();
timelineItem.setText(null);
timelineItem.setHtml(makeHtmlForCard("<p class='text-auto-size'>" + "You said " + noteText + "?</p>"));
timelineItem.setMenuItems(Lists.newArrayList(new MenuItem().setAction("DELETE")));

mirrorClient.timeline().update(timelineItem.getId(), timelineItem).execute();
```

If you watch your Glass closely, you may first see a card with the text of what you said; then seconds later it gets updated with the previous HTML content.

https://developers.google.com/glass/v1/reference/timeline/update shows the complete list of properties you can use for updating a card, which is the same as those for inserting a card. This is because with update, you replace the old card with the new one, so you have to provide all the fields you want to show.

Patch is a partial or small update. Using Patch, you only need to send the data for the specific fields you need to update (add, modify, or delete). Here is a simple example (you'll see how to test this in the "Contacts" section):

```
TimelineItem itemPatch = new TimelineItem();
itemPatch.setText("J.J. Mirror got your photo! " + caption);
mirrorClient.timeline().patch(notification.getItemId(),
                itemPatch).execute();
```

Pagination

If the content for a timeline doesn't fit on a single card, you should enable paginating if the content is HTML. Glass does paginating for you automatically if the content is plain text. Tapping a paginated item will show the "Read more" menu item.

There are two ways to enable paginating for HTML content.

- *The manual way*: As shown in Listing 10-7, use the article tag for each card in a timeline item.

- *The automatic way*: Set the article's class property value to auto-paginate. For example, go to the Java starter project App Engine URL, click the "Insert a card with long paginated HTML" button, and you'll see a card shown in Figure 10-14 inserted.

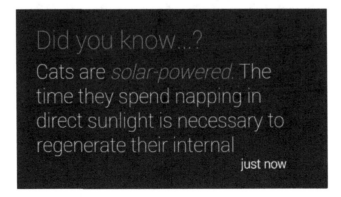

Figure 10-14. A card that supports pagination

Tap it and you'll see "Read more." Tap again to read the rest of content. Swiping is needed if there are more than two pages of content.

The HTML code for the card is as follows, using the auto-paginate class for the article element:

```
<article class="auto-paginate"><h2 class="blue text-large">Did you know...?</h2><p>Cats are
<em class="yellow">solar-powered.</em> The time they spend napping in direct sunlight is necessary
to regenerate their internal batteries. Cats that do not receive sufficient charge may exhibit the
following symptoms: lethargy, irritability, and disdainful glares. Cats will reactivate on their own
automatically after a complete charge cycle; it is recommended that they be left undisturbed during
this process to maximize your enjoyment of your cat.</p><br><p>For more cat maintenance tips, tap to
view the website!</p></article>
```

One last thing to know about paginating for HTML is another CSS class name called cover-only, used to prevent the default behavior of the first card appearing again when you tap "Read more." You can apply cover-only to both cases of enabling paginating: <article class="cover-only"> or <article class="auto-paginate cover-only">.

Bundling

To group related timeline items, call the setBundleId(<id>) method and pass the same <id> to those items. Then a page curl on the top-right corner will appear when those items are inserted, as shown in Figure 10-15.

Figure 10-15. Bundled cards

You'll see an example of this in the NBA Roster app; all the players in the same team are bundled together.

> **Note** Although both pagination and bundling are for presenting related content that won't fit on one screen, their UI and implementation are totally different. You can't tell whether an item has pagination until you tap it. If it does, you'll see "Read more." But you can tell if an item is one of the bundled items right away; it is if there is page curl on the top-right corner.

That's about all you need to know about timeline and static cards. Of course, you should check out the Mirror API guides, the Mirror API reference, the Mirror API Playground, and the Mirror API Java library reference for more details when necessary. With what you've learned here, it's easy and quick to write your own code and then build, deploy, test, and iterate.

Contacts

Chances are you have used contacts without even realizing it. After you take a picture or record a video, there's a Share menu item that lets you share the picture or video to your G+ circles or, if you have installed the apps, to your Facebook, Twitter, Evernote, or Path accounts. This is one of the two typical use cases of contacts: allowing users to share content with your app. To make the sharing possible, a contact needs to be created in the app to represent the app. Then when you tap Share, you'll see a list of contacts you can share the item with.

The other use case of contacts is to share your timeline cards with other apps that have contacts created in the apps. To make it happen, you just need to add the built-in SHARE menu item to the card.

If you expect your app to handle only specific types of content, you should use acceptable MIME types when creating your contact so your app appears only for cards that match the MIME types.

You can also subscribe to timeline notifications if you want to get notified when users share some content with your contact. That way, you can perform any necessary processing on the content. For example, you'll see how image processing can be done with contacts and notifications, in the Mirror API way, later in the chapter.

In the middle of the Java starter project at `https://java-mirror-api.appspot.com/`, there's a Delete Java Quick Start Contact. Click it, and after page reloads, you'll see the button changes to Insert Java Quick Start Contact. The JSP code that does this is as follows:

```
<% if (contact == null) { %>
<form action="<%= WebUtil.buildUrl(request, "/main") %>" method="post">
  <input type="hidden" name="operation" value="insertContact">
  <input type="hidden" name="iconUrl" value="<%= appBaseUrl +
        "static/images/chipotle-tube-640x360.jpg" %>">
  <input type="hidden" name="id"
        value="<%= MainServlet.CONTACT_ID %>">
  <input type="hidden" name="name"
        value="<%= MainServlet.CONTACT_NAME %>">
  <button class="btn btn-block btn-success" type="submit">
    Insert Java Quick Start Contact
  </button>
</form>
<% } else { %>
<form action="<%= WebUtil.buildUrl(request, "/main") %>" method="post">
  <input type="hidden" name="operation" value="deleteContact">
  <input type="hidden" name="id" value="<%= MainServlet.CONTACT_ID %>">
  <button class="btn btn-block btn-danger" type="submit">
    Delete Java Quick Start Contact
  </button>
</form>
<% } %>
```

CONTACT_NAME is set in MainServlet.java. You can change it to any unique string. This is my changed line:

```java
public static final String CONTACT_NAME = "J.J. Mirror";
```

Listing 10-10 handles creating and deleting the contact.

Listing 10-10. Inserting and Deleting a Contact

```java
else if (req.getParameter("operation").equals("insertContact")) {
    if (req.getParameter("iconUrl") == null ||
                req.getParameter("name") == null) {
        message = "Must specify iconUrl and name to insert contact";
    } else {
        Contact contact = new Contact();
        contact.setId(req.getParameter("id"));
        contact.setDisplayName(req.getParameter("name"));
        contact.setImageUrls(Lists.newArrayList(
            req.getParameter("iconUrl")));
        MirrorClient.insertContact(credential, contact);
    }
} else if (req.getParameter("operation").equals("deleteContact"))
    MirrorClient.deleteContact(credential, req.getParameter("id"));
```

After you share a timeline item with the contact, you'll get a notification where you can get the item shared to you (actually, a copy of the shared item is created and inserted to the timeline because your app cannot access the original item) and update the item as you want. The following code from the Java starter project illustrates how to do this:

```java
else if (notification.getCollection().equals("timeline")) {
    TimelineItem timelineItem = mirrorClient.timeline().get
                    (notification.getItemId()).execute();

    if (notification.getUserActions() != null &&
        notification.getUserActions().contains
                        (new UserAction().setType("SHARE"))
        && timelineItem.getAttachments() != null
                && timelineItem.getAttachments().size() > 0) {

                String caption = timelineItem.getText();
                if (caption == null) caption = "";
                TimelineItem itemPatch = new TimelineItem();
                itemPatch.setText("J.J. Mirror got your photo! " + caption);
                mirrorClient.timeline().patch(notification.getItemId(),
                            itemPatch).execute();
        }
}
```

Figure 10-16 shows a picture taken and text added to it after it's shared to my app and processed by the previous code.

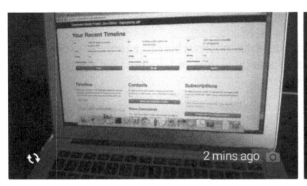

Figure 10-16. Before and after a picture is shared to a contact and patched

Sharing Transcribed Speech

Another neat feature of contacts is that you can use voice commands to share transcribed speech with a contact, with or without a timeline card. Currently there are two commands you can use: "Take a note" and "Post an update." Add one of the following lines of code to Listing 10-10, before the `insertContact` line:

```
contact.setAcceptCommands(Lists.newArrayList(
        new Command().setType("TAKE_A_NOTE")));

contact.setAcceptCommands(Lists.newArrayList(
        new Command().setType("POST_AN_UPDATE")));
```

Now after building, deploying, and launching the app again, when you say "Take a note" or "Post an update" from the OK Glass menu, you can choose your app to send the note or update to. After that, your app will get a notification. If you open the App Engine log, you'll see that both commands' raw notifications are the same.

```
com.google.glassware.NotifyServlet doPost: got raw notification { "collection": "timeline",
"itemId": "79cf7fa7-4d9a-4a90-9bc5-f54c0498083f", "operation": "INSERT", "userToken":
"107295550450648165922", "userActions": [ {    "type": "LAUNCH"   } ]}
```

The code in `NotifyServlet.java` shown here shows how to get the spoken text and update the timeline item with it and a DELETE menu item:

```
if (notification.getUserActions().contains(new UserAction().setType("LAUNCH"))) {
    String noteText = timelineItem.getText();
    timelineItem.setText(null);
    timelineItem.setHtml(makeHtmlForCard("<p class='text-auto-size'>" + "You said "
    + noteText + "?</p>"));
    timelineItem.setMenuItems(Lists.newArrayList(new MenuItem().setAction("DELETE")));
    mirrorClient.timeline().update(timelineItem.getId(), timelineItem).execute();
}
```

In the NBA Roster app, you'll see how to use the voice command feature as a workaround to query for player information.

Subscriptions

You can subscribe to two types of notifications: timeline notifications when an action is taken on a timeline item and location notifications when the user location is updated. In the Java starter project, the code to create and delete a subscription is as follows:

```
MirrorClient.insertSubscription(credential,
    WebUtil.buildUrl(req, "/notify"), userId,
    req.getParameter("collection"));
MirrorClient.deleteSubscription(credential,
    req.getParameter("subscriptionId"));
```

Possible values for both `collection` and `subscriptionId` are `timeline` and `locations`, defined in `index.jsp`. After a subscription is inserted, the app will get notification in `NotifyServlet.java`, as you saw earlier with actions taken on a timeline item, such as SHARE, LAUNCH, and selection on a menu item. You use `notification.getCollection().equals("locations")` and `notification.getCollection().equals("timeline")` to test the notification type, and you use `notification.getUserActions().contains(new UserAction().setType("LAUNCH"))`, `notification.getUserActions().contains(new UserAction().setType("SHARE"))`, and `notification.getUserActions().contains(new UserAction().setType ("CUSTOM").setPayload("<payload>"))` to test for a specific action on a timeline item.

> **Note**   Not all menu item actions will generate a notification. For example, none of the Read loud, Play, or items that launch a GDK app will result in a notification. But Share, Reply, Pin, Delete, Take a note, or Post an update will. One way to find out for sure is via your app's App Engine log.

Again, remember that subscriptions require SSL and won't work on localhost, unless you set up the subscription proxy server; see `https://developers.google.com/glass/tools-downloads/subscription-proxy` for more details.

Locations

It's really easy to get periodic location data. Use the following code in the doPost method of NotifyServlet.java:

```
if (notification.getCollection().equals("locations")) {
    Mirror glass = MirrorClient.getMirror(credential);
    Location location = glass.locations().get
        (notification.getItemId()).execute();
    LOG.info("New location is " + location.getLatitude()
        + ", " + location.getLongitude() + ", address:"
        + location.getAddress() + ", accuracy="
        + location.getAccuracy());
}
```

Click the "Subscribe to location updates" button on the right end of the Java starter project page, and you'll see in your project's App Engine log something like this:

```
com.google.glassware.NotifyServlet doPost: New location is 37.4268091,-122.0808162, address:null,
accuracy=27.951000213623047
```

The accuracy is in meters, but the address is not returned; this seems to be out of your control; however, it's possible to use the Geocoder class and its getFromLocation method, shown in Chapter 8, to get the address information from the latitude and longitude.

See https://developers.google.com/glass/v1/reference/locations#resource for a detailed explanation of the properties of Location, and see https://developers.google.com/resources/api-libraries/documentation/mirror/v1/java/latest/ for a complete list of methods of Location.

Image Processing: The Mirror API Way

Now that I have covered all the basics of the Mirror API, let's consider image processing, a common use of Glass, but this time using the Mirror API. You can reuse the image upload code for social sharing in Chapter 7 to upload a picture that the user selects to a server for any kind of image processing (passing the image URL to a GDK app for processing is another option).

You can add the code in Listing 10-11, with its uploading part mostly copied from Chapter 7, to NotifyServlet.java to upload a picture, which you choose to share to your app, to a server. timelineItem.getAttachments().get(0) returns an Attachment object that has a getContentUrl() method you can use to generate an InputStream object to be uploaded to your server.

Listing 10-11. Uploading Shared Image to Server for Further Processing

```
if (notification.getUserActions().contains(new UserAction().setType("SHARE"))
        && timelineItem.getAttachments() != null && timelineItem.getAttachments().size() > 0) {
        InputStream inputStream = downloadAttachment(mirrorClient, notification.getItemId(),
        timelineItem.getAttachments().get(0));
    try {
        URL url = new URL("http://www.morkout.com/iapps/social/glassupload.php?shareapp=mirror");
        String boundary = "*****";
        String lineEnd = "\r\n";
        String twoHyphens = "--";
        int bytesRead, bytesAvailable, bufferSize;
        byte[] buffer;
        int maxBufferSize = 1 * 1024 * 1024;

        // Open a HTTP  connection to  the URL
        HttpURLConnection conn = (HttpURLConnection) url.openConnection();
        conn.setDoInput(true); // Allow Inputs
        conn.setDoOutput(true); // Allow Outputs
        conn.setUseCaches(false); // Don't use a Cached Copy
        conn.setRequestMethod("POST");
        conn.setRequestProperty("Connection", "Keep-Alive");
```

```
    conn.setRequestProperty("ENCTYPE", "multipart/form-data");
    conn.setRequestProperty("Content-Type", "multipart/form-data;boundary=" + boundary);
    conn.setRequestProperty("Filedata", "jjmirror.jpg");

    DataOutputStream dos = new DataOutputStream(conn.getOutputStream());

    dos.writeBytes(twoHyphens + boundary + lineEnd);
    dos.writeBytes("Content-Disposition: form-data; name=Filedata;filename=jjmirror.jpg"+
    lineEnd);

    dos.writeBytes(lineEnd);

    // create a buffer of  maximum size
    bytesAvailable = inputStream.available();
    bufferSize = Math.min(bytesAvailable, maxBufferSize);
    buffer = new byte[bufferSize];

    // read file and write it into form...
    bytesRead = inputStream.read(buffer, 0, bufferSize);

    while (bytesRead > 0) {
        dos.write(buffer, 0, bufferSize);
        bytesAvailable = inputStream.available();
        bufferSize = Math.min(bytesAvailable, maxBufferSize);
        bytesRead = inputStream.read(buffer, 0, bufferSize);
    }

    // send multipart form data necesssary after file data...
    dos.writeBytes(lineEnd);
    dos.writeBytes(twoHyphens + boundary + twoHyphens + lineEnd);

    // Responses from the server (code and message)
    int serverResponseCode = conn.getResponseCode();
    String serverResponseMessage = conn.getResponseMessage();
    InputStream is = conn.getInputStream();
    int ch;
    StringBuffer b = new StringBuffer();
    while ((ch = is.read()) != -1) {
        b.append((char) ch);
    }

    LOG.info("uploaded file at http://www.morkout.com/iapps/social/uploads/" + b.toString());
    is.close();
    dos.flush();
    dos.close();

} catch (Exception e) {
    LOG.warning(e.getMessage());
}
```

```
public static InputStream downloadAttachment(Mirror service, String itemId, Attachment attachment) {
    try {
        HttpResponse resp = service.getRequestFactory().buildGetRequest
            (new GenericUrl(attachment.getContentUrl())).execute();
        return resp.getContent();
    } catch (IOException e) {
        LOG.warning(e.getMessage());
        return null;
    }
}
```

The server PHP code is the same as that in Chapter 7.

```
<?
if (!isset($_FILES["Filedata"]) || !is_uploaded_file($_FILES["Filedata"]["tmp_name"]) ||
$_FILES["Filedata"]["error"] != 0) {
    echo 0;
}
else {
    $uploaded_filename = "glassupoad-" . md5($_FILES["Filedata"]["tmp_name"] . uniqid("")) . ".jpg";
    move_uploaded_file($_FILES["Filedata"]["tmp_name"], "uploads/" . $uploaded_filename);
    echo $uploaded_filename;
}
?>
```

Now build and deploy the code in Listing 10-11 to App Engine and reload your app. Take a picture, choose the Share menu item, and select your app to share with. Go check your App Engine log in a few seconds, and you'll see the uploaded file URL like this:

```
com.google.glassware.NotifyServlet doPost: uploaded file at
 http://www.morkout.com/iapps/social/uploads/mirror-a89e082e42f6b2895d7c49b52c256fc5.jpg
```

Server-based image or video processing is beyond the scope of the book, but there are a lot of online tutorials and books about the server-based OpenCV and FFmpeg, whose Android libraries I covered in Chapters 4 and 5.

Creating and Testing a New Mirror App in Java

Before I show you a complete example of a Mirror API app, I will first outline the steps to create, deploy, and test a new Mirror API app in Java.

1. Make a copy of the sample Mirror API quick-start Java project.

2. Change the `<artifactId>` value of pom.xml to something different from your other Maven projects in Eclipse and then import the project to Eclipse.

3. Create a new App Engine instance and client ID and secret, as you saw earlier in this chapter. Then update oauth.properties. (If you copy from the original GitHub Java project, you also need to copy the appengine-web.xml file and change the application name, also discussed earlier in the chapter.)

4. Mainly modify `index.jsp`, `MainServlet.java`, and `NotifyServlet.java` for the new app feature implementation.

5. Use the Google Mirror API Playground at `https://developers.google.com/glass/tools-downloads/playground` to choose the template or templates that best fit your app and make any necessary changes to the source HTML code according to your app requirements.

6. Run the `mvn war:war` and `appcfg` commands I discussed earlier to deploy the app to App Engine.

7. Launch the app on App Engine, debug with the App Engine log service, and test on your Glass.

For simplicity purposes, I'll continue to modify the Java starter project to implement the features for the NBA Roster app.

The NBA Roster App

It's May 2014—NBA playoff time! By the time you read the book, the NBA Finals 2013–2014 should already be over, but it doesn't hurt to get some basic facts straight on your Glass, anytime and anywhere.

When I watch NBA games, I often want to get a player's information right away. So, after I owned Google Glass, I hoped to be able to look at the TV screen and zoom in on a player and get the basic information about him with a simple voice command. In this section, let's see how to use the Mirror API to access a player's information. I'll work on the more challenging facial recognition problem in a future GitHub project.

In summary, the features you will implement are as follows:

1. Browse the 16 NBA 2013–2014 playoff teams.

2. Selecting any of the 16 teams will let you see all players' information in the team, including each player's jersey number, name, position, age, height, weight, college if any, and salary.

3. Use a voice command to search for a player and see his information right away.

To implement these features, let's first add in `MainServlet.java` the following constant array consisting of all 16 playoff teams' player information, collected from the Internet and parsed into the Java format. (In a real app, you're more likely to access the data from a back-end database.)

```
public static final String[][] teams = {
    ...
    {"Los Angeles Clippers", "3", "Chris Paul", "PG", "29", "6-0", "175", "Wake Forest",
    "$18,668,431"},
    {"Los Angeles Clippers", "4", "J.J. Redick", "SG", "29", "6-4", "190", "Duke", "$6,500,000"},
    {"Los Angeles Clippers", "8", "Hedo Turkoglu", "SF", "35", "6-10", "220", "", "$473,357"},
```

```
    {"San Antonio Spurs", "21", "Tim Duncan", "PF", "38", "6-11", "250", "Wake Forest",
    "$10,361,446"},
    {"San Antonio Spurs", "20", "Manu Ginobili", "SG", "36", "6-6", "205", "", "$7,500,000"},
    {"San Antonio Spurs", "4", "Danny Green", "SG", "26", "6-6", "215", "North Carolina",
    "$3,762,500"},
    {"San Antonio Spurs", "9", "Tony Parker", "PG", "31", "6-2", "185", "", "$12,500,000"},
    ...
};
```

Now in index.jsp, make the following change after the insertItemAllUsers form (so you'll see a new button called NBA Roster when you reload the app (see https://java-mirror-api.appspot.com for an example):

```
<form action="<%= WebUtil.buildUrl(request, "/main") %>" method="post">
  <input type="hidden" name="operation" value="insertItemAllUsers">
  <button class="btn btn-block" type="submit">
    Insert a card to all users</button>
</form>

<!-- ******** START of NBA Roster 2014 ******** -->

<form action="<%= WebUtil.buildUrl(request, "/main") %>" method="post">
  <input type="hidden" name="operation" value="getNBAPlayerInfo">
  <button class="btn btn-block" type="submit">
    NBA Roster</button>
</form>
</div>
```

To handle the getNBAPlayerInformation operation, add in MainServlet.java the following code:

```
else if (req.getParameter("operation").equals("getNBAPlayerInfo")) {
    TimelineItem timelineItem = new TimelineItem();
    timelineItem.setText("NBA Team Rosters");
    List<MenuItem> menuItemList = new ArrayList<MenuItem>();

    Set<String> names = new LinkedHashSet<String>();
    for (String[] team : teams)
        names.add(team[0]);
    for (String name : names) {
        String words[] = name.split(" ");
        String mascot = words[words.length - 1].toLowerCase();
        List<MenuValue> menuValues = new ArrayList<MenuValue>();
        menuValues.add(new MenuValue().setIconUrl(WebUtil.buildUrl
                    (req, "/static/images/ic_run_50.png")).setDisplayName(name));
        menuItemList.add(new
            MenuItem().setValues(menuValues).setId(mascot).
                setAction("CUSTOM"));
    }
```

```
    timelineItem.setMenuItems(menuItemList);
    timelineItem.setNotification(new NotificationConfig().setLevel("DEFAULT"));
    MirrorClient.insertTimelineItem(credential, timelineItem);
    message = "The NBA Roster item has been inserted.";
}
```

What the previous code does is to collect the names of the 16 teams, use the names as custom menu items' display names, and insert a new timeline item with 16 custom menu items and "NBA Team Rosters" as its content. Notice you use the team's mascot name as its menu item ID, which will be passed and retrieved as the payload when a team (menu item) is selected; for example, if you select Chicago Bulls, you'll see in the App Engine log the following information (payload has the value of bulls, the mascot of Chicago Bulls set in setId(mascot)):

```
com.google.glassware.NotifyServlet doPost: got raw notification { "collection": "timeline",
"itemId": "0cad6dd7-a944-4272-b857-e9cec2ac9e11", "operation": "UPDATE", "userToken":
"107295550450648165922", "userActions": [ {    "type": "CUSTOM",    "payload": "bulls"  } ]}
```

Now you need to handle the tap on each of those names. In NotifyServlet.java, at the end of else if (notification.getCollection().equals("timeline")), add the following:

```
else {
    boolean notificationProcessed = false;
    // get all mascots
    Set<String> mascots = new LinkedHashSet<String>();
    for (String[] team : MainServlet.teams) {
        String words[] = team[0].split(" ");
        String mascot = words[words.length - 1].toLowerCase();
        mascots.add(mascot);
    }
    for (String mascot : mascots) {
        if (notification.getUserActions().contains(new UserAction().setType("CUSTOM").
        setPayload(mascot))) {
            notificationProcessed = true;
            TimelineItem item = new TimelineItem();

            for (String[] team : MainServlet.teams) {
                String words[] = team[0].split(" ");
                if (mascot.equals(words[words.length - 1].toLowerCase())) {
                    String html = "<article><section><div class='layout-figure'>
                    <div class='align-center yellow'><p class='text-auto-size'>" + team[2] + "</p>
                    <p class='green'>Age: " + team[4] + "</p></div><div class='text-normal'>";
                    html += "<p>No. " + team[1] + ", " + team[3] + "</p>";
                    html += "<p>" + team[5] + ", " + team[6] + "lb</p>";
                    html += "<p>" + team[7] + "</p>";
                    html += "<p class='red'>" + team[8] + "</p>";
                    html += "</div></div></section></article>";

                    LOG.info("html="+html);
                    item.setHtml(html);
                    item.setBundleId(mascot);
```

```
            item.setSpeakableText(team[2] + ", Age " + team[4] + ", " + team[5] + ", " +
            team[6] + ", " + team[7] + ", Salary: " + team[8]);

            List<MenuItem> menuItemList = new ArrayList<MenuItem>();
            menuItemList.add(new MenuItem().setAction("SHARE"));
            menuItemList.add(new MenuItem().setAction("READ_ALOUD"));
            menuItemList.add(new MenuItem().setAction("TOGGLE_PINNED"));
            item.setMenuItems(menuItemList);
            MirrorClient.insertTimelineItem(credential, item);
        }
    }

    break;
}
```

Here you first collect the mascots of all the teams and then go through the mascots to determine which team is selected by checking to see whether the notification's action contains CUSTOM as the action type and the mascot as the payload. After the team is found, all its players' information is generated based on a modified FLIGHT template tested in the Mirror API Playground.

Note that you use setBundleId to combine all the players for a team and setSpeakableText to enable READ_ALOUD (because the content is HTML). You also throw in SHARE and TOGGEL_PINNED menu items in case you want to share or save the information. Finally, you insert the timeline item.

To enable search for a player with voice, a workaround using the "Take a note" voice command is used. Because you have the TAKE_A_NOTE command type enabled for the contact inserted in the app (you may want to review the "Sharing transcribed speech" section earlier in this chapter), let's add the following code inside else if (notification.getUserActions().contains(new UserAction(). setType("LAUNCH"))) of NotifyServlet.java:

```
// search for NBA roster info
String noteText = timelineItem.getText();
for (String[] team : MainServlet.teams) {
    if (team[2].toLowerCase().equals(noteText.toLowerCase())) {
        String html = "<article><section><div class='layout-figure'><div class='align-center
        yellow'><p class='text-auto-size'>" + team[2] + "</p><p class='green'>Age: " + team[4] +
        "</p></div><div class='text-normal'>";
        html += "<p>No. " + team[1] + ", " + team[3] + "</p>";
        html += "<p>" + team[5] + ", " + team[6] + "lb</p>";
        html += "<p>" + team[7] + "</p>";
        html += "<p class='red'>" + team[8] + "</p>";
        html += "</div></div></section></article>";

        TimelineItem item = new TimelineItem();
        item.setHtml(html);
        item.setSpeakableText(team[2] + ", Age " + team[4] + ", " + team[5] + ", " + team[6] + ", "
        + team[7] + ", Salary: " + team[8]);
        List<MenuItem> menuItemList = new ArrayList<MenuItem>();
        menuItemList.add(new MenuItem().setAction("SHARE"));
        menuItemList.add(new MenuItem().setAction("READ_ALOUD"));
        menuItemList.add(new MenuItem().setAction("TOGGLE_PINNED"));
```

```
            item.setMenuItems(menuItemList);
            MirrorClient.insertTimelineItem(credential, item);
            break;
    }
}
```

timelineItem is set as mirrorClient.timeline().get(notification. getItemId()).execute() at the beginning of if (notification.getCollection().equals("timeline")), and its getText() returns the transcribed speech.

Now build, deploy, and relaunch the app. Click the NBA Roster button, and you'll see a new card inserted to your Glass. Tap it, and you can swipe to see all 16 playoff teams. Tap your interested team, and a new bundled card will be inserted, as shown in Figure 10-17. Tap the bundled card, and you can swipe to see each player's information in the team.

Figure 10-17. Timeline items showing teams and players in a team

To search for a player among the 16 teams, say "OK Glass." Then say "Take a note with <app contact name>" (I used "J.J. Mirror" as the app contact name, defined in MainServlet.java). Now speak a name like "Chris Paul" or "Tim Duncan," and you'll get their information cards in seconds, as shown in Figure 10-18.

Figure 10-18. Timeline items inserted with voice search

Enterprise Apps

Just Google *google glass healthcare* or *google glass education*, and you'll see lots of exciting results. Innovative startups like Augmedix (http://augmedix.com/about) and Wearable Intelligence (http://wearableintelligence.com) are building Glass apps for healthcare. Doctors are using Glass to get real-time information and interact with back-end systems, tablets, or smartphones with their hands full, and universities are using Glass to educate students where visual and demonstrative content is common. See www.cnet.com/news/google-glass-handed-out-to-all-medical-students-at-uc-irvine/ for an example.

I wish I could provide more examples from the enterprise world in the book. But with what you've learned in this chapter and all the previous chapters on GDK development, I'm sure you'll be able to get up to speed with your project ideas and build great Glass enterprise apps if you're interested, whether in the Mirror API, with the GDK, or in the hybrid way.

Design Principles

Before I write the summary for this last chapter of this book, I do need to say a few words about design. This is a book on Glass development, and I covered little on design. My main goal is to make things work and show you examples that work, but this doesn't mean design is not important; just see what amazing success Apple has achieved in the past years because of its obsession with great design.

On a high level, I completely agree with what Donald Norman said, "Design is understanding people." To develop a great Glass app, you have to really understand your users. Users care most if your apps help solve their problems, save their time, or entertain them. Most users don't care about your brand. Google also offers a set of excellent design principles, some of which are especially for Glass: https://developers.google.com/glass/design/principles. My two favorite ones are as follows:

- *Design for Glass*: Complement your Glass with a smartphone, tablet, or laptop instead of trying to replace those devices.

- *Don't get in the way*: Be there when you need it and out of the way when you don't. (I also believe this is what best friends, parents, or books are like.)

On a detailed UI design level, the templates in the Mirror API Playground and sample GDK apps offer the best illustration of an optimal Glass user experience. You should follow them as closely as possible to bring a familiar and consistent interface to users, unless you have great reasons to be innovative.

> **Note**   Distribution is another topic I won't cover here because `https://developers.google.com/glass/distribute/` and `https://developers.google.com/glass/distribute/best-practices` offer excellent information on the subject.

Summary

In this chapter, I discussed in detail how to set up your environment for Mirror API app development and how to deploy the Glass Mirror API quick-start PHP project to your own server and the Java project to Google App Engine. Then I went through the main building blocks of the Mirror API in detail with many examples, including timeline and static cards, contacts, subscriptions, and locations. I also showed you how to build a hybrid app launching the GDK app from the Mirror app and pass information from the Mirror app to the GDK app if needed. This can be really powerful because you combine the simple, elegant Mirror API with the native, sophisticated GDK. You also reused the Java image-uploading code from the networking chapter in your Mirror app to upload a picture to a server for further processing. Finally, I demonstrated a complete Mirror API app that lets you view and search for any player in the 16 NBA playoff teams.

Before Moving On

It's been a long journey since I started writing the book six months ago. The journey has been full of excitement with one puzzle after another solved, but there are still many areas I wish I could have more time to do better. Overall, I hope I have provided a lot of useful content and examples to help you quickly learn how to develop for Glass, one of the paradigm-shifting wearable devices. Whether you missed the mobile opportunity or not, don't let the wearable opportunity pass you by.

I'm sure the journey ahead for you to build great Glass apps to solve real-world problems and create fun and innovative user experiences for Glass users will be even more exciting. But you have to roll up your sleeves, get your hands dirty, toil and sweat, and work on real projects to make your journey truly rewarding. Let this book inspire you. Let it be a practical tour guide and reference to you. Let it be there when you need it.

Again, if you have any questions or comments, just drop me a line at `jeff.x.tang@gmail.com` and I'd love to get back with you within 24 hours.

Index

Get the eBook for only $10!

Now you can take the weightless companion with you anywhere, anytime. Your purchase of this book entitles you to 3 electronic versions for only $10.

This Apress title will prove so indispensible that you'll want to carry it with you everywhere, which is why we are offering the eBook in 3 formats for only $10 if you have already purchased the print book.

Convenient and fully searchable, the PDF version enables you to easily find and copy code—or perform examples by quickly toggling between instructions and applications. The MOBI format is ideal for your Kindle, while the ePUB can be utilized on a variety of mobile devices.

Go to www.apress.com/promo/tendollars to purchase your companion eBook.

Apress®
THE EXPERT'S VOICE™